AF836201

# New Directions in Expatriate Research

# New Directions in Expatriate Research

Edited by

Michael J. Morley
*University of Limerick*

Noreen Heraty
*University of Limerick*

David G. Collings
*Sheffield University Management School*

palgrave
macmillan

Selection and editorial matter © Michael J. Morley, Noreen Heraty and David G. Collings 2006
Individual chapters © contributors 2006

All rights reserved. No reproduction, copy or transmission of this publication may be made without written permission.

No paragraph of this publication may be reproduced, copied or transmitted save with written permission or in accordance with the provisions of the Copyright, Designs and Patents Act 1988, or under the terms of any licence permitting limited copying issued by the Copyright Licensing Agency, 90 Tottenham Court Road, London W1T 4LP.

Any person why does any unauthorised act in relation to this publication may be liable to criminal prosecution and civil claims for damages.

The authors have asserted their rights to be identified as the authors of this work in accordance with the Copyright, Designs and Patents Act 1988.

First published 2006 by
PALGRAVE MACMILLAN
Houndmills, Basingstoke, Hampshire RG21 6XS and
175 Fifth Avenue, New York, N.Y. 10010
Companies and representatives throughout the world

PALGRAVE MACMILLAN is the global academic imprint of the Palgrave Macmillan division of St. Martin's Press, LLC and of Palgrave Macmillan Ltd. Macmillan® is a registered trademark in the United States, United Kingdom and other countries. Palgrave is a registered trademark in the European Union and other countries.

ISBN-13: 978–1–4039–4297–5 hardback
ISBN-10: 1–4039–4297–8 hardback

This book is printed on paper suitable for recycling and made from fully managed and sustained forest sources.

A catalogue record for this book is available from the British Library.

Library of Congress Cataloging-in-Publication Data

New directions in expatriate research / edited by Michael J. Morley, Noreen Heraty and David G. Collings.
p. cm.
Includes bibliographical references and index.
ISBN 1-4039-4297-8 (cloth)
1. International business enterprises—Personnel management.
2. International business enterprises—Employees. 3. Employment in foreign countries. I. Morley, Michael. II. Heraty, Noreen. III. Collings, David G.

HF5549.5.E45N49 2006
658.3—dc22 2006043252

10 9 8 7 6 5 4 3 2 1
15 14 13 12 11 10 09 08 07 06

Printed and bound in Great Britain by
Antony Rowe Ltd, Chippenham and Eastbourne

# Contents

# List of Tables

# List of Figures

# Notes on the Editors

**Michael J. Morley** is Assistant Dean (Research) and Director of the Graduate Centre of Business at the University of Limerick where he teaches organizational behaviour and international human resource management. He has co-authored/edited some fifteen books including *Global Industrial Relations*, co-edited with Patrick Gunnigle and David Collings (2006), *Human Resource Management in Europe: Evidence of Convergence*, co-edited with Chris Brewster and Wolfgang Mayrhofer (2004) and *New Challenges for European Human Resource Management*, also with Brewster and Mayrhofer (2000). His refereed journal contributions have appeared in sources such as the *International Journal of Human Resource Management*, *Human Resource Management Journal*, *Advances in International Management*, *Industrial Relations Journal*, and *Human Resource Management Review*. He is Consulting Editor of the *Journal of Managerial Psychology* and is a member of the Editorial Board of several international journals including the *International Journal of Cross Cultural Management*, *Management Review*, *Leadership and Organization Development Journal* and the *International Journal of Strategic Change Management*.

**Noreen Heraty** is Lecturer in Human Resource Management and Development in the Department of Personnel & Employment Relations, Kemmy Business School, University of Limerick. She has co-authored/co-edited five books and two monographs, and has produced numerous book chapters and refereed journal articles in sources such as *International Studies of Management and Organization*, *Human Resource Management Review*, *International Journal of Manpower*, *Journal of Managerial Psychology* and *Personnel Review*. Her research interests include the creation and development of learning environments at the organizational level; competency development of HR practitioners and the nature of multinational HR operations across countries.

**David G. Collings** is Lecturer in Human Resource Management and Organization Behaviour at the Sheffield University Management School, Sheffield, UK. His current research interests centre on human resource management and industrial relations in the multinational firm. He is also a co-editor (with Hugh Scullion) of the *Global Staffing* text in the *Global HRM Series* and has published a number of journal articles on industrial relations and HRM in MNCs.

# Notes on the Contributors

**Dr Maike Andresen** is an assistant professor in the Department of Human Resource and International Management of Helmut-Schmidt University in Hamburg, Germany. Her research specializations are diversity management, corporate universities, and working time flexibility. She has published numerous articles in blind-refereed journals and books and presented papers in conferences including the European, Eastern and Western Academy of Management and IHRM Conference. She has been teaching for six years in the field of business administration and is responsible for the Master Programme in European Human Resource Management (EHRM).

**Oliver Breiden** is a Senior Manager working for the international Metro Cash & Carry group in Germany. He completed his Ph.D. research at the University of Bradford (UK) and holds a Master of Business Administration from the University of Cambridge (UK). His research focus is on international human resource management and expatriate management practices.

**Amanda Dunkel** is assistant professor at the Interdisciplinary Department for Management and Organizational Behaviour at Wirtschaftsuniversität Wien, Austria. Her research interests and main areas of expertise include cross-cultural management, international careers and expatriation research. She is consultant and partner of the 5p consulting company.

**Christiane Erten** has worked as research assistant and assistant professor at the University of Economics and Business Administration-Vienna/ Interdisciplinary Department of Management and Organizational Behaviour as well as a consultant in the field of strategic process planning; since 2002 she is managing director of an SME in the field of heating and ventilation and partner of AT Consult Austria. Her research interest lies in cross-cultural management and training (focus on Asian and Islamic countries), expatriation research and IHRM.

**Dr Thomas Hippler** studied business administration at the Fachhochschule Ostfriesland in Germany and the Regional Technical College Galway in Ireland. He graduated with a thesis on relocation support for German expatriates in the Republic of Ireland and is currently a researcher in the Human Resource Management Group at the Kemmy Business

School, University of Limerick. His doctoral thesis explored methodological and conceptual deficiencies in expatriate adjustment research.

**Dr Tina L. Howell** is a lecturer in Human Resource Management and Industrial Relations in the School of Economic and Management Studies at Keele University (UK). She completed her Ph.D. at the Nottingham University Business School (UK) and holds an M.Sc in Occupational Psychology also from the University of Nottingham. Her current research interests are varied and include discourse analysis, expatriation and repatriation, identity management and work/life balance issues.

**Elena Hristozova** is research assistant at the IPA Institute for Human Resource and International Management, Helmut-Schmidt University in Hamburg. Her main research areas are human resource management in consultancies and crisis-driven personnel practices. She is currently working on her thesis on evolution and success of crisis-driven human resource management in German consultancies. She is editor of the volume *Human Resource Management in Consulting Firms* (2006).

**Uta B. Lieberum** is assistant professor at the IPA Institute for Human Resource and International Management, Helmut-Schmidt University in Hamburg. She is also Head of the Faculty for Business Administration at the OTA-Hochschule in Berlin. Her main research areas are special aspects of International Human Resource Management, Gender- and Age-Diversity and Career-Management. She obtained her doctorate from the Helmut-Schmidt University with a thesis on cultural aspects of international alliances.

**Wolfgang Mayrhofer** is professor of business administration and holds a chair for management and organizational behaviour at Wirtschaftsuniversität Wien, Austria. His research interests include international comparative research in human resource management and leadership, careers and systems theory. He regular conducts trainings for both public and private organizations.

**Hafiz R. Mirza** is Professor of International Business and Management at the University of Bradford (UK) School of Management. In addition, he is the Head of Group, Strategy, Economics and International Business (SEIB) and serves as a reviewer for various publishers and international journals. His research interests encompass transnational corporations, regionalization, foreign direct investment and poverty reduction as well as the globalization of multinational enterprises.

**Alexander T. Mohr** is a Lecturer in International Business and Management at the University of Bradford (UK) School of Management. Following his studies at the University of Tübingen, Germany, the University of Edinburgh (UK) and the University of Erlangen-Nuremberg, Germany, he completed a Ph.D. at the University of Erlangen-Nuremberg. In his research, he focuses on international strategic alliances, international human resource management, foreign direct investment in China and eastern Europe and cross-cultural management.

**Yvonne M. McNulty** is a Ph.D. candidate in the Department of Management at Monash University, Australia. Her current research interest is focused on measuring financial and non-financial returns on investment from internationally mobile employees. Her other research interests include the challenges of the trailing spouse on international assignments, and distance education as an international mobility opportunity.

**Solja Paganus** has obtained her doctorate from the Swedish School of Economics and Business Administration in Helsinki. Her study explored Finnish Business Repatriates' Coping Strategies. Her research interests include expatriation, international HRM, and cross-cultural management.

**Michael Schiffinger** works as a research assistant at the Interdisciplinary Department for Management and Organizational Behaviour. His research interests include career research (he commenced his own career as research assistant for the Vienna Career Panel Project), political behaviour, and leadership.

**Professor Phyllis Tharenou** is the Dean of Research in the Division of Business at the University of South Australia. She graduated with a Ph.D. in organizational psychology from the University of Queensland. Her current research interest is in the international mobility of professionals including self-initiated expatriation abroad and repatriation home.

**Dr Marie-France Waxin** is an Assistant Professor at the School of Business and Management, American University of Sharjah (United Arab Emirates), where she teaches International Human Resources Management and Organizational Behaviour. She specializes in International Human Resources, Expatriation, and Cross-cultural Management. Her current research interests are centered around international HRM and the degree of congruency between individual, organizational and cultural values.

# 1

# Introduction: New Directions in Expatriate Research

*Michael J. Morley, Noreen Heraty & David G. Collings*

The successful establishment and continuing prosperity of many companies is dependent upon the performance of the expatriates and yet being an expatriate remains a 'rigorous experience' (Web & Wright, 1996: 38). Faced with unprecedented levels of foreign competition at home and abroad, firms are beginning to recognize not only that international business is high on top management's list of priorities, but that finding and nurturing the human resources required to implement an international strategy is of critical importance (Dowling & Welch, 2004). As MNCs increase in influence and number associated with rapid increases in global activity, so the role of expatriates in those MNCs increases in significance (Black et al., 1999). There are a number of well-articulated advantages associated with the deployment of expatriates in the staffing of international subsidiaries and operations. From their trawl of the extant literature, Paik & Shon (2004: 63) note that compared to their locally hired counterparts, expatriates are generally believed to have a better understanding of overall corporate priorities, an easier acceptance of headquarter-determined rules and a greater commitment to overall corporate goals. Expatriates' familiarity with the corporate culture and the control system of headquarters is also posited as a distinct advantage and something that may result in more effective communication and coordination. Paik and Shon further point to the fact that expatriates are also often seen as effective in replicating the operating procedures of headquarters in their local units, and their assignment to subsidiaries also facilitates the creation of an information network consistent with corporate culture.

Scullion (2001) argues that an understanding of the management of expatriates is of growing importance for several reasons. Prominent among them is the ongoing and rapid globalization of business. In this context, the effective management of expatriates is recognized as a major determinant of success or failure in international business (Black and Gregerson, 1999). Beyond the globalization issue, Harris and Brewster (1999) point to a shift in host location patterns with a decline in the proportion of expatriates going from the developed to the developing world and an increase in assignments and cross-border developments between developed countries and New World trading blocs. They also draw attention to a change in the nature of international organizations themselves, with increasing numbers of joint ventures and alliances and the emergence of small- to medium-sized organizations as key players in global trade, something that historically was less evident. With respect to this latter point, Brewster and Scullion (1997) note that the rapid growth of smaller and medium sized enterprises (SMEs) who have newly internationalized their operations in recent years means that issues of expatriate management are increasingly important in a far wider range of organizations than the traditional giant multinationals. This is likely to prove particularly significant given that many companies, relatively new to the international scene, underestimate the complex nature of HR problems in this international arena. Indeed, Forster (2000) suggests that business failures in this international arena may often be linked to the poor performance of expatriates.

While historically much of the research on the management of expatriates was from research focused on North American multinationals, this has changed in recent years and we are witnessing an extension of the expatriation experience across the globe and especially to the transition economies of the CEE, China and India, giving rise to significant lines of inquiry on the explanatory power of cultural and psychic distance in accounting for variations in intercultural transitional adjustment. Morley et al. (1997) address the extent to which frameworks of international adjustment, developed primarily in the North American context, are applicable in such context. They argue that a detailed understanding of the context of adjustment in each case is necessary in determining which variables are likely to cause problems. Indeed, Cyr and Schneider (1996), in their study of expatriation in central and eastern Europe, found that local managers in these countries often resent the attitude of western expatriate managers who are seen as unwilling to take into account the views of local people. As these economies develop, we are likely to witness continued investigation of the expatriation process in these regions and beyond, most especially in regions of considerable contemporary foreign direct investment.

From an overall perspective, we can see that the study of expatriation has followed the traditional expatriate 'cycle' – selection, training, relocation and adjustment, pay and performance and return – with initial attention on the earlier stage of the assignment and a successively developing focus on the later and more complex issues of performance and repatriation (Scullion and Brewster, 2001). Baruch and Altman (1999) found that much research dealing with expatriation has been concerned with individuals lacking in conceptual work at the organizational or human resources operational level. Linehan (2000), Adler (1997) and Harris (1995) suggest that expatriate management has long been a masculine preserve in the United States and Europe, with little research conducted with European female expatriates, mainly due to their relative scarcity. Indeed Adler (2002) contends that as global competition intensifies, the opportunity cost of relying on the traditional male expatriate escalates. Furthermore, Fisher (1992) cautions that companies can no longer afford to ignore potential talent 'simply because it's wearing a skirt' or because it holds a passport different from that of the founding executives.

Interesting practice differences between North American and European firms are evident in trends in international staffing practices. Recent European research highlights the importance of country specific factors and points to the differences between countries in staffing practices. For example, Scullion (2001) found that UK owned firms tend to use longer assignments and rely more heavily on expatriates to control overseas operations, than do their US counterparts. His findings echo earlier results by Harzing (1999a) which depicted Japan and Germany at one extreme with a high level of expatriate presence while the USA was at the other extreme.

There is some evidence that the 'traditional' expatriate assignment, in terms of nature and duration, is changing, with a diminution of the longer-term assignment in favour of shorter term, frequent flier assignments. The development of travel and technology is making such 'substitute' expatriate activities more common, particularly in Europe. By way of illustration, there is an increasing trend of purchasing and sales activities being conducted by people on short (often, literally flying) visits. Euro commuting or frequent flying is becoming ever more common (Petrovic et al., 2000; Mayrhofer and Scullion, 2002) and the increasing use of video conferencing and real time computer information from around the world has provided alternatives to control by the physical presence of an expatriate. The implications of these developments for the management of expatriates remain largely unresearched, however, though Scullion & Brewster (2001) do note that they may have considerable implications for MNCs.

Turning to the issue of recruitment and selection for expatriate assignment, there is concern that some of the research here is rather prescriptive and has generally been focused on issues such as selection criteria. Studies by Brewster & Harris (1999) highlight that decisions on expatriate selection are usually taken by line managers – who often simply ignore the selection decisions espoused by the HR department. Research also suggests that, compared with their US counterparts, European MNC companies pay closer attention to the selection of expatriates, perhaps reflecting the greater importance of international revenues. Data from Price Waterhouse Europe (1997–8) suggests that the international experience is highly valued in European MNCs, and expatriate assignments are regarded as high status and often integral to the management development process.

Holden (1997) and Mendenhall et al. (2001) reported that very few empirical studies have been conducted on career management issues facing expatriates. Their collective views suggest that an overseas assignment is often a 'haphazard, ill-planned affair' that all too frequently leads to poor job performance and job displacement. Ferner (1994) reported that there are major gaps in empirical research and in the understanding of issues and processes concerning expatriation. Brewster and Scullion (1997) argue that much of the literature on the management of expatriates is still open to the criticisms of Schollhammer (1975), i.e. being mainly descriptive and lacking in analytical rigour; ad hoc and expedient in research design and planning; frequently ignoring the existing research literature; and failing to develop case material. Morley & Heraty (2004) argue that despite these problems, or perhaps because of them, it is important that we redouble our efforts to understand better the nature and value of this international assignment. We must do so in the full knowledge that having a cadre of able and committed women and men willing to take on such roles is critical because a lack of such personnel may act as a significant and ongoing means constraint on the implementation and execution of international strategies.

Clearly, planning and managing the expatriate assignment remains a core concern of international human resource management. Dowling and Welch (2004: 66) suggest 'there are ebbs and flows associated with the number of staff moved internationally' and certainly questioning why multinationals continue their use of expatriates is reasonable because of the common difficulties and challenges seen to surround such assignments. Suutari & Brewster (2001: 555) note that: 'while the use of expatriates can help to overcome some problems for an international enterprise, it also creates several problems' with the consequence that the management of the international assignee remains a critically important, if challenging, task. They highlight several ongoing problems that characterize this aspect of international human resource management. Chief among them are the direct and indirect costs associated with international assignments. High salaries to persuade good individuals to work outside their own country are, they note, compounded by extensive benefits, moving costs, expense accounts and substantial administrative expense for a relatively small, but important, group of employees. Secondly they point to the omnipresent intercultural transitional adjustment issue. In this regard they note that adaptation to any new task or job can be difficult and for new expatriates this problem is exacerbated by the need to perform in a new culture. Consequently, significant adaptation problems are seen to make it difficult to operative effectively, especially in the early part of the assignment.

The whole question of performance measurement and return on investment from the international assignment more generally in multinational companies involves a complex range of issues. Research suggests that European multinationals are more likely to pay close attention to this aspect of expatriation and tend to evaluate managers more on the achievement of long term goals than on the short term measures used by US multinationals (Lindholm et al., 1999). However, rigorous performance appraisal systems for expatriates appear far from universal (Schuler et al., 2004; Brewster and Harris, 1999). This is perhaps surprising given the high costs of expatriate underperformance and the growing tendency to see expatriates as key strategic human assets (Black and Gregerson, 1999). It is increasingly recognized that the human and financial costs of underperformance/failure in the international business area are considerably more severe than in the domestic area. There is also evidence that many companies relatively new to the international scene underestimate the complex nature of HR problems in the international arena and that business failures in the international arena may often be linked to the poor performance of expatriates (Forster, 2000). In addition to this changing context, Harris et al. (2003) suggest that the traditional expatriate profile is also changing. Thus third country nationals, rather than assignees from the headquarters country are increasingly being deployed. So also are more women assignees emerging. While the proportion of female assignees remains small and the barriers to participation remain numerous, the number of women expatriates is on the increase. Bringing with them their own unique challenges, the number of dual career couples has also increased. Finally, in addition to a general increase in the base educational level of the international assignee, there have been a corresponding increase in assignees' expectations concerning the value of the assignment both as a personal and a career development exercise.

The repatriation of expatriates has further been identified as a major problem for MNCs in Europe and North America (Black et al., 1999; Linehan and Scullion, 2002). Tellingly, a recent study by Tung (1998) reported that while a majority of US managers were satisfied with expatriation, the majority were also very unhappy with repatriation. Indeed, concern over re-entry was cited as a significant reason affecting expatriate performance (Scullion, 2001) and North American academics have made a major contribution to our understanding of repatriate adjustment (see Black et al., 1999). Many expatriates leave their company on return with the consequent loss of investment and expertise. This loss of investment and international knowledge has led to calls for a more strategic approach to repatriation (Linehan and Scullion, 2002). Yet, while it is widely accepted that the costs of expatriate turnover are high, very few firms have effective repatriation programmes. There is a widespread assumption by managers in corporate headquarters that re-entry to the home country and home organization is relatively non-problematic or even a non-issue. Yet, research indicates that repatriation can be an even more difficult adjustment than expatriation (Black and Gregersen, 1999; Black and Gregersen, 1998). Scullion and Starkey (2000) argue that the management of repatriation is more complex in decentralized multinational companies and they offer some important insights into how the repatriation process can be used to develop the internationalization of organizations. Research by Black & Gregersen (1998) highlights that between 20 per cent and 50 per cent of all expatriates resign – a significantly higher percentage than among non-repatriate executives. In practice, many organizations continue to adopt an ad hoc, sink or swim attitude in relation to repatriation for employees and their families, and many expatriate managers continue to experience the repatriation process as falling far short of expectations (Stroh et al., 1998).

Overall then, as Yan et al. (2002: 373) point out, 'the challenges involved in these assignments can be high for both the individual and the organisation', an experience which they suggest is often characterized by 'all too familiar and vexing difficulties' (374) and scholars have highlighted the necessity for greater empirical evidence, especially in light of the ongoing increase in the level of internationalization in the business world and associated likely increase in the demand for and deployment of expatriate assignees.

## The contributions to the book

This edited collection brings together eight papers dealing with expatriate assignments. The majority of the papers in our collection are revised contributions originally presented at the 7th Conference on International Human Resource Management held at the University of Limerick, Ireland during June 2003. Conceived of and presented under the theme *International Human Resource Management: Exploring the Mosaic, Developing the Discipline*, the conference took as its point of departure the ever increasing globalization of business and how this brought into sharp relief the need to develop a more in-depth understanding of international human resource management and its associated activities. The contributions to the conference focused on, *inter alia*: the current state of the field of international human resource management; strategy, human resource management and organizational performance; international assignments and global careers; knowledge management and human capital development; multinational corporations and their impact on human resource management, employment relations and collective bargaining. This volume brings together a selection of papers under the theme 'New Directions in Expatriate Research' which combined, seek to extend our understanding of the contribution of and exigencies surrounding such assignments from an organizational and individual perspective. From an organizational standpoint return on investment from such assignments and the relationship with business performance are explored. At the level of the individual a reassessment of our approach to conceptualizing and measuring adjustment, person–work fit, the impact of the expatriate's culture of origin on adjustment, gender diversity and assignment success and the repatriation experience are featured and represent exciting and promising lines of enquiry.

The second chapter, by McNulty and Tharenou, examines the complex issue of expatriate return on investment (ROI) and seeks to extend our understanding of the myriad contextual factors that can influence the degree to which the expatriate assignment is seen to yield a positive ROI. Return on Investment is clearly a critical issue for organizations and yet, surprisingly, there is no published research on examining how expatriate ROI may be calculated and what factors may increase or decrease expatriate ROI for the firm. Adopting a multi-disciplinary approach, McNulty and Tharenou argue that expatriate ROI is a complex phenomenon that needs to be understood from a number of perspectives in order to produce a calculation that has a meaningful rate of return. They persuasively argue that the importance of an expatriate ROI calculation lies not just in determining the rate of return, but also in understanding why rates of return increase and decrease and what influences such rates. Whilst acknowledging that each individual antecedent has the potential to increase or decrease ROI on its own, McNulty and Tharenou contend that understanding the inter-relationship of these antecedents with each other, from a systems perspective, will produce a more accurate and useful ROI calculation in the long-term. However, they do caution against the utility of a 'one best' ROI formula that expects identical costs and benefits to be calculated for every assignment, arguing that an ROI calculation will differ from one assignment to the next because the objectives of each assignment are likely to be different.

Specifically, they propose that expatriate ROI can be best understood as a confluence of the following: First, it must contain a summary of costs and benefits incurred during a long-term international assignment; second, the costs and benefits of a long-term assignment must always be defined within the context of the purpose of the assignment itself; third, the compilation of costs and benefits data must be approached from a systems perspective which avoids investigating only individual costs and benefits at one point in time, and finally, expatriate ROI must be calculated at a time that is appropriate to meeting the assignment's objectives, for example, at the immediate conclusion of an assignment or at some point during repatriation. Given the dearth of empirical studies examining expatriate costs and benefits from a HR systems approach, the authors advance a series of testable hypotheses associated with planning, selection, relocation package, compensation, training and development, performance management, family supports, repatriation, and retention. It is proposed that these offer a useful framework within which scholars and practitioners can advance research in this important area.

The third chapter is by Christiane Erten, Michael Schiffinger, Wolfgang Mayrhofer and Amanda Dunkel and it explores the use of foreign assignments in a number of European countries. Specifically, and using comparative analysis of northern, southern and eastern European countries, the authors explore the relationship between the use of foreign assignments and economic success and business strategy. As a starting point, Erten et al. note that, despite theoretical and practical establishment, international assignments as empirical phenomena undergo constant changes. Here, they point to continuing increase in international business activities, to 'new' forms of international assignments that are increasingly supplementing or partly substituting for 'traditional' patterns of expatriation, and to significant recent developments within the European Union (EU) that have opened up new possibilities for business activities across borders. Moreover, the authors note that the economic aspect of expatriation is becoming increasingly important because of the strong economic pressures that companies face and that this focuses attention on the contributions that foreign assignments can make to overall organizational performance.

Erten and her colleagues argue that the unique context of Europe itself makes an examination of international assignments in Europe a compelling and worthwhile one. Here, they suggest that a combination of historic, cultural, economic and institutional factors contribute to an arguably unique mixture of unifying and dividing elements that can provide fruitful contexts within which to explore the continuing use of the expatriate assignment. Specifically, the authors point to the relative geographic closeness of European countries that allows for greater opportunity to deviate from the traditional relocation expatriation experience, the large differences in economic development that have led to different routes and stages of internationalization, and to the growing number of SMEs at the threshold of internationalization that are only partly covered and explained by theories of internationalization developed from research in large MNCs.

Using data generated from the Cranfield Network on Human Resource Management (Cranet), the authors explore three important issues: the frequency of use of international experience schemes (IES) for managers in for-profit organizations in selected European country clusters, the development of the use of such IES over the past years and the relationship between the use of IES and organizational performance.

Their results suggest a trend of directional convergence towards an increasing use of IES in Europe whereby companies across all country clusters appear to use IES to an increasing extent. While the direction of causality is not clear, there is some evidence that the use of IES is part of an overall business strategy focusing on quality related performance criteria rather than a low-price strategy. The authors suggest that their results underscore the importance of a better understanding of the general link between HR and organizational performance, and propose that the reasons for such a link as well as its direct and indirect effects on various HR activities and areas outside of HR deserves further attention.

The measurement of expatriate adjustment is taken up by Thomas Hippler in Chapter 4. Here, whilst acknowledging the seminal work by Black and others in the field, Hippler suggests that the almost total lack of inductive approaches to the topic of expatriate adjustment may have resulted in overlooking some important factors in the expatriate experience. Specifically he questions whether the 14 items universally used to measure adjustment are, in fact, the most salient or important aspects of the expatriates' host environment, and then whether these items are specific enough to be meaningfully dealt with by the expatriates in a questionnaire survey.

Hippler concludes that the choice of at least some of them may have been somewhat arbitrary and argues that these items are still too broad to be meaningful to the respondents, pointing to the item 'living conditions in general' as particularly susceptible in this regard.

In recognition of this 'potentially shaky ground' Hippler suggests a 'going back to square one' approach. He argues that this is warranted since, given the developmental history of the instruments currently in use to measure expatriate adjustment, it is uncertain whether these are exhaustive or indeed, from the perspective of those concerned, that is the expatriates, relevant. Thus, he advances an exploratory investigation of both expatriate employees and domestic relocates to empirically establish the domains that are seen to matter to the expatriates. Specifically, he sets out to determine in which domains do relocatees, both international and domestic, assigned to a variety of host locations, report experiencing changes when comparing their host environment to their home environment?

Generating data from a large sample of respondents in one organizational setting, Hippler developed a category system for the content analysis that was derived inductively from the data. His results point to some interesting comparisons with extant studies. For example, all of Black and Stephens' facets of adjustment were identified among the answers the international relocatees provided in his study with almost all of them appearing in the upper half of the frequency count table. However, some of the domains that featured prominently in Hippler's frequency count were absent from Black and Stephens' item list. Most notably the distance to the home region, that is contacts to friends, acquaintances and family members back home, anything related to the expatriate's immediate family, that is partner and children, and its cohesion. His results further point to the fact that Black and Stephens' item list only recognizes the expatriate as a social actor in relation to the host environment, that is interacting with and speaking to host nationals. It completely ignores that the expatriate has to adjust to the loss – or at least diminished contact – to friends, acquaintances and family members he or she left behind and thus has to adjust to the loss of an established social support network. This loss is not necessarily transitional and completely compensated for by a newly established circle of friends at the host location. This constitutes an important dimension to be considered in managing the expatriation process.

The nature of managerial work during international assignments is the focus for discussion by Oliver Breiden, Hafiz R. Miraz and Alexander T. Mohr in Chapter 5. Here, the authors concentrate specifically on examining expatriate–assignment fit and its consequences for work adjustment. In the first instance, Breiden et al. note that the costs associated with expatriation has resulted in a continual search to identify the factors that influence career satisfaction, on-the-job performance and workplace adjustment among expatriate managers. Although accepting the multi-faceted nature of expatriate adjustment, they note that adjusting to the work situation encountered abroad has commonly been regarded as a particularly critical and challenging task to be achieved by expatriates during their stays abroad. Even though much emphasis has been placed on the search for factors that can enhance the success of an international assignment, Breiden et al. reflect that little research has been undertaken to examine in greater detail expatriate job characteristics and the nature of managerial work carried out by expatriate managers. Furthermore, they surmise that few investigations have been conducted to determine if expatriate managers derive satisfaction from the work they complete abroad and if the satisfaction levels achieved can help them to reach appropriate levels of work adjustment.

Using survey data collected from 118 German expatriate managers, Breiden et al. examine the nature of managerial work performed by expatriate managers. Here, the data is analysed to determine the workload demands of expatriate managers, to establish the distribution of time allocated to different managerial activities in the foreign workplace, and to examine the skill utilization as well as the perceived job requirements reported by expatriate managers. Breiden et al. argue that a better understanding of the managerial activities and duties that are to be carried out by the expatriate employee is required in order to determine the levels of job satisfaction reported by transferred managers. They propose a model of work adjustment whereby an expatriate manager's work adjustment during an international assignment is related to two distinct facets of satisfaction: (1) task satisfaction and (2) emotional satisfaction. While the degree of task satisfaction is linked to the level of correspondence (or match) between the job requirements and an individual's work-related abilities, emotional satisfaction is regarded as the outcome of an appropriate fit between the reinforcements available in the foreign work environment and the expatriate's expectations and needs. The model further posits that the work adjustment achieved by an expatriate manager can be derived from the levels of task satisfaction and emotional satisfaction reported by the individual. Thus, by assessing the fit between the characteristics of an expatriate manager and the specificities of a foreign assignment, Breiden et al. suggest that it may be possible to make more accurate predictions regarding the level of work adjustment achieved by an expatriate manager sent abroad to complete an international assignment.

The issue of expatriate adjustment is further taken up in Chapter 6 by Marie Waxin, but here she explores the impact of culture of origin on the three facets of expatriates' adjustment (work, interaction and general) and their antecedents. Waxin notes that much of the research on expatriates has focused on adding to the list of antecedents which influence cross-cultural adjustment, but that limited theoretical development for understanding *how* these antecedents impact on cross-cultural adjustment has occurred since the initial work of Black and his colleagues. Specifically she points to the paucity of research on the effect of culture of origin (CO) on expatriates' adjustment.

Set against this backdrop, here Waxin seeks to contribute to our understanding of the expatriate experience through a combination of partial replication of previous research on expatriates' adjustment, and through an examination of the effect of culture of origin on adjustment and its antecedents. Three research questions guide the discussion as follows: What is the relative importance of the antecedents of each adjustment facet? What is the direct effect of culture of origin on each adjustment facet? And what is the moderator effect of culture of origin on the antecedents of each adjustment facet?

Using self-administered questionnaire data from French, German, Korean and Scandinavian expatriated managers in India, and integrating established organizational, individual and contextual variables, Waxin develops a research model of the antecedents of the adjustment process where she introduces culture of origin both as a direct and a moderator variable. The results establish that culture of origin has a direct effect on the three facets of expatriate adjustment and a moderator effect on their antecedents.

Waxin proposes that the results have implications for how the expatriation process is managed, particularly with respect to selection, training and social supports. She acknowledges that further research could fruitfully explore managerial oriented measures, like time to proficiency, or consider the impact of culture on other factors of expatriates' adjustment, i.e. compensation and benefits policies, individual motivation to go abroad, and indeed family/spouse adjustment.

Our focus changes somewhat in the remaining three chapters and zones in on a number of important dimensions of the expatriation process. In Chapter 7, Maike Andresen, Elena Hristozova, and Uta B. Lieberum explore the expatriate assignment through the lens of gender diversity and consider the impact of female foreign assignments on organizational outcomes. They note that, despite the continuing growth in expatriate assignments, the number of female managers pursuing international careers remains considerably lower than that for male managers and, furthermore, that this percentage is disproportionately lower than the comparative rate for women in domestic management. The authors cite a number of positive benefits associated with the implementation of diversity initiatives to achieve gender diversity within a workforce and especially within management ranks including improved recruitment and retention, lower operating costs; enhanced reputations with potential customers; more creativity and better problem-solving capabilities; and strong community and institutional support due to their cultivated diverse workforces.

They also consider that empirical studies generally indicate weak corporate support for woman employees in general and female business expatriates in particular, suggesting that female managers have to overcome more barriers in their progression to (international) management positions than men. As a result of these additional barriers that exist both inside and outside the work environment, women may need more support on the part of the company in developing their (expatriate) careers.

Using data collected from the banking and insurance sectors in Germany, Andersen et al. investigate whether these companies implemented activities to support gender diversity in general and/or promoted this topic by communicating it *internally* to their employees and/or implemented measures to support female expatriation. They found that several companies used external and/or internal information platforms to communicate the goal of gender diversity to the public and/or to their employees. They also make arrangements for specific activities to implement measures to reach the goal of gender diversity. However, few if any organize special activities to increase the number of women placed on foreign assignments. Based on these findings, they propose a model to determine the impact of female management development on organizational success, based on the assumption that female foreign assignments do contribute to a better gender diversity in management ranks. Their model details a number of important aspects specifying the relation between FFA, gender diversity in management ranks and organizational success. The conclude that there remains a need to determine an optimum level of gender diversity in management ranks with respect to its impact on organizational success.

Our attention turns to repatriation in Chapter 8, and here Solja Paganus provides an interesting treatise on Finnish business repatriates' coping strategies at work. Drawing on a qualitatively rich data source, gathered from depth interviews with 22 respondents, she reports on the use of emotion-focused coping strategies or reactive work adjustment mode. Paganus differentiates between emotion-focused and problem-focused adjustment coping strategies. Here cognitive, typically emotion-focused, coping strategies were found to have occurred when the repatriates, working usually as specialists, returned to almost the same position or role and with the same work tasks as before their overseas assignment. Respondents recounted that they felt restricted in that their work role allowed them little scope for making changes in the way they conducted their work and thus their adjustment to work is described as essentially reactive. Specifically it was felt that some elements of absorption strategy were manifested in the repatriates' coping efforts since, in this reactive coping, they mostly assimilated their new skills, social behaviours and frames of references to meet the requirements of their present work situation.

The opposite was found with respect to the managers in her sample. In this respect, Paganus likens their coping strategies to a proactive work adjustment mode that was usual among the managers who were in a better position than the specialists to modify their work roles. Using problem-focused coping strategies, they expressed the repatriates' active strive towards confirmation and reconstruction of their identity. They used a greater number and a greater variety of different forms of problem-focused strategy than emotion-focused strategy. When using these strategies, the repatriates could draw upon their changed identities, increased self-confidence, and rich work experience. These repatriates had more opportunities to define their work tasks and change the structures of their work roles. Thus, their coping efforts included more likely elements of exploration adjustment mode.

The final contribution in this book comes from Tina Howell who presents us with a thought-provoking discursive analysis of expatriates' talk of work after repatriation. Recognized as an area of considerable importance to organizations, she notes that the role of repatriation in the expatriation process and its potential impact on the success of international assignments has often been overlooked and under-researched. Moreover, she cites the lack of studies that approach expatriation and repatriation from the perspective of the individual. Using a constructionist framework and discursive approach to textual analysis, Howell explores emerging issues of expectation, change, and organizational belonging in the context of talk about social identity, repatriation and the experience of short-term assignments among a group of 44 respondents. The focus of her research is on recounting the sometimes problematic nature of short-term repatriation that was evident not only in talk by individuals who had recently returned to work within the 'home' organization, but also emerged as a topic of concern by individuals who had only recently expatriated.

Within the text of her discussion, Howell draws attention to accounts of short-term assignment repatriation that were not only constructed as disconcerting in the final stages of a short-term assignment, but also implied by some as a problematic and issue of concern over the course of the assignment. Moreover, she presents identity formation not as a static entity, but as a continuing and flexible phenomenon that was created in and for the context of social interaction. Hence, accounting for the self as an expatriate-experienced employee in this particular organization varied considerably depending on the background and knowledge that each participant brought with them to the workplace.

Howell's findings provide compelling evidence to suggest that short-term assignments may not necessarily alleviate all of the problems traditionally associated with long-term assignments; rather they have the ability to inherently create their own new and unique set of problems. This theme was particularly evident in talk constructed around the loss of autonomy, unmet or undesired change, and a overwhelming lack of consensus about what is, or should be expected from repatriation by individuals undertaking arguably brief stretches of time away from the 'home' organization. As a result, the findings have relevance by offering some new perspectives and raising fresh questions about the nature of short-term assignments and repatriation embedded within a framework of social identity construction.

## References


Adler, N. J. (1997) *International Dimensions of Organizational Behaviour.* Boston: PWS-Kent.

Adler, N. J. (2002) Global managers: no longer men alone, *International Journal of Human Resource Management* 13(5): 743–60.

Baruch, Y. and Altman, Y. (1999) Expatriation and repatriation in MNCs: a taxonomy, Paper presented at Academy of Management Conference, Chicago, 6–11 August.

Black, J. S. and Gregersen, H. B. (1998) *So You're Going Overseas: a Handbook for Personal and Professional Success,* San Diego: Global Business Publishers.

Black, J. S. and Gregersen, H. B. (1999) The right way to manage expats, *Harvard Business Review,* March/April, 52–63.

Black, J. S., Gregersen, H. B., Mendenhall, M. E., and Stroh, L. K. (1999) *Globalizing People Through International Assignments,* Reading, MA: Addison-Wesley.

Brewster, C. and Harris, H. (eds) (1999) *International HRM: Contemporary Issues in Europe,* London: Routledge.

Brewster, C. and Scullion, H. (1997) A review and agenda for expatriate HRM, *Human Resource Management Journal,* 7(3): 32–41.

Cyr, D. and Schneider, S. (1996) Implications for learning: Human Resource Management in east–west joint ventures, *Organization Studies,* 17(2): 201–26.

Dowling, P. J. and Welch, D. E. (2004) *International Human Resource Management: Managing People in a Multinational Context,* 4th edn, London: Thompson.

Ferner, A. (1994) Multinational companies and human resource management: an overview of research issues, *Human Resource Management Journal,* 4(2): 79–102.

Fisher, A. B. (1992) When will women get to the top? *Fortune,* 21 September: 44–56.

Forster, N. (2000) The myth of the international manager, *International Journal of Human Resource Management,* 11(1): 126–42.

Harris, H. (1995) Women's role in (international) management. In Harzing, A. W. and Van Ruysseveldt, J. (1995) (eds) *International Human Resource Management: an Integrated Approach.* London: Sage Publications, 229–51.

Harris, H. and Brewster, C. (1999) International human resource management: the European contribution, in *International HRM Contemporary Issues In Europe,* ed. C. Brewster and H. Harris, London: Routledge.

Harris, H., Brewster, C. and Sparrow, P. (2003) *International Human Resource Management,* London: Chartered Institute of Personnel & Development.

Harzing, A. W. (1999a) MNE Staffing Policies for the managing director position in foreign subsidiaries. The results of an innovative research method, in Brewster, C. and Harris, H. (eds), *International HRM: Contemporary Issues in Europe,* London: Routledge, 67–88.

Harzing, A. W. – (1999b) *Managing the Multinationals: an International Study of Control Mechanisms,* Cheltenham: Edward Elgar.

Holden, L. (1997) International Human Resource Management, in Beardwell, I. and Holden, L. (eds), *Human Resource Management: a Contemporary Perspective* (2nd edn), London: Pitman publishing.

Lindholm, N., Tahvanainen, M. and Bjorkman, I. (1999) Performance appraisal of host country employees: Western MNEs in China. In C. Brewster and H. Harris (eds) *International HRM: Contemporary issues in Europe.*

Linehan, M. (2000) *Senior Female International Managers: Why So Few?* Aldershot: Ashgate.

Linehan, M. and Scullion, H. (2002) Repatriation of European female corporate executives: an empirical study, *International Journal of Human Resource Management,* 13(2): 254–67.

Mayrhofer, W. and Scullion, H. (2002) All equal? the importance of context – empirical evidence about male and female expatriates from the German clothing industry, *International Journal of Human Resource Management,* 13(5): 815–36.

Mendenhall, M. E., Kühlmann, T. M. and Stal, G. K. (eds) (2001) *Developing Global Business Leaders: Policies, Processes and Innovations,* Westport, CT: Quorum Books.

Morley, M., Burke, C., and O'Regan, T. (1997) The Irish in Moscow: a question of adjustment, *Human Resource Management Journal,* 7(3): 53–66.

Morley, M. and Heraty, N. (2004) International assignments and global careers, *Thunderbird International Business Review,* 46(6): 633–46.

Paik, Y. and Shon, J. D. (2004), Expatriate Managers and MNC's ability to control international subsidiaries: the case of Japanese MNCs, *Journal of World Business*, 39: 61–71.

Petrovic, J., Harris, H. and Brewster, C. (2000) *New Forms of International Working*, Crème Research report, 1/00, Cranfield School of Management, Cranfield University.

Price Waterhouse Europe (1997–98) *International Assignments: European Policy and Practice*. Price Waterhouse International Assignment Services Europe.

Schollhammer, H. (1975) Current research in international and comparative management issues, *Management International Review*, 15(2–3): 29–40.

Schuler, R. S., Budhwar, P. S. and Florkowski, G. W. (2004) International Human Resource Management: review and critique, *International Journal of Management Reviews*, 4(1): 41–70.

Scullion, H. (2001) International human resource management, in J. Storey (ed). *Human Resource Management*, London: International Thompson.

Scullion, H. and Brewster, C. (2001) Managing expatriates: messages from Europe, *Journal of World Business*, 36(4): 346–65.

Scullion, H. and Starkey, K. (2000) The changing role of the corporate human resource function in the international firm, *International Journal of Human Resource Management*, 11: 1061–81.

Stroh, L., Gregersen, H. B. and Black, J. S. (1998) Closing the gap: expectations versus reality among repatriates, *Journal of World Business*, 33(2): 111–24.

Suutari, V. and Brewster, C. (2001) Expatriate management practices and perceived relevance: evidence from Finnish expatriates, *Personnel Review*, 30(5): 554–77.

Tung, R. L. (1998) American expatriates abroad: from neophytes to cosmopolitans, *Journal of World Business*, 33(2): 125–44.

Web, A. and Wright, P. (1996), The expatriate experience: implications for career success, *Career Development International*, 1(5): 38–44.

Yan, A., Zhu, G. and Hall, D. (2002), International assignments for career building: a model of agency relationships and psychological contracts, *Academy of Management Review*, 27(3): 373–91.

# 2

# Moving the Research Agenda Forward on Expatriate Return on Investment

*Yvonne M. McNulty & Phyllis Tharenou*

## Introduction

The costs associated with a long-term international assignment, defined as the relocation of an employee abroad by a firm for a year or more (Cendant, 2002, 2004; Boyacigiller, 2000; Kobrin, 1988; KPMG International, 2003; Mercer Human Resource Consulting, 2003), are high. Some evidence suggests that the costs exceed $1 million per assignee and per assignment, and that the total cost to US multinational corporations (MNCs) is about $75 billion a year (Copeland and Griggs, 1985; Sheridan, 1998). In spite of the costs, a recent industry survey indicated that it is possible that long-term international assignments provide little return on investment (ROI) (GMAC/NFTC/SHRM 2002). As Black, Gregersen, Mendenhall and Stroh (1999: 2) said:

> An international assignment is the single most powerful experience shaping the perspective and capabilities of effective global leaders. It also happens to be the single most expensive per-person investment that a company makes in globalizing their people. It is unfortunate that most firms are getting anemic returns on this substantial investment.

Understanding how to obtain a return on investment from long-term assignments is important. The reporting of expatriate assignment failures, with 44 per cent of MNCs reporting failures in the Asia Pacific region and 63 per cent in Europe (Cendant, 2001), seems to indicate that the direct and non-direct costs associated with expatriation are substantial. Yet industry surveys show that expatriate ROI is not only poorly calculated amongst MNCs but is also not widely used as a tool to reduce expatriate costs (GMAC/NFTC/SHRM 2002). For example, only 30 per cent of respondents in the GMAC/NFTC/SHRM 2002 survey rated their expatriate ROI as 'good' or 'excellent', with only 9 per cent indicating they had specific programmes in place to improve it. In fact, 70 per cent of the respondents rated their ROI as average, fair, or poor. Other industry surveys show that, to avoid the costs of long-term assignments, MNCs use a range of alternatives including virtual assignments and teleworking, short-term assignments, business trips, cross-border commuting, frequent flying, and host country nationals (HCNs) (Cendant, 2002; GMAC/NFTC/SHRM 2002; KPMG International, 2003; PricewaterhouseCoopers, 2001, 2002). Yet, despite the costs, many MNCs continue to use long-term assignments (Cendant, 2004; Mercer Human Resource Consulting, 2003; PricewaterhouseCoopers, 2002) even when cost-effective alternatives are available. This is because the costs associated with expatriation are only one of several factors that are considered when approving international assignments (KPMG, 2004). Determining a return on investment is therefore necessary to justify the continued use of these assignments.

Despite the importance of obtaining a return on investment from long-term assignments, there are no published empirical studies examining expatriate ROI in the academic literature. Only two studies, both surveys by consulting companies, ask HR managers whether their companies estimate expatriate ROI and what HR practices may increase it (GMAC/NFTC/SHRM 2002; KPMG International, 2003). Furthermore, although some past studies have empirically examined the outcomes of some relevant individual HR activities associated with expatriation, including: (1) expatriates' premature return from the assignment (Tung, 1981, 1987), (2) labour turnover rates from repatriation (Stroh, 1995), and (3) expatriate job performance (Caligiuri, 1997), the nature and meaning of expatriate ROI still remains unclear. Past studies have investigated the link of only individual HR activities in relation to the costs and benefits of long-term assignments but not the system of HR activities that may influence it.

Based on the shortcomings of the literature, the purpose of this chapter is to address the following research questions: (1) *What is expatriate ROI and how can it be defined?* (2) *What are the antecedents of expatriate ROI in terms of the HR activities that would increase or decrease ROI?* In answering these research questions, the chapter develops hypotheses as it proceeds to guide future research.

## Developing a definition of expatriate ROI

Despite the importance of expatriate ROI, definitions of the term are difficult to obtain. We therefore borrow concepts and theoretical foundations from other disciplines for explanation.

## Definition of key terms

Return on investment is an accounting term. In its simplest form, Flamholtz (1985) defines ROI as a financial ratio that expresses profit in direct relation to investment. Schachner (1973) further defines ROI as a profitability equation that may be used to calculate past performance (for example, earnings) or future expectations (for example, profitability of a proposed investment). However, scholars in accounting and economic theory (Abdallah and Keller, 1985; Brief and Lawson, 1992; Laitinen, 2003; Spencer, 1999) have cast doubts on the appropriateness of using only traditional accounting methods in determining ROI, because accounting measures indicate only past or future *financial* performance (defined as lagging or leading indicators of financial profitability) to the exclusion of *non-financial* performance indicators.

In the economics literature, ROI is defined within the context of economic profit (EP) (Canibano, Garcia-Ayuso, and Sanchez, 2000; Mills, Rowbotham, and Robertson, 1998). EP combines a value-based approach to measure both past (lagging) and future (leading) returns by including *financial* and *non-financial* data in the ROI calculation. EP is most commonly used in the economic equations of *shareholder value analysis* (SVA) (Rappaport, 1981) and *economic value added* (EVA) (Stewart, 1991). Both SVA and EVA calculate ROI from the perspective of overall value, where value is defined in terms of both financial and non-financial gains and losses.

In terms of defining expatriate ROI from industry surveys, the GMAC (2001) survey concluded that, at that time, there was no universally understood definition of the term. In 2002 the same survey (2002: 55) defined expatriate ROI as the 'accomplishment of the assignment objectives at the expected cost'. Yet in the GMAC (2004) survey only 10 per cent of respondents agreed that they used this definition to measure the ROI of their international assignments. The definition is therefore considered inadequate in comparison to definitions given by scholars in related fields (Canibano et al., 2000; Mills et al., 1998). As Boudreau and Ramstad (1997) asserted, the definition of expatriate costs needs to be more fully explained in terms of both the financial and non-financial gains and losses associated with HR investments. A part of any definition of expatriate ROI is whether the benefit to the MNC outweighs the costs of the international assignment (Kobrin, 1988; Sheridan, 1998).

## The costs and benefits of long-term assignments

From the literature (Downes and Thomas, 1999; Dyer and Reeves, 1995; Kobrin, 1988), we conclude that developing a definition of expatriate

ROI needs to include an estimation of both the financial and non-financial costs and benefits of a specific assignment. In order to understand these costs and benefits, we adopt Williamson's (1985) transaction cost theory which focuses on the combination of: (1) transactions, (2) costs arising from transactions, and (3) the minimization of transaction costs through efficient control structures. We suggest that there are transaction costs arising over the life of the long-term assignment that may reduce ROI (Masten, Meehan, and Snyder, 1999).

With respect to non-financial costs and benefits, labour turnover during repatriation and poor cross-cultural adjustment can generate losses for an MNC. Yet, the non-financial benefits of long-term assignments can also be extensive. For example, Boyacigiller (2000) and Harzing (2001) concluded that an increase in organizational knowledge resulting from a greater knowledge of foreign markets, transfer of a firm's culture and capability, and the development of global managers were a benefit at the firm level. Downes and Thomas (1999) argued that the benefits of international assignments might be linked to a longer-term competitive advantage for MNCs, for example, by developing unique rare capacities through the international competencies of the top management team. This view is consistent with Barney's (1991) resource-based theory of the firm which emphasizes the importance of using employees as a source of competitive advantage to increase a firm's success (Lepak and Snell, 1999; Wright, Dunford, and Snell, 2001).

We therefore conclude that approaches to defining expatriate ROI should include a combination of financial and non-financial costs and benefits. We propose that expatriate return on investment be defined as a calculation in which the financial and non-financial benefits to the MNC are compared to the financial and non-financial costs of the international assignment, as appropriate to the assignment's purpose. We further propose that accurate rates of return are likely to be determined when the benefits are compared to the costs, irrespective of whether a cost is financial (for example, cross-cultural training) and the corresponding benefit is non-financial (for example, improved performance).

## The importance of the purpose of the long-term assignment

One of the themes of this chapter is the importance of calculating expatriate ROI within the context of the purpose of the long-term assignment. Given that MNCs differ greatly in terms of industry, organizational culture, and overall strategic objectives (Boyacigiller, 1990; Dyer and Reeves, 1995), they will have different reasons for using expatriates. Edstrom and Galbraith (1977, 1994) argued that MNCs have three major purposes for using expatriates: (1) to fill international positions when qualified locals are not available, (2) for management development, and (3) to help control, coordinate and assist in the transfer of a firm's culture. These purposes have been more recently validated by several industry surveys in which it was found that the top six reasons for using expatriates were to: (1) fill a skills gap, (2) build management expertise, (3) launch new endeavours, (4) transfer technology, (5) enable managerial control, and (6) transfer corporate culture (Cendant, 2002; GMAC et al., 2004). We therefore contend that if the purpose of a long-term assignment is to control, coordinate, and assist in the transfer of a firm's culture, then expatriates will be selected, trained and compensated differently than if the purpose of the assignment is mostly knowledge transfer. As a result, these

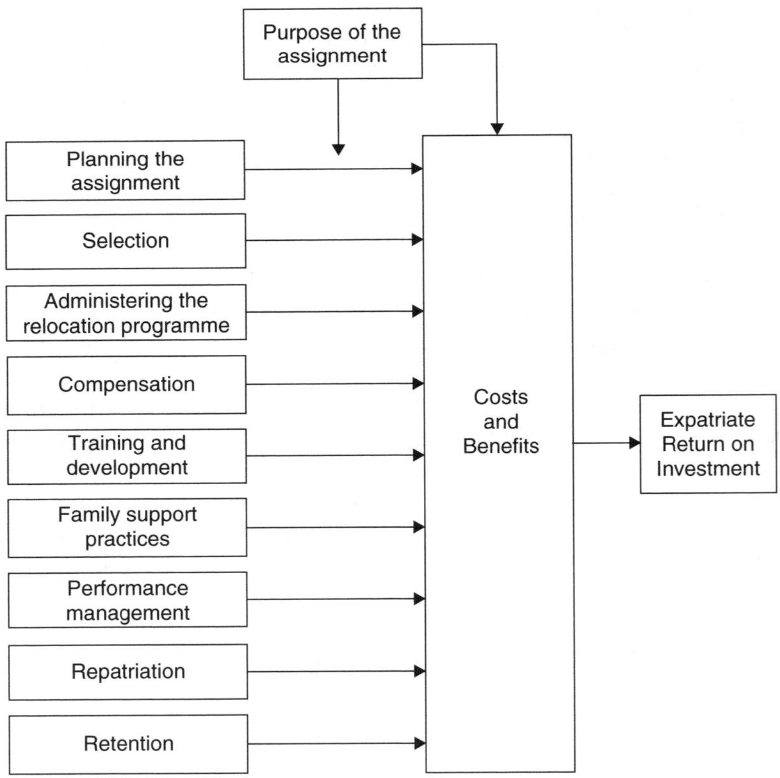


*Figure 2.1:* The system of human resource activities influencing expatriate ROI

differences will lead to varying rates of return from one assignment to the next, as the costs and benefits associated with each assignment's purpose are likely to be different.

## Justifying our definition of expatriate ROI

Overall, we make certain justifications for the definition of expatriate ROI we propose. First, as Kamoche (1997) argued, there should be no 'one best' ROI formula. An ROI calculation will differ from one assignment to the next because the objectives of each assignment are likely to be different. Consequently, these differences in assignment objectives reduce the usefulness of a 'one best' ROI formula that expects identical costs and benefits to be calculated for every assignment. A second justification is that expatriate ROI should be calculated at different times for each international assignment. This is because, as suggested by Bonache, Brewster, and Suutari (2001) and Stroh and Caligiuri (1998), the differences in assignment purpose will not only dictate what is included in the ROI calculation, but also the most appropriate time to do the calculation. For instance, the original purpose of an international assignment may not have included ensuring that the expatriate was repatriated home. Therefore, outcomes such as successfully finding a suitable position in the company for the expatriate upon return or an increase in labour turnover resulting from unsuccessful repatriation would not be included in the ROI calculation, and the calculation could be made as soon as the assignment is completed. Third, we assert that in order to avoid a misleading ROI calculation, a longer-term perspective with regard to an assignment's purpose is necessary. This is because many of the costs and benefits associated with long-term assignments are non-financial in nature and only appear at, or after, the conclusion of an assignment. As Mills and Print (1995) pointed out, accurate calculations of ROI are less likely to be made in the short-term if the long-term benefits cannot be identified in the period during which the calculation occurs.

## The antecedents of expatriate ROI: the system of human resource activities

In order to explore the antecedents of expatriate ROI in terms of HR activities, including the development of hypotheses for future testing, the first theoretical perspective to consider is *transaction cost theory* which examines, amongst other things, the influence of a system of activities taking place during all stages of a contract (Williamson, 1985; Williamson and Masten, 1999). The contract of interest for this chapter is the international assignment, which may be considered as a contract between the MNC and the expatriate. Essentially, transaction cost theory argues that contractual activities have the potential to influence costs and benefits to the firm both *ex ante* (that is, before execution of the contract) and *ex post* (that is, during execution of the contract) (Benito, Tomassen, Bonache-Perez, and Pla-Barber, 2003; Tan and Mahoney, 2003). That is, each contractual activity has the potential to increase or decrease the costs and benefits to the firm *at different times during the life of a contract.*

A second theoretical perspective to consider is *high performance work practices* (HPWP) (Becker, Huselid, Pickus, and Spratt, 1997; Huselid, 1995). HPWP are a group of HR activities which are viewed as a *system* of superior practices that can more fully explain costs and benefits to the firm than individual practices alone. Whereas we believe at this stage in the research it is premature to suggest that a group of HPWP can be developed to influence expatriate ROI, we do believe that approaching expatriate ROI from a systems perspective of HR activities would be an important step forward from the isolated perspectives used in previous studies (Caligiuri, 1997; Stroh, 1995; Tung, 1981, 1987). This is because a system of HR activities can more adequately explain what influences costs and benefits during a long-term assignment than individual activities alone; that is, a system of HR activities represents a group of interrelated practices in which one practice can potentially influence the costs or benefits to be derived from another. We therefore contend that a systems approach to expatriate ROI will enable increases and decreases in rates of return to be more accurately calculated, because, as noted by scholars, although isolated practices (for example, training and development) can improve the likelihood of assignment success, and therefore increase ROI, individual practices are less likely to be an effective substitute for the collective impact of many carefully planned HR activities operating at one time (Bennett, Aston, and Colquhoun, 2000; Farid and Buda, 1998; Huselid, 1995). Yet, empirical studies examining expatriate costs and benefits from a HR systems approach have not been done, therefore, the assumption requires testing in the following hypothesis:

> *Hypothesis 1. An expatriate ROI calculation that evaluates a system of HR activities during all stages of a long-term assignment will produce a more accurate rate of return than an expatriate ROI calculation that evaluates individual HR activities in isolation.*

Figure 2.1 illustrates our proposed system of HR activities and its hypothesized influence on overall expatriate ROI. It groups the system of HR activities occurring during all stages of a long-term assignment and connects the system to the expected costs and benefits from that assignment. The underlying concept is that the expected costs and benefits will be influenced by the system of HR activities and the purpose of the assignment. A calculation of those costs and benefits in turn will result in the ROI of the international assignment.

## The antecedents of expatriate ROI: human resource practices

There are nine major HR activities taking place during a long-term assignment that potentially affect the costs or benefits that may arise from expatriation and thus cause ROI to increase or decrease. The empirical studies, reviews, and surveys of HR activities that may increase or decrease expatriate ROI are classified and listed in Table 2.1.

### Planning the assignment

Scholars (Bonache et al., 2001; Dyer and Reeves, 1995) have suggested that if the purpose of an assignment has not been clearly identified, the assignment may not be able to provide clear benefits to the MNC and may result in unforeseen costs, including failure to achieve specific strategic goals (Torbiorn, 1994; Welch and Welch, 1997). Kamoche (1997) proposed that international assignments should meet clear business needs and have clear business goals in order to increase the benefits to the MNC, including improving the likelihood of assignment success. Hence, the following hypothesis is offered:

> *Hypothesis 2. Linking expatriation to careful planning of the purpose of an international assignment will increase benefits and reduce costs, and increase expatriate ROI.*

### Recruitment and selection of expatriates

Scholars have argued that few companies have adequate recruitment and selection practices to support their global staffing strategies (Harvey, 1996; Porter and Tansky, 1999), which can result in significant costs to MNCs due to not meeting the purpose of the assignment. For example, Tung (1981, 1982) concluded that selecting candidates who did not demonstrate relational abilities or failing to assess a spouse's ability to adapt to a foreign environment could lead to increases in poor performance and

*Table 2.1:* Empirical studies, reviews and surveys of HR activities that may increase or decrease expatriate ROI

| HR activity | Variable(s) influencing ROI | Study |
|---|---|---|
| Planning the assignment | Identifying the purpose of an assignment | Dyer and Reeves (1995)<br>Kamoche (1997)<br>Welch and Welch (1997) |
| Selection | Recruiting suitable candidate(s) | Farid and Buda (1998)<br>Porter and Tansky (1999) |
| Administering the relocation programme | Outsourcing expatriate administration | KPMG (2004)<br>SHRM (2004) |
| Compensation | Linking compensation to assignment objectives | Bonache and Fernandez (1997)<br>Fish and Wood (1996)<br>Gomez-Mejia (1993)<br>Gomez-Mejia and Welbourne (1991)<br>Harvey (1993)<br>Stone (1995) |
| Training and development | Customizing training and development to needs of assignment | Caligiuri, Phillips, Lazarova, Tarique, and Burgi (2001)<br>Eschbach, Parker, and Stoeberl (2001)<br>Shaffer and Harrison (1998)<br>Tung (1982)<br>Vance and Paik (2002) |
| Family support practices | Providing family support to increase assignment success | Black and Gregersen (1991)<br>Harvey (1985)<br>KPMG (2003)<br>Pricewaterhouse Coopers (2000)<br>Shaffer, Harrison, Gilley, and Luk (2001) |
| Performance management | Customizing appraisals according to the assignment's purpose | Gregersen, Hite, and Black (1996)<br>Hendry, Woodward, Bradley, and Perkins (2000)<br>Milliman, Nason, Zhu, and De Cieri (2002) |

(*Continued*)

*Table 2.1:* (*Continued*)

| HR activity | Variable(s) influencing ROI | Study |
|---|---|---|
| | Conducting appraisals during an assignment | Schuler, Fulkerson, and Dowling (1991)<br>Tahvanainen (2000) |
| Repatriation | Planning expatriate re-entry appropriate to an assignment's purpose | GMAC (2004)<br>Gregersen and Black (1995)<br>Lazarova and Caligiuri (2001) |
| Retention | Maintaining functional turnover and functional retention appropriate to an assignment's purpose | Black, Gregersen, and Mendenhall (1992)<br>McEvoy and Cascio (1987)<br>Stroh (1995) |

assignment failure, thereby increasing costs and reducing benefits. Hence, the following hypothesis is offered:

> *Hypothesis 3. Developing recruitment and selection practices that meet the assignment's planned objectives and which result in an appropriate expatriate being selected for the assignment's purpose will increase benefits and reduce costs, and increase expatriate ROI.*

### Administering the relocation programme

It is estimated that administering a relocation programme can cost approximately US$200,000 (Van Pelt and Wolniansky, 1990). To reduce some of these costs many MNCs outsource the administration of the relocation programme (for example, relocation of household goods) to independent specialists as a way to: (1) ensure greater cost savings, (2) gain access to vendor expertise the MNC could not otherwise provide, and (3) allow the MNC to focus on its core business (KPMG, 2004; GMAC/NFTC/SHRM 2002). However, whereas one survey (GMAC/NFTC/SHRM 2002) reported that 56 per cent of respondents used outsourcing to specifically save money and reduce operating costs, it also reported that less than 30 per cent chose to outsource employee relocation, and less than 10 per cent chose to outsource expatriate administration. In light of the above, to the authors' knowledge there has been no empirical work investigating the costs associated with administering either a relocation programme or its impact on ROI. Hence, the following hypothesis is offered:

> *Hypothesis 4. Outsourcing expatriate administration will allow HR staff to focus more on expatriate strategy which will increase benefits and decrease costs, and increase expatriate ROI.*

## Compensation

Expatriate compensation includes base salary, mobility premiums, and hardship allowances (Mercer, 2001) and is a financial cost in expatriation that influences ROI. To avoid some of these costs, many MNC's use standardized compensation packages because they are less costly to administer and control, and give the perception of equity amongst international assignees, thereby reducing the costs associated with unplanned labour turnover (Harvey, 1993; Stone, 1995). But scholars have argued that standardized compensation packages do not take into account differences in assignment objectives or cultural conditions, where expatriate compensation and reward systems are often a critical factor in motivating expatriates to not only accept assignments, but to also perform in difficult locations (Bonache and Fernandez, 1997; Gomez-Mejia and Welbourne, 1991).

Yet, the costs associated with compensation are often outweighed by the benefits, particularly when compensation is linked to the purpose of the assignment, which then result in improvement in organizational performance (Fish and Wood, 1996; Gomez-Mejia, 1993). Hence, the following hypothesis is offered:

> *Hypothesis 5. Linking expatriate compensation packages to facilitate meeting the purposes of the international assignment will increase benefits, and increase expatriate ROI.*

## Training and development

The training and development of expatriates involves cross-cultural preparation and language programmes appropriate to the assignment's location (Black and Gregersen, 1991; Forster, 2000), and represents a significant financial cost to MNCs in the initial stages of expatriation. In contrast to the costs, there are also significant benefits to be gained from training in terms of better performance and cultural adjustment (Eschbach, Parker, and Stoeberl, 2001; Tan and Mahoney, 2003). Shaffer and Harrison (2001) found that pre-departure training (particularly language training) had a positive impact on expatriate and spousal adjustment, which in turn led to improved performance. Some scholars have suggested that training and development programmes that are customized according to an expatriate's past international experience, the assignment's objectives, the intended location, and the needs of the relocating family, are likely to be more effective than generic training and development programmes (Bennett et al., 2000; Caligiuri et al., 2001; Tahvanainen, 2000; Vance and Paik, 2002). Hence, the following hypothesis is offered:

> *Hypothesis 6. Providing expatriates with training and development appropriate to the international assignment will increase benefits and reduce costs, and increase expatriate ROI.*

### Family support practices

Scholars have found that family support practices are often critical during expatriation in order to facilitate the achievement of an assignment's objectives (Caligiuri, 1997; Harvey, 1985; Shaffer et al., 2001; Tung, 1987), which in turn increases benefits and decreases costs. A number of industry surveys (GMAC/NFTC/SHRM 2002; KPMG International, 2003; PricewaterhouseCoopers, 2000) have reported that lack of family support, in terms of spousal adjustment and the dual-career issue, was the most common reason for assignment failure and increases in assignment costs. Black and Gregersen (1991) concluded that when MNCs failed to facilitate an expatriate spouse's general adjustment, increases in failed assignments were likely to occur. Hence, the following hypothesis is offered:

> *Hypothesis 7. Providing support to the expatriate family will increase the likelihood of assignment success which will increase benefits and reduce costs, and increase expatriate ROI.*

### Performance management

Performance management can influence expatriate ROI in two ways. First, it can decrease costs and increase ROI when it is conducted *during an assignment* by: (1) providing MNCs with the ability to assess whether the objectives of an assignment are likely to be met, (2) providing MNCs with an opportunity to address problems before they result in assignment failure, and (3) providing insights into the effectiveness of other HR activities, including training needs and the appropriateness of reward systems and compensation packages, that may be affecting performance (Brewster and Scullion, 1997; Schuler, Fulkerson, and Dowling, 1991; Tahvanainen,

2000). When MNCs are able to monitor their strategic progress *during the assignment* they are able to address issues before the achievement of an assignment's objectives are jeopardized.

Second, performance management can decrease costs and increase ROI when appraisals are *customized*, because customized appraisals can account for differences in an assignment's purpose and the different types of jobs being performed (Gregersen, Hite, and Black, 1996; Hendry, Woodward, Bradley, and Perkins, 2000; Milliman, Nason, Zhu, and De Cieri, 2002). The result is that MNCs will improve employee motivation because performance can be linked to incentive systems, such as compensation and promotion, that are appropriate to the job being performed and the location it is being performed in (Huselid, 1995). The following hypothesis is therefore offered:

> *Hypothesis 8. Customized performance management practices that are linked to an assignment's objectives and that are conducted during all stages of an assignment will increase benefits and reduce costs, and increase expatriate ROI.*

**Repatriation**

Successful repatriation is a potentially critical component in the ROI calculation for two reasons. First, repatriation can deliver considerable benefits to an MNC which, if lost, can significantly affect ROI. For example, scholars (Erdener and Torbiorn, 1999; Gregersen and Black, 1995; Lazarova and Caligiuri, 2001; Stroh, 1995) have argued that repatriated staff can improve strategic capabilities when their international knowledge and expertise is leveraged during repatriation. As a result, MNCs long-term strategic capabilities can be improved, and ROI can be expected to increase. Second, if the purpose of an assignment does not include a repatriation strategy, then any cost and benefit outcomes to be expected from repatriation (for example, the integration, or lack thereof, of intellectual knowledge gained from the assignment) are not likely to impact expatriate ROI. This is because if successful repatriation home is not part of an assignment's objectives, then the activity should not be included in the ROI calculation. To do so would be misleading in terms of the final ROI outcome.

This highlights the importance of context with regard to an assignment's purpose in terms of expatriate ROI; that is, not every HR activity is appropriate to every long-term assignment, nor should every HR activity be automatically included in the ROI calculation. The importance of context also highlights why customizing the ROI calculation for each assignment, rather than applying a standardized formula which expects identical costs and benefits to be calculated across the board, is essential. Consequently, careful consideration as to the inclusion, or exclusion, of repatriation is important to the expatriate ROI calculation. The following hypothesis is therefore offered:

> *Hypothesis 9. Planning and managing repatriation as appropriate to an assignment's purpose will increase benefits and decrease costs, and increase expatriate ROI.*

## Retention

Finally, when all is said and done, if a system of HR activities is perfectly managed yet an MNC is unable to retain the talent in which it has invested a considerable amount of time, money and effort, then ineffective retention practices can be a costly factor in the ROI calculation. For example, Stroh (1995) concluded that the turnover of expatriate staff after repatriation incurs an obvious cost to MNCs when the loss is *unexpected* and an MNC loses key employees considered pivotal to achieving its long-term strategic objectives. However, the unexpected turnover of expatriates *during* an assignment (for example, due to early withdrawals and premature returns) can be equally as costly (GMAC/NFTC/SHRM 2002; Shaffer and Harrison, 1998; Tung, 1988). All can impact returns on investment considerably.

To highlight the significance of retention and its potential impact on ROI, two factors with regard to costs must be considered. First, retention statistics must be interpreted correctly; that is, expatriate retention and the costs associated with it should be defined within the context of the risks associated with losing only *high* performers (Abelson and Baysinger, 1984; Black, Gregersen, and Mendenhall, 1992), whose retention is a specific objective of an international assignment. This is because when poor performers leave an organization, labour turnover may not always be unwelcome or as costly. As such, expatriate retention needs to be approached as a carefully managed combination of functional retention and functional turnover, in which high performers are retained and low performers are lost, as part of a larger strategic plan (Black et al., 1992; McEvoy and Cascio, 1987). Second, when an MNC unexpectedly loses key talent, and in particular those employees upon which it was intending to build the firm's international competencies, labour turnover in these circumstances can be devastating and very costly (O'Connor, 2002). Hence, the following hypothesis is offered:

> *Hypothesis 10. Maintaining functional retention and functional turnover of the expatriate as appropriate to an assignment's purpose will increase benefits and decrease costs, and increase expatriate ROI.*

## Discussion

We contend that expatriate ROI is a complex phenomenon requiring careful examination on many levels in order to produce a calculation that has a meaningful rate of return. Expatriate ROI can therefore be explained by four inter-related approaches. First, it must contain a summary of costs and benefits incurred during a long-term international assignment, and these costs and benefits must be defined both financially (for example, the cost of pre-departure training, processing of immigration documents, or the sales revenue of a particular business unit) and non-financially (for example, the development of global leadership talent, or the transfer of technical knowledge). Second, the costs and benefits of a long-term assignment must always be defined within the context of the purpose of the assignment itself. For example, if an assignment is designated as a one-way transfer for which no post-assignment job guarantees are offered, then the inclusion of any repatriation-related outcomes (such as labour turnover) is not relevant to the expatriate ROI calculation for that assignment. Third, the compilation of costs and benefits data must be approached from a systems perspective which avoids investigating only individual costs and benefits at one point in time (for example, training costs during pre-departure preparation) to the exclusion of a system of HR activities occurring during the entire assignment (for example, the combined effects of expatriate selection, remuneration, repatriation, and retention). Finally, expatriate ROI must be calculated at a time that is appropriate to meeting the assignment's objectives, for example, at the immediate conclusion of an assignment or at some point during repatriation. Determining when to calculate expatriate ROI depends upon the specific purpose of the assignment and requires that a long-term, rather than short-term, view be adopted. This is because costs incurred at the start of an assignment may not be able to be matched to a corresponding benefit until the completion of the assignment years later. The timing of the calculation therefore remains an important step that can help avoid a rate of return that is misleading or incorrect.

Given our explanation of what expatriate ROI is, we argue that expatriate ROI must therefore be defined as a calculation in which the financial and non-financial benefits to the MNC are compared to the financial and non-financial costs of the international assignment, as appropriate to the assignment's purpose. We further contend that accurate rates of return will only be achieved when the benefits are compared to the costs, irrespective of whether a cost is financial (for example, cross-cultural training) and the corresponding benefit is non-financial (for example, improved performance).

Our analysis of the literature thus far has highlighted that the importance of an expatriate ROI calculation is not just in determining the rate of return, but also in understanding why rates of return increase and decrease; that is, what are the antecedents of expatriate ROI? As we have acknowledged, the antecedents of expatriate ROI are, in fact, not new. Many of them have been identified in prior research (as outlined in Table 2.1) and include planning, selection, administering the relocation programme, training and development, compensation, family support, performance management, repatriation, and retention. Yet what is new is the way in which we propose these antecedents be incorporated into expatriate ROI calculations. Therefore, whereas we acknowledge that each individual antecedent has the potential to increase or decrease ROI on its own, as identified in prior research, we contend that understanding the inter-relationship of these antecedents with each other (from a systems perspective which we have adopted in this chapter) will produce a more accurate and useful ROI calculation in the long-term. We therefore believe that identifying and understanding these antecedents is a key step to undertaking ROI calculations because: (1) they can enable more appropriate and relevant costs and benefits data to be compiled for each assignment, thereby improving the accuracy of ROI calculations, and (2) they can give scholars and practitioners greater insight into, and the ability to manage, the HR activities occurring during an assignment that have the potential to affect ROI at the conclusion of an assignment. Of course, these antecedents must only be included in an ROI calculation if they can be linked to the purpose of an assignment (for example, repatriation-related outcomes) and if they occurred during an assignment (for example, labour turnover).

## Conclusion

We recommend that expatriate ROI requires a four-step approach: (1) identifying financial and non-financial costs and benefits; (2) linking the costs and benefits to the purpose of the long-term assignment; (3) identifying the appropriate antecedents from a systems perspective; and (4) conducting the calculation at an appropriate time within the context of the assignment's purpose.

Expatriate return on investment is undoubtedly an important topic, as evidenced by the considerable efforts of MNCs to find cost-reducing alternatives to long-term international assignments. Yet no empirical studies have investigated expatriate ROI. With this in mind, we have approached our initial investigation of this topic with thoroughness and caution in order to be absolutely certain that we have considered all possible explanations for understanding the phenomenon. We have adopted a multi-disciplinary perspective to assist in developing a sound theoretical foundation about what expatriate ROI really is, and we have argued and justified, through an extensive review of the academic literature, the relevant and important points that should help us to not only define expatriate ROI but also to understand its antecedents.

Yet it must be said that in this chapter we have proposed only one methodological approach to calculating expatriate ROI, which now requires testing. But there can be other approaches. We therefore encourage future research to use the approach proposed here as a starting point from which to refine our initial investigation and to extend the theoretical foundation. We also suggest that future research consider applying our approach to other types of assignments (for example, short-term assignments), including domestic relocations. In doing so we believe that scholars and practitioners alike will be better equipped to deal with not only the increasing demands of a more globalized workforce, but also the needs of HR managers who must continue to justify their international mobility programmes to senior management.

## References


Abdallah, W. M., and Keller, D. E. (1985) Measuring the multinational's performance, *Management Accounting*, 67: 26–30.

Abelson, M. A., and Baysinger, B. D. (1984) Optimal and dysfunctional turnover: toward an organizational level model, *Academy of Management Review*, 9: 331–41.

Barney, J. B. (1991) Firm resources and sustained competitive advantage, *Journal of Management*, 17: 99–120.

Becker, B. E., Huselid, M. A., Pickus, P. S. and Spratt, M. F. (1997) HR as a source of shareholder value: research and recommendations, *Human Resource Management*, 36: 39–47.

Benito, G. R., Tomassen, S., Bonache-Perez, J. and Pla-Barber, J. (2003) A transaction cost analysis of staffing decisions in international operations, Paper presented at the Nordic Workshop on Transaction Cost Economics in Business Administration, 20–21 June.

Bennett, R., Aston, A. and Colquhoun, T. (2000) Cross-cultural training: a critical step in ensuring the success of international assignments, *Human Resource Management*, 39: 239–50.

Black, J. S., and Gregersen, H. B. (1991) The other half of the picture: antecedents of spouse cross-cultural adjustment, *Journal of International Business Studies*, 22: 461–77.

Black, J. S., Gregersen, H. B., and Mendenhall, M. E. (1992) Toward a theoretical framework of repatriation adjustment, *Journal of International Business Studies*, 23: 737–58.

Black, J. S., Gregersen, H. B., Mendenhall, M. E. and Stroh, L. K. (1999) *Globalizing People Through International Assignments*, Reading, Mass: Addison-Wesley.
Bonache, J., and Fernandez, Z. (1997) Expatriate compensation and its link to the subsidiary strategic role: a theoretical analysis, *International Journal of Human Resource Management*, 8: 457–75.
Bonache, J., Brewster, C. and Suutari, V. (2001) Expatriation: a developing research agenda, *Thunderbird International Business Review*, 43: 3–20.
Boudreau, J. W., and Ramstad, P. M. (1997) Measuring intellectual capital: learning from financial history, *Human Resource Management*, 36: 343–56.
Boyacigiller, N. A. (1990) The role of expatriates in the management of interdependence, complexity and risk in multinational corporations, *Journal of International Business Studies*, 21: 1–11.
——. (2000) The international assignment reconsidered, In *Readings and Cases in International Human Resource Management*, ed. M. E. Mendenhall, and G. Oddou, 125–132. London: South-Western College Publishing.
Brewster, C., and Scullion, H. (1997) A review and agenda for expatriate HRM, *Human Resource Management Journal*, 7: 31–41.
Brief, R. P., and Lawson, R. A. (1992) The role of the accounting rate of return in financial statement analysis, *Accounting Review*, 67: 411–26.
Caligiuri, P. (1997). Assessing expatriate success: beyond just 'Being There', In *New Approaches to Employee Management*, ed. D. Saunders, and Z. Aycan, 117–40, Greenwich: Conn, JAI Press.
Caligiuri, P., Phillips, J., Lazarova, M., Tarique, I. and Burgi, P. (2001) The theory of met expectations applied to expatriate adjustment: the role of cross-cultural training, *International Journal of Human Resource Management*, 12: 357–72.
Canibano, L., Garcia-Ayuso, M. and Sanchez, P. (2000) Accounting for intangibles: a literature review, *Journal of Accounting Literature*, 19: 102–30.
Cendant (2001) *International Assignment Policies and Practices Survey: Asia Pacific*. Central, Hong Kong: Cendant International Assignment Services.
——. (2002) *Worldwide Benchmark Study: New Approaches To Global Mobility*. Bethesda, Md.: Cendant International Assignment Services.
——. (2004) *Emerging Trends in Global Mobility: the Assignee Perspective*. Danbury, Conn: Cendant Mobility.
Copeland, L., and Griggs, L. (1985) *Going International: How to Make Friends and Deal Effectively in the Global Marketplace*, New York: Random House.
Downes, M., and Thomas, A. S. (1999) Managing overseas assignments to build organizational knowledge, *Human Resource Planning*, 22: 33–44.
Dyer, L., and Reeves, T. (1995) Human resource strategies and firm performance: what do we know and where do we need to go? *International Journal of Human Resource Management*, 6: 656–70.
Edstrom, A., and Galbraith, J. R. (1977) Transfer of managers as a coordination and control strategy in multinational organizations, *Administrative Science Quarterly*, 22: 248–63.
——. (1994) Alternative policies for international transfers of managers, *Management International Review*, 1: 71–82.
Erdener, C. and Torbiorn, I. (1999) A transaction costs perspective on international staffing patterns: implications for firm performance, *Management International Review*, 39: 89–106.
Eschbach, D., Parker, G. and Stoeberl, P. (2001) American repatriate employees' retrospective assessments of the effects of cross-cultural training on their

adaptation to international assignments, *International Journal of Human Resource Management*, 12: 270–87.
Farid, M., and Buda, R. (1998) Enhancing the link between expatriate selection and success: organization commitment to global career development, *International Journal of Management*, 15: 516–24.
Fish, A., and Wood, J. (1996) A review of expatriate staffing practices in Australian business enterprises, *International Journal of Human Resource Management*, 7: 846–65.
Flamholtz, E. (1985) *Human Resource Accounting: Advances in Concepts, Methods and Applications*. San Francisco: Jossey-Bass.
Forster, N. (2000) Expatriates and the impact of cross-cultural training, *Human Resource Management Journal*, 10(3): 63–79.
GMAC Global Relocation Services, National Foreign Trade Council (NFTC), and SHRM Global Forum (2001) *Global Relocation Trends 2001 Survey Report*, New Jersey: GMAC Global Relocation Services.
——. (2002) *Global Relocation Trends 2002 Survey Report*, New Jersey: GMAC Global Relocation Services.
——. (2004) *Global Relocation Trends 2003/2004 Survey Report*, New Jersey: GMAC Global Relocation Services.
Gomez-Mejia, L. (1993) Compensation, organizational strategy, and firm performance, *Personnel Psychology*, 46: 196–205.
Gomez-Mejia, L., and Welbourne, T. (1991) Compensation strategies in a global context, *Human Resource Planning*, 14: 29–41.
Gregersen, H. B., and Black, J. S. (1995) Keeping high performers after international assignments: a key to global executive development, *Journal of International Management*, 1: 3–31.
Gregersen, H. B., Hite, J. and Black, J. S. (1996) Expatriate performance appraisal in U.S. multinational firms, *Journal of International Business Studies*, 27: 711–39.
Harvey, M. (1985) The executive family: an overlooked variable in international assignments, *Columbia Journal of World Business*, 20: 84–92.
——. (1993) Empirical evidence of recurring international compensation problems, *Journal of International Business Studies*, 24: 785–99.
——. (1996) The selection of managers for foreign assignments: a planning perspective, *Columbia Journal of World Business*, 31: 102–18.
Harzing, A.-W. (2001) Of bears, bumble-bees, and spiders: the role of expatriates in controlling foreign subsidiaries, *Journal of World Business*, 36: 366–79.
Hendry, C., Woodward, S., Bradley, P. and Perkins, S. (2000) Performance and rewards: cleaning out the stables, *Human Resource Management Journal*, 10: 46–62.
Huselid, M. A. (1995) The impact of human resource management practices on turnover, productivity, and corporate financial performance, *Academy of Management Journal*, 38: 635–72.
Kamoche, K. (1997). Knowledge creation and learning in international HRM, *International Journal of Human Resource Management*, 8: 213–25.
Kobrin, S. J. (1988) Expatriate reduction and strategic control in American multinational corporations, *Human Resource Management*, 27: 22–9.
KPMG (2003) *Global Assignment Policies and Practices Survey*, New York: KPMG.
——. (2004) *Global Assignment Policies and Practices Survey*, New York: KPMG.
Laitinen, E. K. (2003) Future-based management accounting: a new approach with survey evidence, *Critical Perspectives on Accounting*, 14: 293–323.

Lazarova, M., and Caligiuri, P. (2001) Retaining repatriates: the role of organizational support practices, *Journal of World Business*, 36: 389–401.
Lepak, D. P., and Snell, S. A. (1999) The human resource architecture: toward a theory of human capital allocation and development, *Academy of Management Review*, 24: 31–49.
Masten, S. E., Meehan, J. W. and Snyder, E. A. (1999) The costs of organization, In *The Economics of Transaction Costs*, ed. O. E. Williamson, and S. E. Masten, 256–80. Cheltenham: Edward Elgar.
McEvoy, G., and Cascio, W. (1987) Do good or poor performers leave? A meta-analysis of the relationship between performance and turnover, *Academy of Management Journal*, 30: 744–63.
Mercer Human Resource Consulting (2001) *International Assignments – A Survey of Premiums, Incentives and Company Practices*, New York: Mercer HRC.
——. (2003) *International Assignments Survey*, Switzerland: Mercer HRC.
Milliman, J., Nason, S., Zhu, C. and De Cieri, H. (2002) An exploratory assessment of the purposes of performance appraisals in North and Central America and the Pacific Rim, *Human Resource Management*, 41: 87–102.
Mills, R., and Print, C. (1995) Strategic value analysis, *Management Accounting*, 73: 35–7.
Mills, R., Rowbotham, S. and Robertson, J. (1998) Using economic profit in assessing business performance, *Management Accounting*, 76: 34–8.
O'Connor, R. (2002) Plug the expat knowledge drain, *HR Magazine*, 47: 101–07.
Organizational Resources Counselors (ORC) (2002) *Worldwide Survey of International Assignment Policies and Practices*, New York: ORC.
Porter, G., and Tansky, J. W. (1999). Expatriate success may depend on a 'learning orientation': considerations for selection and training, *Human Resource Management*, 38: 47–60.
PricewaterhouseCoopers (2000) *International Assignments: European Policy and Practice Key Trends 1999/2000*, London: PricewaterhouseCoopers.
——. (2001) *Managing a Virtual World: Key Trends 2000/2001*, London: PricewaterhouseCoopers.
——. (2002) *Managing Mobility Matters – A European Perspective*, London: PricewaterhouseCoopers.
Rappaport, A. (1981) Selecting strategies that create shareholder value, *Harvard Business Review*, 59: 139–49.
Schachner, L. (1973) Return on investment: its values, determination and uses, *CPA Journal*, 43: 277–81.
Schuler, R. S., Fulkerson, J. R., and Dowling, P. J. (1991) Strategic performance measurement and management in multinational corporations, *Human Resource Management*, 30: 365–93. From International assignments: work, non-work, and family influences, *Personnel Psychology*, 51: 87–118.
——. (2001) Forgotten partners of international assignments: development and test of a model of spouse adjustment, *Journal of Applied Psychology*, 86: 238–54.
Shaffer, M. A. and Harrison, D. A. (1998) Expatriates psychological withdrawal from international assignments: work, non-work and family influences, *Personnel Psychology*, 51: 87–118.
Shaffer, M. A., Harrison, D. A., Gilley, K. M. and Luk, D. M. (2001) Struggling for balance amid turbulence on international assignments: work/family conflict, support and commitment, *Journal of Management*, 27: 99–121.

Sheridan, W. R. (1998) Expatriates: moving from cost management to ROI, *ACA News*, 41: 6–7.

SHRM (2004) *Human Resource Outsourcing Survey Report*, Virginia: Society for Human Resource Management.

Spencer, S. (1999) Value-based international assignments, *Benefits and Compensation International*, 29: 36–41.

Stewart III, G. B. (1991) *The Quest For Value: a Guide For Senior Managers*, New York: HarperBusiness.

Stone, R. (1995) Expatriate remuneration practices: a survey of Australian multinationals, *International Journal of Management*, 12: 364–72.

Stroh, L. K. (1995) Predicting turnover among repatriates: can organizations affect retention rates? *International Journal of Human Resource Management* 6: 443–56.

Stroh, L. K., and Caligiuri, P. (1998) Increasing global competitiveness through effective people management, *Journal of World Business*, 33: 1–16.

Tahvanainen, M. (2000) Expatriate performance management: the case of Nokia Telecommunications, *Human Resource Management*, 39: 267–75.

Tan, D., and Mahoney, J. T. (2003) Explaining the utilization of managerial expatriates from the perspectives of resource-based, agency, and transaction costs theories, *Advances in International Management*, 15: 179–205.

Torbiorn, I. (1994) Operative and strategic use of expatriates in new organizations and market structures, *International Studies of Management and Organization*, 24: 5–17.

Tung, R. L. (1981) Selection and training of personnel for overseas assignments, *Columbia Journal of World Business*, 16: 68–78.

——. (1982) Selection and training procedures of US, European and Japanese multinationals, *California Management Review*, 25: 57–71.

——. (1987) Expatriate assignments: enhancing success and minimizing failure, *Academy of Management Executive*, 1: 117–26.

——. (1988) *The New Expatriates: Managing Human Resources Abroad*, Cambridge, Mass: Ballinger.

Van Pelt, P., and Wolniansky, N. (1990) The high cost of expatriation, *Management Review*, 79: 40–1.

Vance, C. M., and Paik, Y. (2002) One size fits all in expatriate pre-departure training? Comparing the host country voices of Mexican, Indonesian and US workers, *Journal of Management Development*, 21: 557–71.

Welch, D. E., and Welch, L. S. (1997) Pre-expatriation: the role of HR factors in the early stages of internationalization, *International Journal of Human Resource Management*, 8: 402–13.

Williamson, O. E. (1985) *The Economic Institutions of Capitalism*, New York: Free Press.

Williamson, O. E., and Masten, S. E. (1999) *The Economics of Transaction Costs*, Cheltenham: Edward Elgar.

Wright, P. M., Dunford, B. B., and Snell, S. A. (2001) Human resources and the resource based view of the firm, *Journal of Management*, 27: 701–22.

# 3

# The Use of Foreign Assignments and their Relationship with Economic Success and Business Strategy: a Comparative Analysis of Northern, Southern and Eastern European Countries

*Christiane Erten, Michael Schiffinger, Wolfgang Mayrhofer & Amanda Dunkel*

## Introduction

International assignments are an established part of human resource management (HRM). Usually labelled as expatriation, the management of expatriates and its various aspects is an essential part of international HRM practices. The literature dealing with the different aspects of expatriation flourishes. Examples include textbooks giving an introduction into this subject and defining it as a core element of international human resource management (e.g., Dowling & Welch, 2004), overall studies of expatriate management (e.g., Brewster, 1991) and global managers and leaders (e.g., Suutari, 2003; Mendenhall, Kühlmann & Stahl, 2000), theoretical and empirical analyses as well as practitioner oriented 'hands-on' recommendations in the areas of expatriation patterns (e.g., Mayrhofer, 2001), recruitment and selection (e.g., Guthrie, Ash & Stevens, 2003; Stone, 1991), preparing expatriates for their foreign assignment (e.g., Thomas & Hagemann, 1992; Mendenhall, Dunbar & Oddou, 1987), adaptation and acculturation processes (e.g., Ward, 1996; Black, Mendenhall & Oddou, 1991) or repatriation (e.g., Linehan & Mayrhofer, 2005; Stroh, Gregersen & Black, 1998). In addition, aspects such as the specific situation of MNCs and their handling of expatriation issues (e.g., Baruch & Altman, 2002; Bird & Mukuda, 1989), the situation of females at the global level (e.g.,

Taylor, Napier & Mayrhofer, 2002) or the role of expatriates in the process of internationalization (e.g., Bonache & Cervino, 1997) are discussed.

Despite this theoretical and practical establishment, international assignments as empirical phenomena undergo constant changes. A number of factors are responsible for this.

First, over the past decades, the amount of international business activities has constantly increased. For example, in Europe exports at current prices in the EU-15 countries more than doubled from 403.4 to 985.3 billion Euro between 1991 and 2001 (source: Eurostat Yearbook 2003, section 'International Trade'). Similar developments can be observed at a global level, too.

Second, 'new' forms of international assignments increasingly supplement or partly substitute 'traditional' patterns of expatriation. To be sure, a great number of organizations still use the latter for a number of reasons, especially to fill local know-how gaps, to provide a stronger link between the local unit and the headquarter, and for personnel development reasons (Mayrhofer, 1996). However, there is also a growing debate about the significance of expatriation beyond the 'traditional' form: This does not mean the international assignments will diminish in frequency – rather that their form will change. The development of international managers in the future will involve more frequent cross-border job swops, short assignments or assignments to multi-cultural project teams (Forster, 2000: 138). The reasons for this development are manifold. Core causes include a growing organizational cost consciousness leading to a reduction of expensive measures such as expatriation, resistance of individuals to relocate for longer periods of time due to dual career couple situations and quality of life concerns, better travel opportunities and communication links and different forms of career development such as rotation across several countries or regions (Evans, Pucik & Barsoux, 2002: 119).

Third, the developments within the European Union (EU) and the two steps of enlargement in 1995 and 2005 have opened up new possibilities for business activities across borders. The introduction of the common market and the efforts of the EU to reduce barriers between its member states leading to the four major freedoms – flow of people, goods/services, capital, and entrepreneurship – have widened the scope for economic activities. In turn, this has increased the number of organizations that undertake cross-border business transactions. Especially small companies relying on personalized control mechanisms and companies in early stages of the internationalization process (for a general view on the internationalization process see Jones & Coviello, 2005; Perlmutter, 1969) rely on people sent abroad as representatives of the core business, often in the 'classical' form of expatriation. Thus, the new population of companies in international business increase the use of expatriation.

Fourth, European countries and regions differ in their degree of internationalization. Due to the structure of their industries, their local markets and their economic, social and political history and conditions, the number of companies doing business across borders differs markedly. Traditionally, there is a north–south difference in terms of internationalization with the north of Europe being more involved in cross-border business transactions. Prominent Scandinavian multi-national corporations (MNCs) such as Nokia (Finland), ABB (Sweden) or Carlsberg (Denmark) as well as other global players from the Northern part of Europe such as BP (Great Britain), Unilever (Great Britain/Netherlands) or Bertelsmann (Germany) with their global operations are prominent parts of the tip of the iceberg. Especially interesting is the case of Central and Eastern European countries belonging to the block of former communist countries radically transformed in the early 1990s. Their rapid transformation from central planning to a market economy with all the social and economic problems and achievements makes them a special group within Europe. Among others, the companies in these countries also seem to develop their own path of internationalization. In the early years of transformation, they were mainly the target of foreign direct investment (FDI). Investment incentives by local governments and authorities as well as cheap labour were major attractors for foreign companies. In due course, however, companies from these countries themselves have begun to expand and increase their foreign operations within Europe and beyond.

International assignments are not only constantly changing and developing, they are also embedded into the specific organizational context. Expatriation usually is an integral part of an overall HR configuration that balances various elements of HR. In addition, in profit-oriented companies expatriation has to be balanced against economic performance considerations. Regarding the former, HR practices vary systematically across European countries. Evidence suggests that in terms of culture European countries can be grouped into different cultural clusters (see, e.g., Trompenaars, 1994; Hofstede, 1980). Beyond that, systematic differences in terms of approaches to HRM exist (see, e.g., Filella, 1991; Brewster & Larsen, 2000; Brewster, Larsen & Mayrhofer, 1997). The economic aspect of expatriation becomes increasingly important because of the strong economic pressures that companies face. This has at least two effects. First, the costs of expatriation are under close scrutiny because of its relative size and the constant search for cost reduction opportunities. Second, and maybe more important, the costs have to be weighed against potential benefits. On the one hand, this affects the immediate consequences of the expatriation in terms of goals set. On the other hand, and at a broader level, this targets the contributions that foreign assignments can make to the overall organizational performance.

Given this situation, this chapter will address three intertwined issues: the frequency of use of international experience schemes (IES) for managers in for-profit-organizations in selected European country clusters, the development of the use of such IES over the past years and the relationship between the use of IES and organizational performance. By addressing these three issues, this chapter tries to reflect core developments in expatriation outlined above. In particular, it adopts a comparative angle and includes the specific situation of Eastern European countries.

## International assignments

This section identifies major developments in international assignments as well as specifics of the European situation and their consequences for international assignments.

### Major developments

There is little evidence of international assignments declining in number and importance. Due to an increase in cross-border business activities and the advantages of an internationally minded workforce, sending people abroad still is 'standard practice' in many companies operating across national borders. Traditionally, such assignments on average last between 2–5 years, are long-term and labelled as expatriation. Usually a combination of three major reasons triggers expatriate assignments (see, e.g., Mayrhofer, 1996; Harris, Brewster & Erten, 2005). First, there can be local skill shortages and know-how gaps. People from abroad, often from headquarters or a global competence centre, are used to solve such deficits. Second, by sending people abroad central units can aim at controlling a local unit. Such personalized control mechanisms can be used instead of or in addition to other forms of controlling and coordinating mechanisms such as, for examples, budgets and reports. Third, expatriation can be used as part of systematic personnel development activities. Through a foreign assignment people can develop their technical and personal competencies.

The comparatively well developed expatriation literature (for a general overview see, e.g., Brewster, 1991; Black, Gregersen & Mendenhall, 1992; Suutari, 2003) has analysed various aspects of going abroad at the individual and organizational level. Its implicit point of reference is the 'traditional' foreign assignment, i.e., expatriation, with its basic pattern of 'selection-training-assignment-return' within a 2–5 years period. However, recent empirical evidence suggests a changing picture: 'traditional' expatriation is supplemented and, possibly, partly replaced by other forms of international assignments.

'Traditional' expatriation has a number of problematic characteristics. Most prominently, heavy financial costs for the company, the strong impact on personal lives of employees, the problems linked with recruitment and selection of employees and their reintegration after repatriating them, and the problems of integrating expatriates into the local environment and workforce can be mentioned. For example, studies report companies' negative experiences with shortcomings in the selection of these persons, improper preparation of them, and consequential language and mentality problems of expatriates (Mayrhofer & Scullion, 2002) as well as impaired relations with corporate headquarters (Stahl, 2000). Hence, it is not surprising that Harris et al. (2005) conclude that organizations by and large are not managing the mix of the various forms of international working strategically, that they have very little control over the costs and almost no idea about how to measure the benefits of the different types of foreign assignments (Harris, Brewster & Erten, 2005: 287).

Given these difficulties, it is understandable that organizations and individuals are actively searching for alternatives to 'traditional' expatriation. In particular, two developments have supported the exploration of alternative approaches.

First, the rapid progression in the field of technological developments such as the increasing use of e-mail, telephone/video conferencing and real-time computer information from around the world has made contact and coordination between employees and units all around the globe much easier. In addition, the improvement of travel possibilities increasingly offer the possibility for frequent short-term visits as alternatives to the traditional form of long-term expatriation (Scullion & Brewster, 2001).

Second, the increasing importance of diverse forms of organization also has effects for the type of foreign assignment chosen. Project-dominated organizational forms can serve as an example: There are consultants specializing in different world regions who can even take the lead, for example, in the establishment of subsidiaries in a particular country. Thus, such a project is executed by specialists who are not even part of the company itself. The parent company only supervises this process by frequent visits to the operation site (Harris, 2000). Another example relates to merging companies from different countries which sometimes have no need to set up own operations in foreign countries. They are already well established through their new partners (Scullion & Brewster, 2001: 349). Thus, managerial control as one of the three most predominant reasons for long-term assignments might become obsolete or clearly less important for them. A final example aims at changing staffing strategies. Instead of 'importing' people from other countries, local positions are filled with local people. For example, a study conducted in Austrian export-oriented companies reveals that representative offices are increasingly staffed by host country nationals (Erten-Buch & Strunk, 2000).

Given these developments, a number of alternatives to classical expatriation have gained importance within international assignments over the past years. 'Quasi-expatriation' such as international commuting, frequent travelling or short-term assignments has begun to establish itself as a legitimate and frequently used form of international assignments (for a more detailed view on this see Harris, Brewster & Erten, 2005).

Evidence from case studies conducted in the German (Mayrhofer & Scullion, 2002) and in the Spanish clothing industry (Bonache & Cervino, 1997) gives interesting examples of industries operating successfully with a large number of 'quasi-expatriates'. An ongoing study of new forms of international working carried out among 65 MNCs by the Centre for Research into the Management of Expatriation (CReME), based at the UK's Cranfield School of Management, and Organization Resources Counsellors (ORC) Inc., reveals more supporting results. Compared to the traditional long-term assignments, a higher increase can be observed in the proportion of short-term assignments (67%), and international commuter assignments as well as frequent flyer assignments (52%) in the companies investigated (Harris, 2000). The reasons for this development are complex. People seem increasingly less willing to move their families or disrupt their spouse's career (Harris, 2000). This goes hand in hand with companies failing to provide an adequate framework for their expatriation processes, e.g., not integrating the partners in the decision making processes or failing to support their job search. In addition, there is a tendency for career oriented persons to remain near headquarters for fear of being bypassed by those closer to the organizational power centres and because of poor career planning (Stahl, 2000) and the neglect of relationships between headquarters and subsidiaries (Scullion & Brewster, 2001: 352). In turn, this reduces the organizational pool for foreign assignments. This illustrates that the value a company puts on international experience and its effective management of repatriation (Peltonen, 1997) is critical to its ability to attract, keep, and motivate the 'right' people for their management pool.

These alternative forms of international assignments do overcome some of the problems linked with 'traditional' expatriations. However, new problems emerge. For example, international commuters often encounter problems handling cultural differences, perhaps partly because of an understandable lack of commitment to the host country. In a similar vein, frequent flyers often have to cope with problems of 'burnout' (Harris, Brewster & Erten, 2005: 283).

## Specifics of the European situation and their consequences

Most of the expatriation literature is general or assumes a US context only. Only a small number of researchers focus on the European context (e.g., Scullion, 1992; Brewster & Mayrhofer, 1996; Suutari & Brewster, 1998; Suutari & Brewster, 1999; Scullion & Brewster, 2001; Linehan & Scullion, 2002). However, there are a number of European specifics that influence international assignments in Europe. These specifics do not only come from the specific make up of the continent with its area of 9,839 mill. square kilometres (the US: roughly the same area, i.e. 9,809 mill. square kilometres), roughly 800 mill. inhabitants (the US: less than half, approximately 295 mill.), 45 nation states and more than 70 languages. Historic, cultural, economic and institutional factors contribute to an arguably unique mixture of unifying and dividing elements.

Historically, a long and often belligerent relationship between European countries created a tradition of tension and rivalry. This does include large European states like the UK, France, Spain, Germany or Italy as well as tensions and war-like conflicts between smaller European states or ethnic groups. Culturally, major studies grouping countries according to basic cultural dimensions find great differences within Europe (see, e.g., Hofstede, 1980; Trompenaars, 1994). Findings indicate that various cultural clusters such as a Nordic, an Anglo-Saxon, a Romanic and a Germanic cluster with deeply rooted cultural differences at the level of values/norms and basic assumptions can be identified. Economically, large differences at the country and individual level exist. Rich countries with a comparatively high GDP such as Germany (2,712.3 billion dollars) or the UK (1,402.6) or Italy (1,240.6) are in clear contrast to countries comparable in terms of population with only a fraction of these values such as Turkey (215.1) or Poland (179.9), not to mention smaller countries such as the Slovak Republic with 26.2 billion dollars (source: OECD main economic indicators, Feb. 2004; all figures for 2003). At the individual level and concerning per capita income, a similar situation exists. On the one hand, countries such as Luxembourg, Norway,

Switzerland, Denmark, Iceland, Austria, Ireland and the Netherlands have a purchasing power parity ranging from 27,470 (the Netherlands) to 51,060 (Luxembourg) international dollars.[1] On the other hand, countries such as Albania (4,040), the Ukraine (4,650), Romania (6,290) and also countries that recently entered the European Union such as Latvia (8,940) or Poland (10,130) are much worse off (source: World Development Indicators Database, World Bank, July 2003). Institutionally, great heterogeneity exists. For example, European countries have a great variety of differences in labour related regulations and institutions such as protection of employees, the degree of regulation of the world of work or type of industrial relations and the role of trade unions and employers' associations.

The European Union has partly changed this picture, creating a more unified context for organizations to operate in (Brewster, 1995). Nevertheless, national institutions and individual countries still play an important role. Such a situation also has a number of consequences for international assignments in the European context.

First, international assignments do not necessarily demand to cover large geographic distances or a transition into a culturally unknown territory. For example, from Vienna you can reach nearly all major European cities within three hours flight time. Despite cultural differences, many Europeans have ample experience with visiting other European countries. Among others, such a situation makes 'traditional' expatriation in general easier (for a more detailed discussion see Brewster & Mayrhofer, 1996). In addition, it also encourages other forms of international assignments since commuting, frequent travelling or short-term assignments are feasible with comparatively little cost. Many internationally operating companies make use of such arrangements in the European setting. For example, the head of HR of OMV, an Austrian oil company that recently acquired Petrom, the major Romanian oil company, divided his working week between Vienna and several sites in Romania during the first time after the acquisition.

Second, the large differences in economic development lead to different routes and stages of internationalization. More than 30 years ago, Perlmutter described different basic options in the process of internationalization (Perlmutter, 1969), differentiating between ethnocentric, polycentric and regiocentric approaches. During the early stages of internationalization, an ethnocentric style seems to be more appropriate. For international assignments this primarily means the use of 'traditional' expatriation, i.e., sending people from headquarters to local subsidiaries. In later stages, other forms are also appropriate, which include avoiding international assignments by filling positions locally. Economically, especially the Eastern European countries can be expected to be in a different situation from the rest of Europe. Due to their heritage of former political frameworks in the Eastern European countries (e.g. Pawlowsky & Wilkens, 2001; van Brabant, 1999) as well as the transformation processes, the typical economic developments of Eastern countries took place later and in different forms. In addition, cultural differences can contribute to a different pace of development in some countries.

Third, the growing number of SMEs at the threshold of internationalization influences international assignments. SMEs' market entry strategies are, at the most, only partly covered and explained by theories of internationalization developed from research in large MNCs (Scullion, 1999). Although their size and stage of internationalization would point towards more traditional forms of international assignment, they often can hardly afford expatriation either in terms of money or in terms of personnel and know-how.

## Core questions and hypotheses

Given these general developments in international assignments and the European specifics and their consequences, this chapter empirically analyses international assignments for managers in European companies and addresses three core questions.

First, we look at the number of international assignments in European companies. Specifically, we ask: How frequent is the use of international experience schemes (IES) for managers in for profit-organizations in selected European countries, i.e. Northern European, Southern European and Eastern European countries? Here our main interest is the difference between Eastern European countries on the one hand and the other two country clusters. Hence, our first hypothesis:

> *H1: International experience schemes for managers are more frequently used in for-profit organizations in Northern European and Southern European countries than in Eastern European countries.*

We argue that companies in different regions are at different stages of internationalization. Eastern European countries are delayed due to the transformation process and the specific routes of internationalization they take (e.g., Markoczy, 1994: 5) In addition, a north–south gap of internationalization exists. However, the differences between Northern and Southern Europe combined and Eastern Europe are presumably more important than between Northern and Southern Europe.

Second, we take a more dynamic perspective and look at developments over time: How has the use of these schemes developed in Northern and Southern European countries over the past 10 years and how do these developments compare to the developments in Eastern European countries? Our main interest here is to analyse whether the increasing internationalization in terms of business activities has left its traces in the use of IES in the 1990s. Again, the situation in Eastern European countries is compared to the developments in the Northern and Southern European cluster. This leads to our second hypothesis:

> *H2: Over the past 10 years, the use of international experience schemes for managers has increased in Eastern European countries, but decreased in Northern European and Southern European countries.*

As Perlmutter (Perlmutter, 1969) and later Heenan/Perlmutter (Heenan & Perlmutter, 1979) have pointed out, companies at a more advanced stage of internationalization tend to favour a 'polycentric staffing approach' using increasingly locals instead of people from 'foreign' countries. Such a stage should apply, by and large, to companies in Northern and Southern Europe. In contrast, companies based in Eastern Europe should be more frequently being in an early stage of internationalization. On a more micro level we find that companies increasingly consider expatriates as the most expensive employees; cost cutting, dual-career couples concerns and a growing importance of quality of life lead to a growing resistance towards international assignments among part of the high potentials. Both developments point into the direction of a reduced number of international assignments in Northern and Southern European countries.

Third, we analyse the relationship between the use of international experience schemes and organizational outcome criteria: In which way does the use of international experience schemes relate to various criteria of company success and is there any evidence that international experience schemes are linked with specific types of business strategies? Regarding expatriation as a success factor of companies, we assume that the extensive use of international experience schemes is in some way related to better performance values of companies compared to others that do not use IES. This leads to our third hypothesis:

> *H3a: Companies using international experience schemes achieve better performance values than those which do not.*
> *H3b: Companies using international experience schemes have a business strategy that emphasises quality-related performance measures.*

While the discussion about the direction of causality between various HR activities and organizational performance is not yet decided, there is substantial evidence that under specific circumstances a link between HR and organizational performance exists (for an overview of the HR-performance debate see, e.g., Bowen & Ostroff, 2004; Gelade & Ivery, 2003; Wright, Gardner & Moynihan, 2003; Fey & Bjorkman, 2001; Huselid, Jackson & Schuler, 1997). In the current business environment with its various opportunities at an international scale, the use of international experience schemes allows companies to better exploit these opportunities.

## Data source and methods of analysis

The data used for our analysis has been generated by the Cranfield Network on Human Resource Management (Cranet), a research network established in 1989. Today it consists of 23 European and 12 non-European countries and has more than 25,000 organizations with more than 200 employees in its database built during five major survey rounds. The network is dedicated to analysing developments in the area of HRM in public and private organizations with more than 200 employees in a national, cross-national and quasi-longitudinal way (see Brewster & Hegewisch, 1994; Brewster, Mayrhofer & Morley, 2000; Brewster, Mayrhofer & Morley, 2004). Through the Cranet survey a national sample of organizations with more than 200 employees is questioned on a regular basis on various aspects of HRM via questionnaires. The two most important objectives of this international, comparative survey were, at the outset: (1) to research whether a pattern of 'Europeanization', i.e. convergence to a common pattern could be found over time, and (2) to identify whether changes in personnel policies towards a more strategic approach ('strategic HRM') have occurred. 'Thus, the general objective was to extend the range of internationally comparable evidence about particular policies

*Table 3.1:* Countries included and year of survey

| | 1992 | 1995 | 2000 |
|---|---|---|---|
| 1. Sweden | • | • | • |
| 2. Denmark | • | • | • |
| 3. Norway | • | • | • |
| 4. Finland | • | • | • |
| 5. Greece | • | | • |
| 6. Portugal | • | | • |
| 7. Turkey | • | • | • |
| 8. Spain | • | • | • |
| 9. Czech Republic | • | | • |
| 10. Bulgaria | | | • |

and practices that have been seen as relevant to the concept of HRM' (Brewster, Tregaskis, Hegewisch & Mayne, 1996: 593).

The database used for this analysis includes nine European countries where we have at least two measurement points in time during the five major European survey rounds between 1992 and 2000 (see Table 3.1), and Bulgaria with one measurement point. Furthermore, the analysis is restricted to private sector for-profit organizations with more than 200 employees. Thus, overall more than 1,000 companies were included in this analysis. For the following analyses the countries are split into three country clusters:

- Northern European cluster consisting of Denmark, Norway, Sweden, and Finland.
- Southern European cluster consisting of Spain, Portugal, Greece, and Turkey.
- Eastern European cluster consisting of the Czech Republic and Bulgaria.

## Scales and methods

The Cranet questionnaire contains a question about the regular use of international experience schemes: 'Do you regularly use any of the following . . . ?' Among the six options is 'International experience schemes for managers'. In the 1992 and 2000 surveys, the question could be answered with yes or no; in the 1995 survey there was only a checkbox for 'yes'.

In 2000, economic performance was measured by a rating of the company by the respondents on the following criteria: (1: top 10%, 2: upper half, 3: lower half):

- Service quality
- Productivity

- Profitability
- Product to market time
- Rate of innovation
- Stock market performance.

Furthermore, respondents were asked to rate the following criteria of their core products/services according to their perceived importance for the company's business (1: very important, 2: somewhat important, 3: not important):

- Price
- Quality
- Product variety, customization
- Service (availability, delivery time)
- Innovation.

The use of IES and possible differences between the country clusters and/or the development over time is analysed by frequency tables and Chi-square or Fisher tests. Differences in performance between companies that reported using IES and those that did not are tested via a Mann-Whitney U-Test.

## Results and discussion

This section presents the hypotheses, the statistical analysis as well as the results related to the three main research questions that have been described above.

### Hypothesis 1

The first hypothesis assumes that international experience schemes for managers are more frequently used in companies located in Northern European and Southern European countries than in Eastern European countries. Table 3.2 shows the respective proportions of companies using international experience schemes (IES) as of 2000. About one-third of the observed companies in Northern and Southern Europe but only about one-fourth of the companies in Eastern Europe regularly use IES. The difference between the proportion of companies that reported using IES for Northern and Southern Europe combined and the percentage for Eastern Europe (based on valid cases) is also statistically significant at the 5%-level (Fisher test, one-tailed). Therefore, H1 is supported by the data.

*Table 3.2:* Use of IES in the Northern, Southern, and Eastern European cluster

| Country cluster (incl. respective number of valid responses/total respondents) | Number of companies reporting use of IES* |
|---|---|
| Northern Europe; n = 443 (553) | 158 (35.7%) |
| Southern Europe; n = 458 (576) | 168 (36.7%) |
| Eastern Europe; n = 123 (148) | 34 (27.6%) |

* Percentages are based on the number of valid responses. The respective proportions of the total number of respondents are 28.6% (Northern Europe), 29.2% (Southern Europe), and 23% (Eastern Europe) (see also Figure 3.1; the small deviation for Eastern Europe is due to the exclusion of Bulgaria mentioned in the text).

## Hypothesis 2

Our second hypothesis postulated that over the past 10 years the use of international experience schemes for managers has increased in Eastern European countries, but decreased in Northern European and Southern European countries. In order to examine the development of the use of IES throughout our country clusters data had been taken from three survey rounds (1992, 1995, 2000) conducted by Cranet. Before presenting the results, some caveats have to be mentioned. First, Bulgaria could not be included into the analysis, as data from this country were only available for 2000. Second, the 'Southern European' cluster only contains Spain and Turkey for 1995, so these results should be taken with caution. Third, the number of participating companies varies considerably between the three survey years. Furthermore, the data for 1995 do not allow to differentiate between respondents who answered the question concerning IES with no and those who left it blank. Therefore, unlike for hypothesis 1, the percentages here are based on the total number of respondents.

Figure 3.1 shows the results. First, the collected data show a remarkable slump in the use of IES in 1995 in all three clusters, least so in Southern Europe. Second, between 1992 and 2000, the proportion of companies that report using IES has risen in all three clusters, although the difference between those years is only significant in the Northern European cluster (as marked by the thicker lines in Figure 3.1; all differences were tested using the Fisher test, two-tailed, $\alpha = 0.05$). The increase has therefore been most remarkable in Northern Europe (where IES were least used in 1992). In Southern Europe, the percentage of companies using IES is consistently highest and least affected by the 1995 slump. Eastern Europe is in between as far as both percentage rates and development (1995

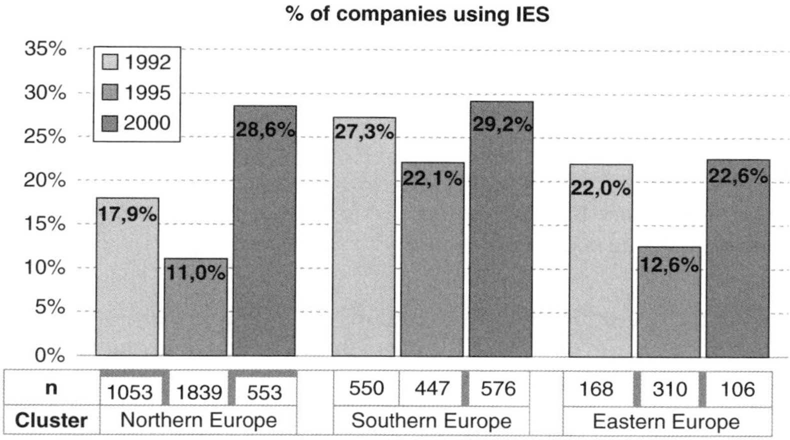


*Figure 3.1:* Development of use of IES in the Northern, Southern, and Eastern European clusters

decline) are concerned, but currently has the lowest share of companies that report using IES. In Eastern Europe, only the 1992 vs. 1995 difference and the 1995 vs. 2000 difference were significant; in Southern Europe it was just the 1995 vs. 2000 difference (illustrated again by thicker lines). We therefore have to state that hypothesis 2 is clearly not supported by the data.

The picture given by our empirical results is unexpected and interesting. In line with our arguments we find that in 1995 (with the exception of Southern Europe) and 2000 less Eastern European companies use IES than in the two other clusters. In the beginning of the nineties, shortly after the opening of the Eastern Bloc, this has not been the case. We may assume – but of course this has to be examined further – that during this phase, being the very initial phase of internationalization of the Eastern European companies, the use of IES was especially important. In the following years we find a comparatively lower level of use of IES in these countries in line with the hypothesis.

As for the steady increase within the two other country clusters we can see that despite all problems and negative experiences on both sides, the side of the company as well as on the side of the expatriates, the need for IES in our global economy is evident. This again shows that the effective management of international employees is a major determinant of success or failure in international business.

### Hypothesis 3

The third hypothesis states that companies using international experience schemes achieve better performance values than those which do not and have a business strategy that emphasizes quality-related performance measures.

> *H3: Companies that use IES achieve better performance values than those which do not.*

The Cranet questionnaire also contains self-reported data on various economic performance values. Although one might question the reliability of these self-report ratings, there is considerable evidence that there is a sufficiently strong link between subjective and objective measures of company performance (see the overview in Wall et al., 2004).

Table 3.3 indicates the respective median values calculated for grouped data[2] for companies that report using IES in 2000 vs. those that report not using IES. The differences are tested for significance using a U-Test, the results of which are also presented in the table.

It is apparent that those companies reporting the use of IES also report better performance measures compared to their counterparts without regular use of IES. For the whole sample, this is the case for all performance indicators. The results remain stable when controlling for company size. These results are quite clearly in accordance with H3.

The picture largely remains the same when analysing the clusters separately. In all clusters and for all performance measures, the companies using IES report better performance indicators on average, except for service quality in the Northern European cluster. In the Southern European cluster, all observed differences in performance ratings are statistically significant. In the Northern European cluster, significant differences emerge only for rate of innovation and stock market performance. In Eastern Europe, the opposite is the case: significant differences are found for all performance measures except these two.

Although these results are quite clear-cut, they invite us to investigate possible reasons for these differences. The assumption that the use of IES (which is just a minor aspect of a more comprehensive business strategy) is directly linked to economic performance measures is probably hard to argue. Instead we try to identify a typology of fundamental business strategy decisions (being best vs. being cheapest) and to investigate whether the use of IES might be part of such a 'general strategy' that may in turn be linked to business performance.

*Table 3.3:* Use of IES and performance ratings (lower values mean better ratings, see methods section)

| **Use of IES** | | **Service quality** | **Productivity** | **Profitability** | **Product to market time** | **Rate of innovation** | **Stock market performance** |
|---|---|---|---|---|---|---|---|
| no | median | 1.50 | 1.73 | 1.82 | 1.89 | 1.83 | 1.87 |
| | n | 606 | 592 | 588 | 511 | 529 | 292 |
| yes | median | 1.39 | 1.56 | 1.64 | 1.74 | 1.62 | 1.65 |
| | n | 337 | 328 | 322 | 293 | 310 | 173 |
| | U-Test | ** | ** | ** | ** | ** | ** |

** $p < 0.01$ (one-tailed).

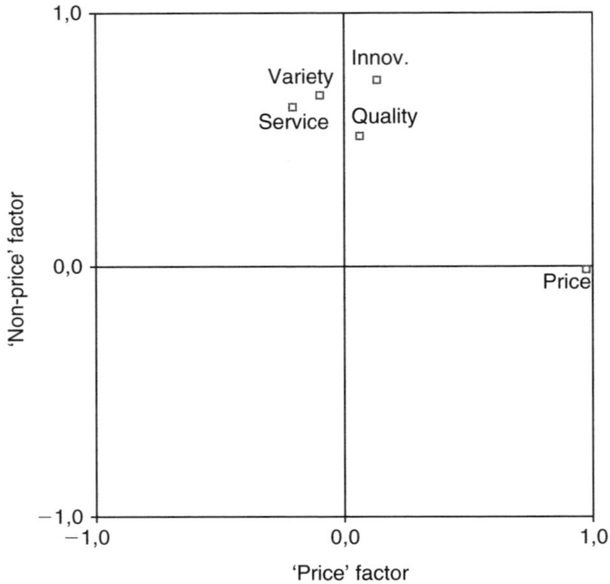


*Figure 3.2:* Two-factor solution plot (rotated) for the core criteria

In a first step, the criteria that are rated according to their importance for the core business (price, quality, product variety, customization, service (availability, delivery time), innovation; see methods section) are analysed with regard to their underlying structure. A principal components analysis of these five items results in a very clear-cut two-factor solution, with one factor being formed by price alone, while the other one unites all other criteria ('non-price' or 'quality' criteria). Figure 3.2 shows the factor loadings for the Varimax-rotated two-factor solution.

Although this result implies that price and the 'quality' (i.e., non-price) criteria form two independent dimensions and are not two ends of a one-dimensional continuum, in practice a company will probably have to focus on either 'being best' or 'being cheapest', at least to some extent.

But how are these two factors related to economic performance? In general, the results suggest that valuing the 'non-price' criteria seems to pay off in terms of business performance, while emphasizing price has no or rather negligible effects. Table 3.4 presents the bivariate correlations between the two factors and the above-mentioned performance measures.

*Table 3.4:* Rank correlations between the two identified factors and performance measures

| Spearman's rho | 'Non-price' factor | 'Price' factor |
|---|---|---|
| Service quality (n = 1016) | 0.19** | −0.08 ** |
| Productivity (n = 989) | 0.24** | −0.02 |
| Profitability (n = 981) | 0.23** | −0.03 |
| Product to market time (n = 896) | 0.23** | −0.05 |
| Rate of innovation (n = 927) | 0.31** | 0.01 |
| Stock market performance (n = 495) | 0.21** | 0.01 |

** $p < 0.01$ (two-tailed).

Again, the results remain consistent across all clusters, except that stock market performance was not significantly correlated with valuing the 'non-price' factor in Northern Europe. Controlling for company size does not alter the results either.

Coming back to the core idea of our third research question we also have to examine whether these two 'strategy factors' are related to the use of IES. In order to investigate this question, the respective factor values of companies using IES are compared to their counterparts which forbear from employing IES by a t-test. The result is interesting and in line with practical experiences in consultancy work: on average, companies that reported using IES put more emphasis on the 'non-price' factor and less on the 'price' factor. However, only the first difference is statistically significant. On the other hand it is striking that a separate analysis for the three clusters and controlling for company size does again not change the results.

All in all, the results allow the assumption that using IES is part of a company strategy that emphasizes 'being best' (instead of 'being cheapest'), a strategy that also pays off in terms of business performance.

## Limitations

Our study has some limitations. The Cranet-E data is obtained through a translated questionnaire in various countries. Therefore, in a way it combines the problematic aspects of both postal and cross-cultural surveys, for example uncontrolled response situation, response bias, trans-cultural accuracy of translated questions, or limits of interpreting findings in another culture. Although there are some precautions taken against these problems (for a more detailed view see Tregaskis, Mahoney & Atterbury, 2004), the database is not ideal. Furthermore not all countries are represented in each survey round.

Apart from that a well-developed theoretical framework for the connection between national culture and HRM is missing. Therefore, our research could not use a common framework but had to build on pieces of research fitting to the areas of interest addressed in the paper. Beyond our results, there are several lines of arguments concerning the interplay between culture and HRM that appear when analysing our results.

It is obvious that the national environment, most notably culture, seems to play an important role in the HR field. A number of cultural dimensions or – to be more precise – operational measures of the culture construct can be related to the practice of HR in European companies. But it is clear from the theoretical point of view that culture does not have a direct causal effect on HRM. This is very much like the well-known discussion in organization theory about the role the environment plays in the configuration of the organization (see, e.g. Burns & Stalker, 1961; Kieser & Kubicek, 1992). Although contingency research empirically links environmental characteristics with specific organizational configurations, it is theoretically clear that it is not 'the environment' that 'directly influences' the organizational structure. Environmental characteristics are a frame within which certain configurations do have a higher chance to be realized, often because of efficiency advantages. In a similar way, we would suggest to describe the effect culture has on organizational practices in the area of HRM. The data we have and the kind of data analysis that can be applied here certainly limited our progress in this respect.

## Concluding remark

Based on the available literature, previous empirical research and our own empirical results we can assume a trend of directional convergence (for different types of convergence see Mayrhofer, Müller-Camen, Ledolter, Strunk & Erten, 2004) towards an increasing use of IES in Europe: Companies across all country clusters seem to use IES to an increasing extent. While the few measurement points in time and the decreasing value in 1995 in all country clusters allow no strong empirical conclusion, this claim is very much in line with much of the expatriate literature and scattered empirical evidence. In addition, there seems to be a positive link between the use of IES and organizational performance measures. While the direction of causality is not clear, there is some evidence that the use of IES is part of an overall business strategy focusing on quality related performance criteria rather than a low-price strategy. These results – while tentative due to data limitations and a lack of theoretical models linking various HR activities and organizational performance – have some consequences for the management of international assignments.

Although it seems to be increasingly difficult for companies to recruit and find people willing to go on an international assignments of different sorts, companies are clearly searching for employees taking on such an assignment – and, it seems, increasingly so. Thus, for organizations as well as individuals the improvement in the management of the expatriation becomes crucial.

For organizations, making full use of an expensive and highly visible HR measure does not only make sense in the light of the immediate reasons of the international assignment such as filling local know-how gaps, coordination and control, or personal development. The link between IES and organizational performance dimensions makes these assignments an economically important issue. Even if the causality of the link remains to be further analysed, the potential positive effects of IES demand the devotion of enough resources to these efforts.

For individuals, the results underscore the well-known importance of handling international assignments in a professional way. If such assignments diversify in form and, as it seems to be the case, do not lose but rather gain importance in terms of number and business consequences, the pressure on individuals increases. Thus, support from the side of the organization becomes even more important.

As always, more research is needed. Two areas deserve special emphasis. First, the integration of IES into an overall HR and business strategy has to be further explored. While the evidence seems to indicate that certain business strategies are linked with the use of IES, the picture is by far not entirely clear. For example, the reasons for such a link as well as its direct and indirect effects on various HR activities and areas outside of HR deserve attention. Second, the research presented here underscores the importance of a better understanding of the general link between HR and organizational performance. While this area has already received considerable attention in the past, much remains to be done in order to analyse cause and effects. Most important, the link between HR and other management areas such as internationalization strategies, production types or marketing efforts and the combined effects of these approaches on organizational performance are essential – not only for a better understanding of international experience schemes.

## References


Baruch, Y., & Altman, Y. (2002) Expatriation and repatriation in MNC: a taxonomy, *Human Resource Management*, 41(2): 239–59.

Bird, A., & Mukuda, M. (1989) Expatriates in their own home: A new twist in the human resource management strategies of Japanese MNCs, *Human Resource Management*, 28(4): 437–53.

Black, J. S., Gregersen, H. B., & Mendenhall, M. E. (1992) *Global Assignments: Successfully Expatriating and Repatriating International Managers*, San Francisco: Jossey-Bass.

Black, J. S., Mendenhall, M., & Oddou, G. (1991) Toward a comprehensive model of international adjustment: an integration of multiple theoretical perspectives, *Academy of Management Review*, 16(2): 291–317.

Bonache, J., & Cervino, J. (1997) Global integration without expatriates, *Human Resource Management Journal*, 7(3): 89–100.

Bowen, D. E., & Ostroff, C. (2004) Understanding HRM-firm performance linkages: The role of the 'strength' of the HRM system, *Academy of Management Review*, 29(2): 203–21.

Brewster, C. (1991) *The Management of Expatriates*, London: Kogan Page.

Brewster, C. (1995) Towards a 'European' model of Human Resource Management, *Journal of International Business Studies*, 26(1): 1–21.

Brewster, C., & Hegewisch, A. (eds) (1994) *Policy and Practice in European Human Resource Management. The Price Waterhouse Cranfield Survey*, London, New York: Routledge.

Brewster, C., & Larsen, H. H. (2000) The Northern European dimension. A distinctive environment for HRM. In C. Brewster, & H. H. Larsen (eds) *Human Resource Management in Northern Europe*, 24–38. Oxford: Blackwell.

Brewster, C., Larsen, H. H., & Mayrhofer, W. (1997) Integration and assignment: a paradox in Human Resource Management, *Journal of International Management*, 3(1): 1–23.

Brewster, C., & Mayrhofer, W. (1996) Ethnocentric staffing policies in European multinationals, *International Executive*, 38(6): 749–78.

Brewster, C., Mayrhofer, W., & Morley, M. (eds) (2000) *New Challenges in European Human Resource Management*, Basingstoke: Macmillan – now Palgrave Macmillan.

Brewster, C., Mayrhofer, W., & Morley, M. (eds) (2004) *Human Resource Management in Europe. Evidence of convergence?* Oxford: Elsevier/Butterworth-Heinemann.

Brewster, C., Tregaskis, O., Hegewisch, A., & Mayne, L. (1996) Comparative research in human resource management: a review and an example, *International Journal of Human Resource Management*, 7(3): 585–604.

Burns, T., & Stalker, G. M. (1961) *The Management of Innovation*, London.

Dowling, P. E., & Welch, D. E. (2004) *International Human Resource Management* (4th edn) London: Thomson Learning.

Erten-Buch, C., & Strunk, G. (2000) *Exportorientierung und Personalmanagement im europäischen Vergleich*, Vienna: Research Study for the Vienna bfi-Euroteam/Europäische Wirtschafts- und Unternehmensführung.

Evans, P., Pucik, V., & Barsoux, J.-L. (2002) *The Global Challenge: frameworks for international human resource management*, New York: McGraw-Hill/Irwin.

Fey, C. F., & Bjorkman, I. (2001) The effect of human resource management practices on MNC subsidiary performance in Russia, *Journal of International Business Studies*, 32(1): 59–75.

Filella, J. (1991) Is there a Latin model in the management of human resources? *Personnel Review*, 20(6): 14–23.

Forster, N. (2000) The myth of the 'international manager', *International Journal of Human Resource Management*, 11(1): 126–42.

Gelade, G. A., & Ivery, M. (2003) The impact of human resource management and work climate on organizational performance, *Personnel Psychology*, 56(2): 383–404.

Guthrie, J. P., Ash, R. A., & Stevens, C. D. (2003) Are women 'better' than men? Personality differences and expatriate selection, *Journal of Managerial Psychology*, 18(3): 229–43.

Harris, H. (2000) *New Forms of International Working*, Cranfield: Center for Research into the Management of Expatriation.

Harris, H., Brewster, C., & Erten, C. (2005) Auslandseinsatz, aber wie? Klassisch oder alternative Formen: neueste empirische Erkenntnisse aus Europa und den USA. In G. Stahl, W. Mayrhofer, & T. M. Kühlmann (eds) *Internationales Personalmanagement. Neue Aufgaben, neue Lösungen*: 275–92. München: Hampp.

Heenan, D. A., & Perlmutter, H. V. (1979) *Multinational Organization Development*, Reading, Mass.: Addison-Wesley.

Hofstede, G. (1980) *Culture's Consequence. International Differences in Work-Related Values*, Newbury Park: Sage Publications.

Huselid, M. A., Jackson, S. E., & Schuler, R. S. (1997) Technical and strategic human resource management effectiveness as determinants of firm performance, *Academy of Management Journal*, 40(1): 171–88.

Jones, M. V., & Coviello, N. E. (2005) Internationalisation: conceptualising an entrepreneurial process of behaviour in time, *Journal of International Business Studies*, 36(3): 284–303.

Kieser, A., & Kubicek, H. (1992) *Organisation* (3.Aufl. ed.). Berlin, New York: de Gruyter.

Linehan, M., & Mayrhofer, W. (2005) International careers and repatriation. In H. Scullion, & M. Linehan (eds) *International Human Resource Management*: 131–55. Basingstoke and New York: Palgrave Macmillan.

Linehan, M., & Scullion, H. (2002) Repatriation of European female corporate executives: An empirical study, *International Journal of Human Resource Management*, 13(2): 254–67.

Markoczy, L. (1994) Modes of organizational learning. Institutional change and Hungarian joint ventures, *International Studies of Management and Organizations*, 24(4): 5–30.

Mayrhofer, W. (1996) *Mobilität und Steuerung in international tätigen Unternehmen. Eine theoretische Analyse*, Stuttgart: Schäffer-Poeschel.

Mayrhofer, W. (2001) Organisational international career logics (OICLs). A conceptual tool for analysing organisational expatriation patterns and their consequences for the management of organisations, *Thunderbird International Business Review*, 43(1): 121–44.

Mayrhofer, W., Müller-Camen, M., Ledolter, J., Strunk, G., & Erten, C. (2004) Devolving responsibilities for human resources to line management? An empirical study about convergence in Europe, *Journal for East European Management Studies*, 9(2): 123–46.

Mayrhofer, W., & Scullion, H. (2002) Female expatriates in international business. Empirical evidence from the German clothing industry, *International Journal of Human Resource Management*, 13(4): 815–36.

Mendenhall, M. E., Dunbar, E., & Oddou, G. R. (1987) Expatriate selection, training and career pathing: a review and critique, *Human Resource Management*, 26(3): 331–45.

Mendenhall, M. E., Kühlmann, T. M., & Stahl, G. (2000) *Developing Global Business Leaders: Policies, Processes, and Innovations*, New York: Quorum Books.

Pawlowsky, P., & Wilkens, U. (eds) (2001) *Zehn Jahre Personalarbeit in den neuen Bundesländern : Transformation und Demographie*, München, Mering: Hampp.

Peltonen, T. (1997) Facing the rankings from the past: a tournament perspective on repatriate career mobility, *International Journal Human Resource Management*, 8(1): 6–23.

Perlmutter, H. V. (1969) The tortuous evolution of the multinational corporation, *Columbia Journal of World Business*, 4(Jan.): 9–18.

Scullion, H. (1992) Strategic recruitment and development of the international managers: Some European considerations, *Human Resource Management Journal*, 3: 57–69.

Scullion, H. (1999) International HRM in medium-sized MNEs: evidence from Ireland. In H. Harris (ed.) *International HRM: Contemporary Issues in Europe*: 48–63. London: Routledge.

Scullion, H., & Brewster, C. (2001) The management of expatriates: Messages from Europe? *Journal of World Business*, 36(4): 346–65.

Stahl, G. K. (2000) *Between Ethnocentrism and Assimilation: An Exploratory Study of the Challenges and Coping Strategies of Expatriate Managers*, Paper presented at the Academy of Management, Toronto, Canada.

Stone, R. J. (1991) Expatriate selection and failure, *Human Resource Planning*, 14(1): 9–18.

Stroh, L. K., Gregersen, H. B., & Black, J. S. (1998) Closing the gap: Expectations versus reality among repatriates, *Journal of World Business*, 33(2): 111–24.

Suutari, V. (2003) Global managers: career orientation, career tracks, life-style implications and career commitment, *Journal of Managerial Psychology*, 18(3): 185–207.

Suutari, V., & Brewster, C. (1998) The adaptation of expatriates in Europe: evidence from Finnish companies, *Personnel Review*, 27(2): 89–103.

Suutari, V., & Brewster, C. (1999) International assignments across European borders: no problems? In C. Brewster, & H. Harris (eds) *International Human Resource Management: Contemporary Issues in Europe*: 183–202. London: Routledge.

Taylor, S., Napier, N. K., & Mayrhofer, W. (2002) Women in global business, *International Journal of Human Resource Management*, 13(4): 160–6.

Thomas, A., & Hagemann, K. (1992) Training interkultureller Kompetenz. In N. Bergemann, & A. L. J. Sourisseaux (eds) *Interkulturelles Management*: 174–99. Heidelberg: Physica.

Tregaskis, O., Mahoney, C., & Atterbury, S. (2004) International survey methodology: experiences from the Cranfield network. In C. Brewster, W. Mayrhofer, & M. Morley (eds) *European Human Resource Management – Evidence of Convergence*, London: Butterworth-Heineman.

Trompenaars, F. (1994) *Riding the Waves of Culture. Understanding Diversity in Global Business*, Chicago, Ill.: Irwin.

van Brabant, J. M. (ed.) (1999) *Remaking Europe: the European Union and the Transition Economies*, Lanham, Md.: Rowman & Littlefield.
Wall, T. D., Michie, J., Patterson, M., Wood, S. J., Sheehan, M., Clegg, C. W., & West, M. (2004) On the validity of subjective measures of company performance, *Personnel Psychology*, 57(1): 95–119.
Ward, C. (1996) Acculturation. In D. Landis, & R. S. Bhagat (eds) *Handbook of Intercultural Training*, 2nd edn: 124–47. Thousand Oaks: Sage.
Wright, P. M., Gardner, T. M., & Moynihan, L. M. (2003) The impact of HR practices on the performance of business units, *Human Resource Management Journal*, 13(3): 21–36.

# 4

# Another Scandal in Bohemia? A Look Back on how we Measure Expatriate Adjustment

*Thomas Hippler*

## Introduction

In his story 'A Scandal in Bohemia', Arthur Conan Doyle lets his protagonist Sherlock Holmes warn his assistant Dr Watson, 'I have no data yet. It is a capital mistake to theorize before one has data. Insensibly one begins to twist facts to suit theories instead of theories to suit facts' (Doyle, 1930: 5). This quote has become a classic in the debate on research paradigms (see, for example, Gummesson, 1991). What has happened in expatriate adjustment research may serve as a case in point.

In 1991, Black, Mendenhall and Oddou, in a comprehensive review of the literature on expatriate adjustment, concluded that 'although international adjustment has received increased scholarly attention, the majority of the writing has been anecdotal in nature, and few scholars have rigorously investigated the phenomenon, empirically or theoretically' (p. 293). Some would argue that this has changed over the past ten to twenty years, most notably through the work of Black and his colleagues (for example Black, 1988; Black, 1990a; Black, 1990b; Black, 1992; Black and Gregersen, 1991a; Black and Gregersen, 1991b; Black and Gregersen, 1991c; Black and Stephens, 1989; Gregersen and Black, 1990; Gregersen and Black, 1992). However, although the view is being held that 'more rigorous empirical studies are now being conducted' (Caligiuri, 2000: 63), some shortcuts may have been taken. Stahl (1998), in his study of the challenges faced by German expatriates in Japan and the US and their attendant coping behaviour, points out that in the history of research into foreign assignments 'the stage of exploratory research was [ . . . ] omitted right from the start in favour of questionnaire-based surveys' (p. 5) (translation by the current author). The measures and underlying concepts of these questionnaires have almost exclusively been arrived at by literary deduction (Ady, unpublished manuscript). And while 'moving from theory to proposition and to operational definition makes excellent deductive sense and constitutes good science' (Ady, unpublished manuscript: 10), the almost total lack of inductive approaches to the topic of expatriate adjustment may have resulted in overlooking some important factors in the expatriate experience.

According to Black (1988), one has to focus on the following three dimensions in order to understand the process of expatriate adjustment:

- the facet (or domain) of adjustment
- the mode of adjustment
- the degree of adjustment.

The facet or domain of adjustment refers to the question of *what* the expatriate has to adjust to, the mode of adjustment refers to the question of *how* the expatriate adjusts to these domains and the degree of adjustment refers to the question of *how successful* that adjustment has been.

The concept of 'adjustment' was borrowed by psychologists who renamed the concept known as 'adaptation' in biology (Lazarus, 1976). In Darwin's theory of evolution species have to adapt to the natural environment in order to survive. In psychology the individual has to 'survive' or rather 'get along' in his or her social and physical environment (Lazarus, 1976). So when the question of adjustment is concerned, the environment, by definition, is of paramount importance. The number of environmental features potentially requiring adjustment, however, is infinite. Hence when it comes to the study of adjustment, the researcher is faced with the challenge of determining which environmental aspects (or domains) to enquire about, as it is obviously impossible to cover an infinite number of variables.

There have been numerous attempts to break an individual's experience of his or her environment down into a set of domains. The results of these attempts vary widely in terms of their number and their nature (for a review of the domain sets found in the literature see Ady, 1995). Over the past decade, research into the adjustment of expatriates has been predominantly led by John Stewart Black and his colleagues. He identifies three broad domains of adjustment (Black, 1988):

1. adjustment to work
2. adjustment to the interaction with host nationals
3. adjustment to the general nonwork environment.

Black and Stephens (1989) used 14 items to represent these domains (Black and Stephens, 1989: 542). These items were:

1. Living conditions in general
2. Housing conditions
3. Food
4. Shopping
5. Cost of living
6. Entertainment/recreation facilities and opportunities
7. Health care facilities
8. Socializing with host nationals
9. Interacting with host nationals on a day-to-day basis
10. Interacting with host nationals outside of work
11. Speaking with host nationals
12. Specific job responsibilities
13. Performance standards and expectations
14. Supervisory responsibilities.

All or part of these items were adopted by numerous researchers in the field of expatriate adjustment (for example Caligiuri, 2000; Ditchburn, 1996; Florkowski and Fogel, 1999; Gregersen, 1992; Gregersen and Stroh, 1997; Harrison et al., 1996; Kraimer et al., 2001; Newman and Leatherwood, 2001; Nicholson and Imaizumi, 1993; Parker and McEvoy, 1993; Selmer, 1996; Selmer, 1997; Selmer, 1998; Selmer, 2000; Selmer, 2001; Shaffer and Harrison, 1998; Shaffer et al., 1999; Sinangil and Ones, 1997; Sinangil et al., 1997; Tsang, 2001). Black's work and that of those working in his tradition has undoubtedly influenced the research into the adjustment of expatriates to a large degree. It has advanced the knowledge about the subject and has introduced very welcomed rigour to the study of expatriate adjustment. The list of items they used, however, begs two important questions:

1. How were these 14 items identified as the most salient or important aspects of the expatriates' host environment?
2. Are these items specific enough to be meaningfully dealt with by the expatriates in a questionnaire survey?

When tracing these items back to their source, one has to come to the conclusion that the choice of at least some of them is somewhat arbitrary. The first seven items, for example, are, according to Black (1988: 283), based on the work by Torbiörn (1982), who in his book states, 'I selected certain aspects of "living conditions" for evaluation, on a basis of general assumption about people's needs and more or less disregarding the specific place of residence' (Torbiörn, 1982: 110). So the validity of these items rests on plausibility considerations. (The other seven items were designed by Black (1990a + b). He does not, however, identify the process of item generation.)

The issue of domain generality vs. domain specificity was raised by Ady (unpublished manuscript). Adjustment can be conceptualized as the general satisfaction with one's life in the new environment. When adjustment is thus conceptualized and operationalized, the responses of those surveyed seem to be unstable and open to situational influences (Ady, 1995). Black, for example, has addressed the problem of the over-generality of this question by breaking it down into the three broad domains mentioned and then further subdividing it into the 14 items given above. It could be argued, however, that these items are still too broad to be meaningful to the respondents. The item 'living conditions in general' seems particularly susceptible to this.

Summarizing the research into establishing which factors of the host environment are most salient or significant in an expatriate's experience, one has to conclude with Ady (unpublished manuscript: 10) that '[g]iven the largely atheoretical nature of adjustment literature – and adjustment domain literature in particular – what emerges, then, is what appears to be a tradition of referencing rather than an operational approach grounded in what sojourners themselves report'. The almost total lack of inductive-exploratory approaches to this question means that despite the wide acceptance some of the measures of expatriate adjustment – and those used by Black and his colleagues in particular – have achieved, no assessment of their validity can be made. This is not to say that, for example, Torbiörn's plausibility considerations are in any way faulty or wrong. It simply means that one cannot know whether or not with these he has captured the essence of the expatriate experience and that without such knowledge, one should be very careful to base too elaborate a theory building on these potentially shaky grounds. What is called for, then, is an exploratory approach, an attempt to establish the domains that matter to the expatriates empirically.

In order to make the results of this study as broadly applicable as possible, it was decided to survey not only expatriate employees, but domestic relocatees as well. This was intended to provide a basis for relocation adjustment studies in both a domestic and an international context. It was also designed to lay the ground for comparative studies of the adjustment of international and domestic relocatees. Thus, the present study tries to answer the following question: 'In which domains do relocatees, both international and domestic, assigned to a variety of host locations, report experiencing changes when comparing their host environment to their home environment?'

This 'going back to square one' proposed here seems well warranted. Given the developmental history of the instruments currently in use to measure expatriate adjustment, it is uncertain whether these are exhaustive or indeed, from the perspective of those concerned, that is the expatriates, relevant. Data collected in an open, exploratory manner 'reflect more strongly the subjective reality of the respondent and less the researcher's view or methodological constraints' (Stahl, 1998: 124) (translation by the current author).

Many of the points discussed here have been raised before by Ady (unpublished manuscript) and have indeed led him to conducting a study that according to him was 'to this writer's knowledge, the first attempt to generate an empirically grounded picture of the domains of adjustment' (Ady, unpublished manuscript: 10). Unfortunately, Ady's sample was one of convenience, as he himself readily admits (Ady, unpublished manuscript: 19). In his total sample of 185, 129 or almost 70 per cent were students. And whereas at least 28 different home countries were included in his sample, it was heavily biased towards the United States with more than 55 per cent of all participants originating there. Japanese, as the second largest group, only accounted for little over 6 per cent of the total sample.

Ady used a questionnaire with open-ended questions, the answers to which he subjected to a content analysis with the categories for the analysis inductively derived from the answers. The strong bias towards students obviously influenced the development of the category set. In a set of 39 categories Ady arrived at a rather broad category labelled 'work/job/assignment', which he acknowledges is even broader than the three-item measure Black (1988) used (Ady, unpublished manuscript). Ady himself accepts that '[ . . . ] discrete sojourn types would require more work on domain specification' (unpublished manuscript: 19). This is clearly being called for in the case of expatriate or domestically relocated employees as it is most unlikely that among this group only one domain in 39 would be work related. While acknowledging the very valuable conceptual contribution of Ady's work, the present author therefore decided that the results of Ady's study, that is the category set he arrived at, could not be used as presented in the context of expatriate employees and that a replication of Ady's undertaking was necessary.

## Methodology

### Data collection instrument

One of the obvious applications of the data resulting from this study is using them as input for the development of more sophisticated, standardized research instruments, which can then be used for surveying relocatees being assigned to a variety of host environments. In order to preserve the largest possible geographical spread of the research population and at the same time overcoming the lack of direct access (in the form of face-to-face interviews) to the research subjects due to prohibitive costs, it was decided to use a mailed survey questionnaire with an open, little structured response format.

The questionnaire contained three questions, two of which were unrelated to the present study. The question relating to this study was printed on a single page, followed by ten numbered lines, which provided space for the respondents to formulate their answers. It was outlined to them that the ten lines were just a guideline and that they were free to provide more or fewer answers. The question, as put to the international relocatees, is reproduced in Box 4.1. The wording of the version for domestic relocatees was slightly different, reflecting the fact that their relocation was domestic rather than international.

**Box 4.1 Question for eliciting domain nominations**

As a consequence of your international assignment your environment has changed considerably. Most likely you had to get used to certain things that you experienced as being unfamiliar or different. I would like to ask you to nominate those domains of your life that you experienced or still experience as being different when you compare your old to your new environment and which you feel needed or still need some adjustment.

The term 'domain of your life' is used here in the broadest possible sense and thus comprises your new work environment as well as your personal environment outside work. It comprises task-related aspects as well as social aspects or changes in the natural environment. I would also ask you to consider 'inner' changes, for example in your feelings, your attitudes, your state or awareness.

In short: What is – in the broadest possible sense – different, when you compare your old to your new living environment?

### Sample

The research subjects of the present study were employees of one large German multinational company. In this author's view, the limitations to the external validity of the study, which result from a one-company design, are far outweighed by the gains in internal validity. By ensuring that all subjects were of the same nationality, had been subjected to the same corporate culture, the same selection process and the same predeparture training (as far as the international relocatees are concerned), the author factored out certain external cultural and societal variables.

To be included in the research population the relocatees had to meet a number of criteria (for example the transfer originating in Germany, the move involving geographical relocation, the move being an intraorganizational one (that is no externally recruited movers) and the relocatees being of German nationality) aimed at ensuring the largest possible degree of homogeneity in the sample.

#### Response rates, description of the sample and nonresponse bias

The number of potential respondents was 454 for the international relocatees and 279 for domestic relocatees. Questionnaires were administered through corporate headquarters, that is being distributed and returned through company internal mail. Incidentally, the overall response rate of 69.8 per cent was the same for both the international (317 out of 454) and the domestic relocatees (195 out of 279). Tables 4.1 and 4.2 will give a detailed description of the sample's geographical distribution per country[1] and world region[2] or state. These parameters indicate that the sample is an almost perfect representation of the population.

## Analysis

The domains nominated by the respondents were subjected to a qualitative and quantitative content analysis. Content analysis is an empirical method for the systematical and intersubjectively replicable identification of specified characteristics of communication content.[3] One research objective content analysis can serve is to find out which constructs appear relevant to a population in a particular context and how many respondents retrieve a particular issue (Lazarsfeld and Barton, 1951).

Given the format of the questionnaire, most responses were provided in the form of bullet points, ranging from single words to lengthy paragraphs. Each of these bullet points was usually dealing with only one domain. Where a statement contained more than one domain, it was split. For

*Table 4.1:* Representation of international relocatees

| Country* | Population | Percentage | Sample | Percentage |
|---|---|---|---|---|
| South Africa (1/1) | 5 | 1,1% | 2 | 0,6% |
| ***Africa (1/1)*** | ***5*** | ***1,1%*** | ***2*** | ***0,6%*** |
| ***Australia (1/1)*** | ***9*** | ***2,0%*** | ***8*** | ***2,5%*** |
| France (9/9) | 39 | 8,6% | 32 | 10,1% |
| Spain (6/6) | 36 | 7,9% | 30 | 9,5% |
| Great Britain (3/4) | 11 | 2,4% | 7 | 2,2% |
| Italy (3/3) | 9 | 2,0% | 7 | 2,2% |
| Portugal (4/4) | 9 | 2,0% | 6 | 1,9% |
| Switzerland (1/2) | 9 | 2,0% | 6 | 1,9% |
| Belgium (3/3) | 7 | 1,5% | 4 | 1,3% |
| Austria (2/2) | 5 | 1,1% | 5 | 1,6% |
| Denmark (1/1) | 5 | 1,1% | 3 | 0,9% |
| The Netherlands (1/2) | 3 | 0,7% | 1 | 0,3% |
| EuroWest1 (1/1) | 1 | 0,2% | 1 | 0,3% |
| EuroWest2 (1/1) | 1 | 0,2% | 1 | 0,3% |
| ***Europe (West) (35/38)*** | ***135*** | ***29,7%*** | ***103*** | ***32,5%*** |
| Czech Republic (4/4) | 26 | 5,7% | 19 | 6,0% |
| Russia (1/3) | 12 | 2,6% | 4 | 1,3% |
| Hungary (2/2) | 3 | 0,7% | 3 | 0,9% |
| Poland (2/2) | 2 | 0,4% | 2 | 0,6% |
| ***Europe (East) (9/11)*** | ***43*** | ***9,5%*** | ***28*** | ***8,8%*** |
| Turkey (2/3) | 7 | 1,5% | 5 | 1,6% |
| NearEast1 (1/1) | 1 | 0,2% | 1 | 0,3% |
| NearEast2 (0/1) | 1 | 0,2% | 0 | 0,0% |
| NearEast3 (0/1) | 1 | 0,2% | 0 | 0,0% |
| ***Near East (3/6)*** | ***10*** | ***2,2%*** | ***6*** | ***1,9%*** |
| India (1/1) | 12 | 2,6% | 11 | 3,5% |
| ***Middle East (1/1)*** | ***12*** | ***2,6%*** | ***11*** | ***3,5%*** |
| Japan (6/6) | 29 | 6,4% | 21 | 6,6% |
| Korea (4/4) | 22 | 4,8% | 14 | 4,4% |
| China (6/7) | 17 | 3,7% | 9 | 2,8% |
| Malaysia (1/1) | 8 | 1,8% | 8 | 2,5% |
| Singapore (1/1) | 6 | 1,3% | 3 | 0,9% |
| Hongkong (1/1) | 3 | 0,7% | 2 | 0,6% |
| FarEast1 (1/1) | 2 | 0,4% | 2 | 0,6% |
| FarEast2 (1/1) | 1 | 0,2% | 1 | 0,3% |
| FarEast3 (1/1) | 1 | 0,2% | 0 | 0,0% |
| ***Far East (22/23)*** | ***89*** | ***19,6%*** | ***60*** | ***18,9%*** |
| Mexico (3/3) | 25 | 5,5% | 17 | 5,4% |
| Mid America1 (1/1) | 1 | 0,2% | 1 | 0,3% |

(*Continued*)

*Table 4.1:* (*Continued*)

| Country* | Population | Percentage | Sample | Percentage |
|---|---|---|---|---|
| ***Middle America (4/4)*** | ***26*** | ***5,7%*** | ***18*** | ***5,7%*** |
| USA (18/22) | 105 | 23,1% | 67 | 21,1% |
| ***North America (18/22)*** | ***105*** | ***23,1%*** | ***67*** | ***21,1%*** |
| Brazil (3/3) | 17 | 3,7% | 12 | 3,8% |
| SAmerica1 (1/1) | 1 | 0,2% | 1 | 0,3% |
| SAmerica2 (1/1) | 1 | 0,2% | 1 | 0,3% |
| SAmerica3 (0/1) | 1 | 0,2% | 0 | 0,0% |
| ***South America (5/6)*** | ***20*** | ***4,4%*** | ***14*** | ***4,4%*** |

* First number in parentheses indicates the number of locations responses were received from; second number indicates the number of locations questionnaires were sent to.

*Table 4.2:* Representation of domestic relocatees

| State* | Population | Percentage | Sample | Percentage |
|---|---|---|---|---|
| Baden-Württemberg (14/16) | 119 | 42,7% | 83 | 42,6% |
| Lower Saxony (3/4) | 42 | 15,1% | 29 | 14,9% |
| Bavaria (7/7) | 41 | 14,7% | 28 | 14,4% |
| North Rhine-Westphalia (6/7) | 26 | 9,3% | 18 | 9,2% |
| Berlin (1/1) | 17 | 6,1% | 12 | 6,2% |
| Hesse (1/1) | 12 | 4,3% | 10 | 5,1% |
| Saarland (1/1) | 10 | 3,6% | 7 | 3,6% |
| Thuringia (1/1) | 6 | 2,2% | 4 | 2,1% |
| Saxony (2/2) | 5 | 1,8% | 3 | 1,5% |
| Mecklenburg-Vorpommern (1/1) | 1 | 0,4% | 1 | 0,5% |

* First number in parentheses indicates the number of locations responses were received from; second number indicates the number of locations questionnaires were sent to.

example, a statement 'I have less contact with my family and my friends back home' was split into the two statements 'I have less contact with my family back home' and 'I have less contact with my friends back home'. Combining the transcripts for the international and domestic relocatees resulted in a total of 4537 domain nominations.[4] Thus, based on the total of 512 participants in the survey, each respondent nominated an average of 8.9 domains (ranging from 1 to 27 nominations).

In line with the exploratory nature of this study the category system for the content analysis was developed inductively from the data. The general objective of inductive category development is to represent the whole range of manifestations of the variable under investigation (for example the whole range of domains present in the responses) and at the same time to drastically reduce the diversity of responses given (Stahl, 1998: 139). The present study's category creation process was based on a model by Mayring (1997), who describes the process of inductive category creation as one of paraphrasing, selection and omission, generalization and integration. The investigator started with the first line of the relevant communication content's transcript. The first recording unit[5] identified provided the kernel for a first tentative category. The second recording unit identified was then judged as semantically similar or dissimilar to the first recording unit. If it was judged semantically similar, it was subsumed under the first tentative category. Otherwise, it provided the kernel for a second tentative category and so on. The recording units were not noted down as presented in the original communication content, but in a paraphrased form. All elements of a text passage that were not content-bearing were eliminated and recording units were summarized into a descriptive term or short sentence. After the entire transcript had been processed in this manner, redundant paraphrases (that is paraphrases expressing identical content) were omitted. It was then attempted to generalize from those paraphrases that were semantically close but not identical in meaning. Depending on these generalizations' level of abstraction, they were either accepted as a tentative description of a category or were combined (integrated) to higher-level paraphrases, which then provided a tentative description of a category.

Domains were grouped into predominantly professional domains, predominantly private domains and domains spanning both the professional and private sphere. The rationale behind this grouping is the potential relevance for companies. For them it is important to know whether adjustment domains are located in the professional sphere and can therefore be addressed by the company or whether they are located in the private sphere where the influence a company can bring to bear is much more limited or non-existent. In organizing the domain nominations in this manner, this study follows Stahl (1998).

Following the outlined procedure, the researcher arrived at a set of 68 categories. In the present study, an 'ambiguous'-category (code '99') was added to the category set. This code was to be assigned if a recording unit was covered by the category set *in principle*, its presentation, however, was too unspecific to be assigned to any particular category.

It needs to be pointed out that the necessity of introducing the code '99' was not owed to the ambiguity of the recording instructions, but to the inherent ambiguity of the communication content itself. The following domain nomination may serve as an example: 'separation from the family'. It remains unclear whether the respondent refers to the nuclear family (spouse or partner and children) or the extended family (parents, siblings, other relatives). For both, the nuclear and the extended family, there is a precisely defined category. The response provided, however, does not allow any definite conclusion as to which segment of his or her family is being referred to. It was therefore assigned a code '99'. In order not to bias the 'research results in the direction of easily describable phenomena' (Krippendorf, 1980: 75), all recording units assigned to category '99' were analysed for potential effects on the outcome of the analysis. In the case of the sample answer above and its paraphrases, for example, it was asked: 'how does the overall result change if all of them were treated as referring to the nuclear family?' and 'how does the overall result change if all of them were treated as referring to the extended family?'

Two coders, one of them being the investigator himself, independently coded each domain nomination. Initial inter-coder reliability[6] was $R = 0.71$. As Friede (1981) and Krippendorf (1980) have pointed out, the level of inter-coder agreement required depends on the study's purpose. If a study's results have immediate policy implications, the level required is higher than in a merely exploratory study. According to Krippendorf, it comes down to a cost–benefit analysis, '[ . . . ] standards for data reliability [ . . . ] must be related [ . . . ] to the costs of drawing wrong conclusions. [ . . . ] If it is an exploratory study, the level may be relaxed considerably, but it should not be so low that the findings can no longer be taken seriously' (Krippendorf, 1980: 147). Following his own advice, Krippendorf accepts inter-coder reliability levels from 0.67 upward for 'highly tentative and cautious conclusions' (Krippendorf, 1980: 147). Against this background, the inter-coder reliability coefficient attained in the present study is deemed acceptable.

In resolving non-agreement, this study followed Bos and Straka (1989), Herzberg et al. (1959) and Ady (unpublished manuscript). The two coders discussed their non-agreements and sought a final consensus. Thus each recording unit could eventually be placed into a category and entered into the frequency count accordingly.

## Examination and explication of results

The examination of the present analysis' findings takes place at two levels, the nominal level and the ordinal level. At the nominal level it is a profiling exercise. Each category needs an explicit *description* (as opposed to *definition*, which was paramount in the process of category creation). This explication of a category's *empirical* (as opposed to *conceptual*) meaning is necessary as, in Mayntz et al.'s (1974: 158) words, 'in the end, the real meaning of a category is determined by the totality of all linguistic units assigned to it' (translation by the current author). The category profiles state the category's meaning more precisely and take into account empirically emerging emphases, sometimes by spinning off lower order categories from more generic ones provided they account for a considerable proportion of the total number of recording units assigned to that particular category.

The more recording units are assigned to a category, the more stable and meaningful the profiling is. If, for example, only eleven recording units have been assigned to a category and they all refer to different aspects of that category, they will all be included in the category's profile, even if they occur only once. If, on the other hand, 70 recording units have been assigned to a category, only 'semantic clusters' will be included in the profile; single mentions, however, will be disregarded. This is necessary in order not to 'swamp' the salient issues with lots of 'noise'. So category profiles are best read in conjunction with the frequency count provided further down.

The explication of all categories used in the present study can be found in Table 4.3. In presenting these category descriptions, a few modifications have been made to the original category set. For example, all categories with fewer than ten recording units assigned to it (which equals about 0.2 per cent of the total domain nominations) were omitted. The rational behind this decision is that there is hardly enough material for 'profiling'. Others were merged or split according to emerging emphases.

At the ordinal level, a frequency count was conducted. It indicates how salient an environmental change is or was across the entire relocatee population. Whereas a reasonable amount of trust can be put into the nominal categories presented above, the findings of the frequency count are *highly* tentative. One must not be deceived by the apparent precision of the figures presented in Table 4.3. Rather than relying on the precise numbers, one should rather interpret a considerably higher number as 'more than' and a smaller number as 'less frequent'. These relative terms do more justice to the nature of the data and this is why this second level of analysis is being called 'ordinal' here. The reason for this caution is the 'ambiguous'-category, which accounts for a substantial part of the coding decisions. The recording units assigned to this category were intended to be valid answers to the investigator's question. It was just not possible for the coders to reconstruct the meaning the sender had attached to them unambiguously. In practical terms, this means that a domain appearing at the top of the frequency count table will always be near the top of the table, regardless of whether or not its portion 'hidden' in category '99' is added or not. However, it may fall, for example, from rank three to rank six. In the context of the present study,

*Table 4.3:* Explication of domain categories

| | |
|---|---|
| CHANGES IN THE PREDOMINANTLY PRIVATE SPHERE | |
| *Infrastructure* | |
| **Health care** | The availability and quality of health care (for example distance to doctors or hospitals, the quality of the equipment of doctors' practices and hospitals, the existence of emergency services, the commitment of doctors and medical personnel or the training and qualification of doctors and medical personnel). Further, the new relationship between doctor and patient, that is the personal trust in the new doctor or doctors. |
| **Cultural infrastructure** | The availability and kind of cultural infrastructure, for example theatres, cinemas, concert halls, exhibitions, and so on. |
| **Opportunities for spending one's leisure time** | The availability and quality of leisure time facilities and the opportunity to continue leisure time activities (for example hobbies, sports or evening classes) practised before relocating or to start new ones (including the existence of clubs and societies) as well as the general recreational value of the new environment. |
| **Shopping** | The range of goods on offer (including food) and the way of arriving at a price (for example haggling instead of fixed prices) as well as opening hours and customer orientation and the manner and qualification of the staff. |
| **Housing conditions** | The characteristics of the self-inhabited accommodation, for example the size of the flat or house, the type (for example detached, flat, apartment complex, closed compound, and so on), the quality and condition of the structure, the location (for example close to a beach), the comfort, the noise pollution, the density of the buildings or accommodation units, the security and the neighbourhood. |
| *Family* | |
| **Partner** | The changes encountered by the relocatee's partner, especially the loss or change of employment and the resulting consequences (for example lack of intellectual challenge, adaptation to the role of a housewife, difficulties in creating 'a meaningful life', diminishing self-esteem, loss of an own income) and a much increased workload in terms of childcare as well as the loss of the familiar social environment and the integration into a new social environment. |
| **Children** | The situation of the relocatee's children at the new place of residence (for example the existence of a circle of friends), the care for and education of the children (for example the |

(*Continued*)

*Table 4.3: (Continued)*

| | |
|---|---|
| | school and the school-system or the kindergarten) as well as the general standing of children in the society. |
| **Family cohesion** | The relationship among the family members (partner and children). This includes the time they have for each other and the intensity of the contact. Among the possibly critical aspects are, for example, problems in the relationship, which originate in the new role of the partner at the new place of work and residence or in the change or discontinuation of his or her employment. |
| **Commuting** | The remaining behind of the family (partner and children) at the former place of work and residence and all ensuing consequences, for example separation from the family, possible loneliness after work, lack of family support, diminishing intensity of contact with the family, the necessity to maintain a second home, the travel time and travel distance between first and second home. |
| *Social life* | |
| **Friends and other private social contacts at the new place of residence** | The existence, the quality and the intensity of friendships and other private social contacts at the new place of residence, for example the number of new friends and acquaintances, the depth of these friendships and acquaintances, the frequency of contact, private contact with colleagues (expatriates and locals), and so on. |
| **Contacts to friends, acquaintances and family members back home** | The distance to and the contact with friends, acquaintances and family members (non-core, for example parents, siblings or other relatives) who stayed behind. |
| *Other* | |
| **Character and size of the community** | The population and the resulting character of the new place of residence, for example city, metropolis or conurbation or else town, village, country or rural area. |
| CHANGES ENCOMPASSING BOTH THE PROFESSIONAL AND THE PRIVATE SPHERE | |
| ***Features of the new country, the new region or city*** | |
| *Infrastructure* | |
| **Distances** | The distance between all relevant locations in the new region (for example between workplace, school, accommodation, friends, shopping facilities and business |

(Continued)

*Table 4.3:* (*Continued*)

| | |
|---|---|
| | partners as well as suppliers and customers) and the amount of time that is needed to overcome these distances. |
| **Public transport and access to the traffic network** | The availability, the type and the quality of public transport as well as the connection of the new place of work and residence to the local and long-distance traffic network (for example motorways or air-traffic). |
| **Banking** | The banking system and the way money transactions are being conducted. |
| **Utilities** | The reliability of the water and electricity supply and the existence of sewerage. |
| *Administrative environment* | |
| **Authorities** | Dealing with institutions of public administration (for example departments and offices) and with authorities of the state (for example the police). This includes bureaucracy and corruption. |
| **Legal environment** | The legal system and its laws, guidelines, rules and regulations. |
| *Social interaction* | |
| **Communication** | The communication in the private and in the professional sphere in spoken or written language of the host country or in a spoken or written third language (for example English) as well as the success of the communication efforts. This includes the ability to understand as well as being able to make oneself understood (that is active and passive language competence). |
| **Role as foreigner** | The reaction of the environment to the role of a foreigner, for example in the form of specific expectations or specific treatment (for example that as a foreigner one is cheated or else treated with exceptional courtesy, that one encounters racial prejudice or that one is always 'the exception' when dealing with institutions of public administration). |
| **Role as an expatriate** | The reaction of the environment to the role of an expatriate, for example in the form of specific expectations or specific treatment. These can manifest themselves, for example, in that one is seen as a competence bearer (expert), that one enjoys preferential terms compared to local employees (for example |

(*Continued*)

*Table 4.3: (Continued)*

| | |
|---|---|
| | holidays, salary), that one is seen as an 'ambassador' of Germany and the company, that one functions as the link between the domestic operations and the foreign subsidiary ('serving two masters'), that one is attributed the role of a model for others to follow, or that the company, the local subsidiary or the local employees exert a particular pressure on the expatriate to succeed and perform. In the private sphere the role of being an expatriate can manifest itself in belonging to the socially or materially privileged of the host country society. |
| **New role at work (for domestic relocatees)** | The reaction of the new subordinates, colleagues and superiors to one's new role, for example in the form of specific expectations or specific treatment. These can manifest themselves, for example, in that one is seen as a competence bearer (expert), that one is attributed the role of a model for others to follow, or that the company, the local subsidiary or the local employees exert a particular pressure on the relocatee to succeed and perform. |
| *Other* | |
| **Climate** | The climatic conditions at the new place of work and residence (for example the temperature, the humidity, the frequency of rainfall, foehn weather conditions or extreme seasons). |
| **Pollution and environmental protection** | The quality and the pollution of the natural environment as well as the attitude towards the environment and environmental protection. Pollution includes, for example, air pollution (for example exhaust fumes and smog), water pollution, noise pollution, toxins in the food or the overexploitation of natural resources. |
| **Nature** | The landscape and its characteristics (for example the absence or presence of, for example, mountains, plains, forests, rivers or the sea) as well as the wildlife and the vegetation. Further the altitude of the new living environment and the hours of daylight. |
| **Road traffic** | The road traffic conditions at the new place of residence and work, for example the behaviour towards other road-users, the traffic flow (congestion), the volume of traffic, the road safety (accidents) and the rules of road conduct and their ambiguity. |

*(Continued)*

*Table 4.3:* (*Continued*)

| | |
|---|---|
| **Hygiene** | The hygiene conditions at the new place of residence and work, especially fear of food poisoning and other illnesses caused by germ-contaminated food or water. |
| **Personal safety** | Threats to one's bodily integrity or one's material basis or property by crime (for example robbery, assault and mugging, theft or abduction), the risk of war or forces of nature (for example earthquakes or typhoons). |
| **Social situation** | The social situation and the distribution of material wealth in the host country society, for example extremely uneven distribution of wealth or the commonness of poverty. |
| **Cost of living** | The cost of living at the new place of residence, especially price levels and rent. |
| **Balance of private and professional live** | The balance of private and professional life, for example a stronger focus on professional matters, less leisure time and a closer integration of professional and private life or a dilution of the boundary between working week and the weekend. |
| ***Cultural characteristics of the population in the target company*** | |
| **Conflict behaviour** | The ability to criticize and to accept criticism, the extent to which criticism is kept factual or directed at the person and emotionalism vs. matter-of-factness in conflict. Further the directness or indirectness of criticism and the ritualization of conflict behaviour. |
| **Negotiation style and decision making** | The way in which negotiations are being conducted and decisions are being arrived at in the new living and working environment, especially the efficiency of the discussion style and the decision-making process. |
| **Predictability and reliability** | The predictability of human behaviour in the host country. This refers to the presence of rules of conduct and the stringency with which these are applied and enforced. It also includes, for example, reliability, meeting deadlines, punctuality, committing oneself and keeping appointments. |
| **Dealing with each other** | The way in which people in the host country society deal with each other and how they behave and act towards foreigners, strangers and newcomers. This includes, for example, how friendly, open, direct or polite people are in dealing with each other, how helpful and hospitable they are, whether they are rather loyal and feel solidarity with each other or whether they are rather egoistical and |

(*Continued*)

*Table 4.3:* (*Continued*)

| | |
|---|---|
| | whether it is a society that is more inclined to integrating or excluding foreigners, strangers and newcomers. |
| **Mentality** | The general attitude of mind and the general way of thinking of the people at the new place of residence and work. This includes the role-understanding of the sexes and the social status of women and children, the importance of the family, the society's regard for age, the division of the society into classes and the class relations and the presence of different races in the society and the race-relations. It also means the attitude towards the aspiration to property and material goods, patriotism, achievement-orientation and the acceptance of elites. Further the understanding of hierarchy and authority as well as the short-term or long-term orientation of the people. |
| **Food and gastronomic culture** | The national cuisine as well as the conventions related to eating (for example the eating times), further the role eating plays (that is its status) and the eating instruments (for example cutlery, chopsticks, and so on). |
| CHANGES IN THE PREDOMINANTLY PROFESSIONAL SPHERE | |
| *Social work environment* | |
| **Cooperation and work climate** | The relocatee's cooperation and dealings with subordinates, colleagues and superiors as well as their cooperation and dealings with each other. This includes rivalry or cooperativeness, coordination with colleagues, the closeness or distance to colleagues, subordinates and superiors and appreciation, respect and acceptance among and by colleagues, subordinates and superiors. Further the attitude towards cooperation (for example departmental egoism or the attitude towards teamwork) and the general work climate (for example tense or relaxed) as well as the way male and female employees treat each other. |
| **Leadership behaviour** | The management style, the management methods and instruments and their application at the new place of work and the reaction to them of those they are applied to. This includes the management style, the management methods and instruments the relocatee applies him- or herself as well as those he or she encounters or is subjected to at the workplace. |

(*Continued*)

*Table 4.3:* (*Continued*)

| | |
|---|---|
| **Colleagues' characteristics** | The working method, motivation and satisfaction of the employees in the new company or organizational unit as well as the basic convictions, values and attitudes that are shared by a majority of employees. This includes, for example, the interest in the work, the attitude towards work (or the work ethos), the work mentality, the working style, the work methodology, 'ownership' of one's tasks, the goal-orientation of the employees, the quality-consciousness, the openness towards innovation and the identification of the employees with the company. |
| *Target company unit* | |
| **The new site or plant** | The characteristics of the new site or plant. This includes, for example, the corporate culture (for example a different divisional or site culture, 'the unwritten rules', the size of the new site or plant, the standing of the site in the group, its organization structure and future perspective as well as the age structure and the level of training and the qualification of colleagues and subordinates. |
| **Workplace** | The relocatee's immediate workplace and its surroundings, for example single-room offices or open-plan offices with or without cubicles, the provision of IT (hard- and software), the age and condition of equipment and furnishings as well as the presence or absence of windows or air-conditioning. |
| *Task* | |
| **Task contents** | The contents of the new task or area of responsibility or expertise. Further the diversity and complexity of the area of responsibility. |
| **Responsibility and autonomy** | The extent of responsibility (for personnel and/or budget) in the new job as well as the autonomy and freedom of decision-making in carrying out one's tasks. |
| **Job-related contacts** | The number of job-related internal and external contacts, for example with customers, other departments, sites or companies. |
| **Travel** | The amount of business travel. |
| *Other* | |
| **Working hours** | The length of the working hours as well as their structure (for example flexitime) and their position in the day (for example earlier or later start of work or earlier or later end of work). |

(*Continued*)

*Table 4.3:* (*Continued*)

| | |
|---|---|
| **Work load** | The physical and psychological burden at the new place of work caused by, for example, the intensity or the volume of the work. |
| **Contact to HQ and management** | The distance and contact to the parent company, the respective head office or group headquarters as well as the quality of this contact. This includes, for example, the cooperation and coordination with the parent company or group headquarters, the supply of information, the opportunity to exercise influence on decisions made in the parent organization or group headquarters as well as appreciation of one's performance by the parent company or group headquarters. |
| **Opportunities for professional development** | The increase or decrease of opportunities for professional development in the new position. |
| OTHER | |
| **Contract** | The contractual conditions such as income, working hours and fringe benefits. |

this level of accuracy is sufficient. In order to obtain a more precise assessment of the relevance of each of these domains, they will have to be re-presented to the research population in a subsequent investigation. Table 4.4 presents the frequency count for the domain changes as perceived by the international relocatees.

## Discussion

Examining the results presented above, one immediately notices the large proportion (23.3 per cent) of recording units that have been assigned to the 'ambiguous'-category '99'. This figure could have been significantly reduced by 'technical' changes to the category set, such as the merger of two categories. But while this technical trick would have resulted in an – on the surface – better looking outcome, it would also have resulted in a less meaningful one. Rather than deploring the large proportion of recording units assigned to category '99', one can take some encouragement from the fact that the ratio of recording units stemming from expatriates to those originating from domestic relocatees is close to one (1.01). This indicates that inherently ambiguous domain nominations were equally spread among international and domestic relocatees and one may draw

*Table 4.4:* Count of domain changes: international relocatees

| Category | Count | Percentage | Cumulated |
|---|---|---|---|
| 99 Ambiguous | 616 | 23,3% | 100,0% |
| 13 Friends/Private social contacts | 135 | 5,1% | 76,7% |
| 24 Communication | 132 | 5,0% | 71,6% |
| 3 Leisure time | 111 | 4,2% | 66,6% |
| 49 Corporate culture (specific) | 104 | 3,9% | 62,3% |
| 41 Dealing with each other | 100 | 3,8% | 58,4% |
| 47 Cooperation and work climate | 87 | 3,3% | 54,6% |
| 58 Responsibility/Autonomy | 71 | 2,7% | 51,3% |
| 62 Working hours | 69 | 2,6% | 48,6% |
| 46 Other cultural characteristics | 65 | 2,5% | 46,0% |
| 9 Children | 64 | 2,4% | 43,6% |
| 25 Roles | 58 | 2,2% | 41,1% |
| 14 Distance to the home region | 53 | 2,0% | 38,9% |
| 6 Housing conditions | 51 | 1,9% | 36,9% |
| 11 Coherence | 51 | 1,9% | 35,0% |
| 8 Partner | 47 | 1,8% | 33,1% |
| 53 Other features of the target company unit | 41 | 1,6% | 31,3% |
| 26 Climate | 40 | 1,5% | 29,7% |
| x Other (Not covered by category set) | 38 | 1,4% | 28,2% |
| 4 Shopping | 38 | 1,4% | 26,8% |
| 10 Family | 38 | 1,4% | 25,3% |
| 63 Workload | 37 | 1,4% | 23,9% |
| 31 Safety | 37 | 1,4% | 22,5% |
| 34 Balance of professional and private life | 36 | 1,4% | 21,1% |
| 48 Leadership behaviour | 34 | 1,3% | 19,7% |
| 39 Uncertainty tolerance | 29 | 1,1% | 18,4% |
| 45 Mentality | 25 | 0,9% | 17,3% |
| 15 Character and size of community | 24 | 0,9% | 16,4% |
| 1 Health care | 24 | 0,9% | 15,5% |
| 27 Pollution/Environmental Protection | 24 | 0,9% | 14,6% |
| 29 Road traffic | 20 | 0,8% | 13,7% |
| 55 Task contents | 19 | 0,7% | 12,9% |
| 61 Other (Task) | 19 | 0,7% | 12,2% |
| 32 Social situation | 18 | 0,7% | 11,5% |
| 20 Authorities | 17 | 0,6% | 10,8% |
| 37 Negotiation style and decision making | 17 | 0,6% | 10,2% |
| 28 Nature | 17 | 0,6% | 9,5% |
| 38 Concept of hierarchy | 16 | 0,6% | 8,9% |
| 21 Legal environment | 14 | 0,5% | 8,3% |

(*Continued*)

*Table 4.4:* (*Continued*)

| Category | Count | Percentage | Cumulated |
|---|---|---|---|
| 56 Number and diversity | 14 | 0,5% | 7,7% |
| 17 Distances | 13 | 0,5% | 7,2% |
| 64 Contact to HQ or management | 12 | 0,5% | 6,7% |
| 52 Workplace | 12 | 0,5% | 6,3% |
| 30 Hygiene | 12 | 0,5% | 5,8% |
| 36 Conflict behaviour | 11 | 0,4% | 5,3% |
| 33 Cost of living | 10 | 0,4% | 4,9% |
| 2 Cultural infrastructure | 10 | 0,4% | 4,5% |
| 19 General infrastructure | 10 | 0,4% | 4,2% |
| 65 Opportunities for professional development | 10 | 0,4% | 3,8% |
| 66 Contract | 9 | 0,3% | 3,4% |
| 18 Public transport and access to traffic network | 8 | 0,3% | 3,1% |
| 57 Attractiveness of the task | 8 | 0,3% | 2,8% |
| 40 Social structure | 8 | 0,3% | 2,5% |
| 12 Commuting | 7 | 0,3% | 2,2% |
| 50 Corporate culture (global) | 7 | 0,3% | 1,9% |
| 43 Patriotism | 7 | 0,3% | 1,6% |
| 16 Religion | 6 | 0,2% | 1,4% |
| 59 Number of professional contacts | 4 | 0,2% | 1,1% |
| 60 Travel (task-related) | 4 | 0,2% | 1,0% |
| 5 Availability of information | 4 | 0,2% | 0,8% |
| 67 Financial situation | 3 | 0,1% | 0,7% |
| 42 Materialism | 3 | 0,1% | 0,6% |
| 54 Task clarity | 2 | 0,1% | 0,5% |
| 22 Tax environment | 2 | 0,1% | 0,4% |
| 23 Type of state | 2 | 0,1% | 0,3% |
| 35 Time horizon | 2 | 0,1% | 0,2% |
| 44 Achievement orientation | 2 | 0,1% | 0,2% |
| 51 Size (of target company unit) | 1 | 0,0% | 0,1% |
| 7 Travel destinations within reach | 1 | 0,0% | 0,0% |
| **Total** | **2640** | **100,0%** | |

NB: Category 68 (inner changes) is excluded from this presentation.

the tentative conclusion that the communication content was sufficiently homogeneous to be meaningfully dealt with as one corpus. The same reassurance can be drawn from the use of the category 'x', which represents recording units that constitute valid answers to the question put to the respondents but were not accommodated by the category set. Although the proportion of recording units assigned to this category stemming from domestic relocatees was somewhat higher than for international relocatees, the absolute level of recording units originating from domestic relocatees was very low (2.1 per cent).

With few exceptions (for example the 'Top Two'), the increase in usage from one category to the next, more frequently used one, is incremental. This suggests that there is no small set of easily identifiable domains that are *the* domains relevant in a relocation context. Although in the course of this study, the 'potentially infinite number' of environmental domains has been narrowed down significantly, it is still formidable and probably has to be in order to adequately and exhaustively represent the subjective reality the relocatees are encountering upon arriving in their new working and living environment.

Looking at those categories to which at least 1 per cent of all recording units were assigned, one notes that neither domains of the private sphere nor those of the professional sphere take clear precedence. Nine categories belong to the private sphere, seven to the professional sphere and eight refer to changes encompassing both the private and the professional sphere. Among these categories the social element takes a prominent position. Top of the list are friends and private social contacts, communication, leisure time,[7] corporate culture (specific) (that is colleagues' characteristics), dealing with each other, co-operation and work climate, not far down followed by distance to home region (that is friends and acquaintances left behind). Another strong position is held by the family, adding up the frequency counts for the family related categories 8 to 11 (=7.5 per cent).

Comparing the 14 facets or domains in which adjustment is assessed as they appeared in Black and Stephens (1989: 542) vis-à-vis the corresponding domains and their saliency as identified in the present study, one can make at least three observations. Apart from domains that are too broad or generic to be compared meaningfully (for example living conditions in general), all of Black and Stephens' facets can also be identified among the answers the international relocatees provided in the present study. With the exception of the cost of living, all of these appear in the upper half of the frequency count table. Most notably, Black and Stephens' items comprise the three most frequently nominated domains of socializing/private social contacts (although confined to host nationals), speaking with host nationals/communication and entertainment/recreation facilities and opportunities/leisure time. So the items they use all appear to be at least reasonably relevant to the expatriate population.

Some of the domains that featured prominently in this study's frequency count are absent from Black and Stephens' item list. Most notably the distance to the home region (category 14), that is contacts to friends, acquaintances and family members back home and anything related to the expatriate's immediate family, that is partner and children (categories 8, 9, 10), and its cohesion (category 11), all of which appear in the top third of the present study's frequency count table. The latter is easily explained as Black and Stephens investigated spouse adjustment separately and then related it to the expatriates' adjustment.

The other void reflects the fact that Black and Stephens' item list only recognizes the expatriate as a social actor in relation to the host environment, that is interacting with and speaking to host nationals. It completely ignores that the expatriate has to adjust to the loss – or at least diminished contact – to friends, acquaintances and family members he or she left behind and thus has to adjust to the loss of an established social support network. This loss is not necessarily transitional and completely compensated for by a newly established circle of friends at the host location. Friendships established in early life, for example at secondary school or at third level education institutions, tend to be more durable that friendships established later in life. The proverbial 'childhood friend' is not easily replaceable. This may be particularly true if the stay at the host location is known to be temporary from the start. Against this background, the commitment to newly established relationships might be limited.

The comparison of the items used by Black and Stephens with the results of the present study is somewhat hampered by the fact that sometimes one can only guess what individual items are referring to. For example, what kind of interaction had the authors in mind when asking for adjustment to 'interacting with host nationals on a day-to-day basis'. This daily interaction will take place at work and outside of work. So it entails dealing with one's superiors, colleagues and subordinates, and possibly comprises encountering other road-users, shop-keepers, one's neighbours, civil servants, and so on. What is probably asked for is a composite judgement, averaging out one's experiences over all these interactions. This immediately points to the problem of domain generality vs. specificity referred to earlier. Maybe these items are specific enough to be meaningful to the respondents and to provide stable answers. Maybe they are not. Since the process of item generation is not being made explicit, it is not possible to assess the reasoning behind the decision for the particular level of generality or specificity employed. Even where a domain appears among Black's items and the present study's results, it is not clear whether they mean the same thing. In the case of the shopping-domain, for example, the present study's profile explicates that this domain entails the range of goods on offer, the way prices are arrived at, the opening hours, customer orientation and the manner and qualification of the staff. All these are constituent parts of the shopping experience. An individual customer may be more than happy (and thus be perfectly adjusted to) with shops being open for 24 hours a day. The same customer, however, may be deeply unhappy about what is on offer (and thus not at all be adjusted to the available goods). So unless the expatriate-customer has indicated that he or she feels confident making a composite judgement about the shopping experience, he or she will be faced with a dilemma when being asked 'how well have you adjusted to shopping?'

Comparing this study's results to those obtained by Ady (unpublished manuscript) vindicates the present author's decision to replicate Ady's study rather than using his domain set as presented. The content analysis of the answers provided in response to Ady's 'Adjustment Domain Questionnaire' yielded the 39 categories presented in Table 4.5. Since his work also produced frequencies for the domain nominations, these are also given in per cent of the total number of domain nominations.

The heavy bias towards a student population comes out clearly in these results. While a number of seemingly identical or very similar domains emerged in both studies, the frequencies with which these appear sometimes differ considerably. The combined family domains (children, partner, family and its cohesion), for example, were identified as much

*Table 4.5:* Adjustment domains

| | |
|---|---|
| 1) Language (7.8) | 21) Politics (1.7) |
| 2) Values/ethics/morals (7.4) | 22) Eating/drinking (1.6) |
| 3) Food (6.4) | 23) Male–female relationships (1.5) |
| 4) Climate/weather (6.2) | 24) Media (1.5) |
| 5) Affective states (6.0) | 25) Chronemics (1.4) |
| 6) Transportation (5.2) | 26) Religion/spirituality (1.4) |
| 7) Etiquette (4.5) | 27) Shopping (1.3) |
| 8) Culture (4.5) | 28) Cleanliness/sanitation (1.2) |
| 9) Entertainment (4.2) | 29) Bathroom/hygiene (1.2) |
| 10) Work/job/assignment (4.1) | 30) Currency/monetary transactions (1.1) |
| 11) Interpersonal relationships (3.7) | 31) Crowdedness (1.0) |
| 12) Physical well-being (3.1) | 32) Family (1.0) |
| 13) Dress/clothes (2.4) | 33) Cost of living (0.8) |
| 14) Education (2.3) | 34) Personal growth (0.7) |
| 15) Outgroupness (2.3) | 35) Man-made environment (0.6) |
| 16) Friendship (2.2) | 36) Privacy (0.5) |
| 17) Isolation (2.1) | 37) Legal matters (0.5) |
| 18) Living quarters (2.1) | 38) Sex (0.5) |
| 19) Verbal communication (1.7) | 39) Material goods (0.3) |
| 20) Non-verbal communication (1.7) | |

Adapted from: Ady (unpublished manuscript).

more prominent in the present study (7.5 per cent vs. 1.0 per cent in Ady's study). The number of married respondents and respondents with children will be disproportionately higher among expatriate employees than it is among graduate and, particularly, undergraduate students. The most obvious consequences of the differences in sample composition can be seen in the 'work/job/assignment' domain. As anticipated, a much more detailed picture of this domain emerged in the present study, comprising 14 sub-domains at the profiling stage. These accounted for more than one-fifth of all recording units and thus highlight the saliency the work environment has in an expatriate's experience.

The third study relevant in the present context is that of Stahl (1998). He investigated the problems German expatriates in Japan and the US encounter and their attendant coping behaviour. He did this by personally interviewing 116 current German expatriates, comprising two subsamples of 58 in each country. What distinguishes Stahl's work from the present study is that he confined himself to problems the expatriates encountered. He thus only sought to extract domains that impacted negatively on the expatriates. The present study, on the other hand, was aimed at obtaining a complete picture of all changes the expatriates experienced, irrespective of whether this experience was positive or negative.

The particular value of Stahl's work with regard to the present study is that he too used content analysis for arriving at his domain set and that both studies involved a sample of German expatriates, which may be very different from samples of US-American expatriates, which have dominated much of the expatriation research over the past decades. He arrived at a total of 24 'problem classes', which are reproduced in Table 4.6.

*Table 4.6:* Problem classes on expatriate assignments

| | |
|---|---|
| 1) Working hours/work load | 13) Discrimination |
| 2) Job content and work processes | 14) Daily hassles |
| 3) Personnel/leadership | 15) Threats to one's existence |
| 4) Relationships with colleagues | 16) Deficits in support |
| 5) Expatriate role | 17) Repatriation/future |
| 6) Headquarters relations | 18) Settling in |
| 7) Business practices | 19) Children |
| 8) Professional success | 20) Spouse/partner |
| 9) Situation of the company | 21) Host country contacts |
| 10) Law/bureaucracy | 22) Expatriate community |
| 11) Language/communication | 23) Quality of life |
| 12) Cultural barriers | 24) Home country contacts |

Adapted from: Stahl, 1998: 157 (translation by the current author).

Comparing these findings with those of the present study, one notes that they are almost identical at the nominal level, albeit at different levels of aggregation. Whereas, for example, Stahl singled out 'the situation of the company', it was subsumed under 'other features of the target company unit' in the present study. In the case of Stahl's 'quality of life' domain, the situation is reversed in that the present study gives a more detailed account of domains (leisure time, cultural infrastructure, housing conditions, distances, shopping, social situation and climate) constituting his higher order domain. The differences in aggregation levels may have been directed by the differing study purposes. Stahl was seeking to establish 'problem domains', whereas the present study was trying to establish 'environmental domains'. Depending on one's research purpose, one can deem one a subset of the other. The difference in research purpose becomes most obvious where domains did not at all emerge in the present study, for example 'return/future'. While it is easily conceivable that this constitutes a 'problem domain' it is not an 'environmental domain' in any conventional sense.

The overlap between the two studies may be due to two factors. Even if the present study is looking for changes in general (positive, negative and neutral), negatively perceived changes are clearly a subset thereof and in some cases clearly dominate the domain nominations, for example in the case of 'distance to the home region'. So even if on the surface one study was dealing with 'problem domains' and the other with 'environmental domains', these sometimes mean the same thing. Secondly, as was mentioned before, in organizing the domain categories into predominantly professional domains, predominantly private domains and those spanning both the professional and private sphere, this study deliberately followed Stahl's lead. It can therefore not be said that both category sets were arrived at completely independently. This highest order structure may have influenced the subsequent category formation to an extent that similarities between the two studies were inevitable. Nonetheless, the fact that Stahl derived his category set from German expatriates in only two countries and via a different data collection technique and still arrived – at least at the nominal level – at domains very similar (if the different levels of aggregation are taken into account) to those established in the present study, leads to both studies cross-validating each other to some degree.

## Conclusion

This study set out to fill the empirical and exploratory void with regard to environmental domains relevant in relocatee adjustment left by the almost exclusive use of literary deduction in previous research. It was thus aiming at reflecting the subjective reality of domestic and international relocatees. The broad spectrum of environmental domains unearthed suggest that it is one of the richest and most in-depth study of these issues to date, second only to work based on in-depth personal interviews. As the latter is necessarily restricted in its geographical reach, the present study provides an important complement to this work. While relinquishing some depth, it traded it in for far greater geographical dispersion. What emerged is a very detailed and differentiated picture of environmental domains that, to the best of the author's knowledge, goes beyond all representations found in any single published study so far. The outcome of this exploration provides an important interim result that, when welded to a proper adjustment theory in a subsequent investigation, promises highly relevant results, due to its established content validity.

## References

Ady, J. C. (1995) Toward a differential demand model of sojourner adjustment, *International and Intercultural Communication Annual*, 19, 92–114.

Ady, J. C. (unpublished manuscript) Empirically-defined domains of sojourner adjustment: new findings and advances.

Black, J. S. (1988) Work role transitions: a study of American expatriate managers in Japan, *Journal of International Business Studies*, 19, 277–94.

Black, J. S. (1990a) Factors related to the adjustment of Japanese expatriate managers in America, in Ferris, G. R. and Rowland, K. M. (eds) *Research in Personnel and Human Resources Management*. Supplement 2, 109–25.

Black, J. S. (1990b) The relationship of personal characteristics with the adjustment of Japanese expatriate managers, *Management International Review*, 30 (2), 119–34.

Black, J. S. (1992) Coming home: the relationship of expatriate expectations with repatriation adjustment and job performance, *Human Relations*, 45 (2), 177–92.

Black, J. S. and Gregersen, H. B. (1991a) Antecedents to cross-cultural adjustment for expatriates in Pacific Rim assignments, *Human Relations*, 44 (5), 497–515.

Black, J. S. and Gregersen, H. B. (1991b) When yankee comes home: factors related to expatriate and spouse repatriation adjustment, *Journal of International Business Studies*, 22 (4), 671–94.

Black, J. S. and Gregersen, H. B. (1991c) The other half of the picture: antecedents of spouse cross-cultural adjustment, *Journal of International Business Studies*, 22 (3), 461–77.

Black, J. S., Mendenhall M. and Oddou, G. (1991) Toward a comprehensive model of international adjustment: an integration of multiple theoretical perspectives, *Academy of Management Review*, 16 (2), 291–317.

Black, J. S. and Stephens, G. K. (1989) The influence of the spouse on American expatriate adjustment and intent to stay in Pacific Rim overseas assignments, *Journal of Management*, 15 (4), 529–44.

Bos, W. and Straka, G. A. (1989) Mulitvariate Verfahren zur heuristischen Analyse kategorialer Daten: Eine Inhaltsanalyse von Lesebüchern der chinesischen Grundschule, in Bos, W. and Tarnai, C. (eds) *Angewandte Inhaltsanalyse in Empirischer Pädagogik und Psychologie*. Münster: Waxmann Wissenschaft, 211–28.

Caligiuri, P. M. (2000) Selecting expatriates for personality characteristics: a moderating effect of personality on the relationship between host national contact and cross-cultural adjustment, *Management International Review*, 40 (1), 61–80.

Ditchburn, G. J. (1996) Cross-cultural adjustment and psychotism, *Personality and Individual Differences*, 21 (2), 295–6.

Doyle, A. C. (1930) *Adventures of Sherlock Holmes*. New York: Doubleday, Doran & Company, Inc.

Florkowski, G. W. and Fogel, D. S. (1999) Expatriate adjustment and commitment: the role of host-unit treatment, *International Journal of Human Resource Management*, 10 (5), 783–807.

Friede, C. K. (1981) Verfahren zur Bestimmung der Intercoderrelabilität für nominalskalierte Daten, *Zeitschrift für Empirische Pädagogik*, 5, 1–25.

Früh, W. (1989) *Inhaltsanalyse*. 2nd edn, Munich: Verlag Ölschläger.

Gregersen, H. B. (1992) Commitments to a parent company and a local work unit during repatriation, *Personnel Psychology*, 45, 29–54.

Gregersen, H. B. and Black, J. S. (1990) A multifaceted approach to expatriate retention in international assignments, *Group & Organization Studies*, 15 (4), 461–85.

Gregersen, H. B. and Black, J. S. (1992) Antecedents to commitment to a parent company and a foreign operation, *Academy of Management Journal*, 35 (1), 65–90.

Gregersen, H. B. and Stroh, L. K. (1997) Coming home to the arctic cold: antecedents to Finnish expatriate and spouse repatriation adjustment, *Personnel Psychology*, 50, 635–55.

Gummesson, E. (1991) *Qualitative Methods in Management Research*. Newbury Park: Sage.

Harrison, J. K., Chadwick, M. and Scales, M. (1996) The relationship between cross-cultural adjustment and the personality variables of self-efficacy and self-monitoring, *International Journal of Intercultural Relations*, 20 (2), 167–88.

Herzberg, F., Mausner, B. and Snyderman, B. B. (1959) *The Motivation to Work*. New York: John Wiley & Sons.

Holsti, O. R. (1969) *Content Analysis for the Social Sciences and Humanities*. Reading, Mass.: Addison-Wesley

Kraimer, M. L., Wayne, S. J. and Jaworski, R. A. (2001) Sources of support and expatriate performance: the mediating role of expatriate adjustment, *Personnel Psychology*, 54, 71–99.

Krippendorf, K. (1980) *Content Analysis: An Introduction to Its Methodology*. Beverly Hills: Sage.

Lazarsfeld, P. F. and Barton, A. H. (1951) Qualitative measurement in the social sciences: classification, typologies, and indices, in Lerner, D. and Lasswell, H. D. (eds) *The Policy Sciences: Recent Developments in Scope and Method*. Stanford: Stanford University Press, 155–92.

Lazarus, R. S. (1976) *Patterns of Adjustment*. 3rd edn., New York: McGraw-Hill.
Mayntz, R., Holm, K. and Hübner, P. (1974) *Einführung in die Methoden der empirischen Soziologie*. 4th edn., Opladen: Westdeutscher Verlag.
Mayring, P. (1997) *Qualitative Inhaltsanalyse: Grundlagen und Techniken*. 6th edn., Weinheim: Deutscher Studien Verlag.
Newman, L. V. and Leatherwood, M. L. (2001) Expectations and the adjustment process of cross-culture transitioners: a comparision with same-culture transitioners. Paper submitted to the International Division of the Academy of Management, January.
Nicholson, N. and Imaizumi, A. (1993) The adjustment of Japanese expatriates to living and working in Britain, *British Journal of Management*, 4, 119–34.
Parker, B. and McEvoy, G. (1993) Initial examination of a model of intercultural adjustment, *International Journal of Intercultural Relations*, 17 (3), 355–79.
Selmer, J. (1996) General adjustment, interaction adjustment, work adjustment and subjective well-being of Western expatriate managers in China, *BRC Papers on Cross-Cultural Management*. No. CCMC 96010, November. Hong Kong: Business Research Centre, School of Business, Hong Kong Baptist University.
Selmer, J. (1997) The difficulty of adjusting to a similar culture: ethnic Chinese vs. Western expatriates in the PRC, *BRC Papers on Cross-Cultural Management*. No. CCMC 97001, January. Hong Kong: Business Research Centre, School of Business, Hong Kong Baptist University.
Selmer, J. (1998) Expatriation: corporate policy, personal intentions and international adjustment, *International Journal of Human Resource Management*, 9 (6), 996–1007.
Selmer, J. (2000) International adjustment of business expatriates: the impact of age, gender and marital status, *BRC Papers on Cross-Cultural Management*, No. CCMP 200008. Hong Kong: Business Research Centre, School of Business, Hong Kong Baptist University.
Selmer, J. (2001) Coping and adjustment of Western expatriate managers in Hong Kong, *Scandinavian Journal of Management*, 17, 167–85.
Shaffer, M. A. and Harrison, D. A. (1998) Expatriates' psychological withdrawal from international assignments: work, nonwork, and family influences, *Personnel Psychology*, 51, 87–118.
Shaffer, M., Harrison, D. A. and Gilley, K. M. (1999) Dimensions, determinants, and differences in the expatriate adjustment process, *Journal of International Business Studies*, 30 (3) 557–81.
Sinangil, H. K. and Ones, D. S. (1997) Empirical investigations of the host country perspective in expatriate management, in Saunders, D. M. (series ed.) and Aycan, Z. (volume ed.) *New Approaches to Employee Management, Vol. 4: Expatriate Management: Theory and Research*. Greenwich, Conn.: JAI Press, 173–205.
Sinangil, H. K., Ones, D. S. and Rhoades, D. (1997) The role of spouse and family in expatriate adjustment, stay intentions and job performance. Paper presented at the annual conference of the American Psychological Association, Chicago, Illinois.
Stahl, G. K. (1998) *Internationaler Einsatz von Führungskräften*. Munich: Oldenbourg.
Torbiörn, I. (1982) *Living Abroad: Personal Adjustment and Personnel Policy in the Overseas Setting*. Chichester: John Wiley & Sons.
Tsang, E. W. K. (2001) Adjustment of mainland Chinese academics and students to Singapore, *International Journal of Intercultural Relations*, 25, 347–72.

# 5

# The Nature of Managerial Work During International Assignments: Examining Expatriate–Assignment Fit and its Consequences for Work Adjustment

*Oliver Breiden, Hafiz R. Mirza & Alexander T. Mohr*

## Introduction

Clearly, for multinational organizations it is vital that managers who are sent abroad to complete international assignments are capable of pursuing the work-related objectives that are linked to their new jobs abroad. Yet, frequently it has been noted that expatriate managers experience a lack of job satisfaction, suffer from a decline in motivation and show signs of low performance on the job in their host-country organizations (Black and Gregersen, 1999). Due to the considerable costs associated with an international assignment which probably reflect 'the single largest expenditure most companies make on any one individual except for the CEO' (Black and Gregersen, 1999: 53), practitioners and management researchers have been particularly interested to identify the factors that influence career satisfaction, on-the-job performance and workplace adjustment among expatriate managers.

As it has been illustrated, a mismatch between the employee's expectations and the realities of the job abroad has frequently been associated with adjustment problems on the part of the expatriate manager (Osland, 2000; Caligiuri, Phillips, Lazarova, Tarique et al., 2001; Suutari and Brewster, 2001). Based on an analysis of the responses obtained from 117 German expatriate managers, Horsch (1995) notes that the expectations of expatriates differ significantly from the goals identified by human resources directors of their respective organizations. While the need to accomplish an immediate organizational task or objective – e.g. the transfer of know-how or the co-ordination of work abroad – is emphasized by personnel directors, managers who have been selected for

*Table 5.1:* Comparison of the expectations of firms and expatriates

| **Reasons for the organization (n = 117)** | **Personnel managers of German firms** | **Reasons for the expatriate** | **Expatriate managers of German firms** |
|---|---|---|---|
| Transfer of know-how | 43% | Enhanced career prospects | 54% |
| Human resources development | 32% | Interest in greater responsibility | 31% |
| Co-ordination/Control | 14% | Salary increase | 15% |
| No local staff available | 11% | Personal development | 0% |

*Note:* Multiple responses were possible; the ranking shows the recalculated relative frequency of the top-ranked reason only.
*Source:* Based on Horsch (1995).

international assignments are primarily motivated by career expectations when accepting a position abroad (see Table 5.1). Similarly, commenting on the results of a survey conducted among American expatriate managers, Light (1997) points out that respondents consistently stress two main reasons for accepting a foreign assignment: 'higher pay and the opportunity to advance their careers' (p. 20). Yet, it has been suggested that the mismatch between the demands of the organization and the expectations stated by individual managers can create conflict and lead to performance problems during the assignment. When investigating satisfaction and adjustment among Irish expatriate managers, Morley, Burke and O'Regan (1997) identified two additional areas where a mismatch between employee expectations and the conditions encountered by the transferred manager could have negative consequences for the assignment. In addition to providing expatriates with more defined jobs abroad, they found that '[a] strong relationship existed between the quality of respondents' working environment and both their effectiveness and satisfaction at work' (Morley, Burke and O'Regan, 1997: 63).

In the subsequent sections, the nature of managerial work performed by expatriate managers is investigated and the job situations encountered by transferred managers are critically examined. More specifically, it is argued that a better understanding of managerial activities and duties that are to be carried out by the expatriate employee is required in order to determine the levels of job satisfaction reported by transferred managers. Furthermore, it is held that adjustment to the foreign workplace can only be achieved if the individual is satisfied with the tasks performed in the host-country firm and if the expatriate is emotionally satisfied with the workplace conditions encountered abroad. Relying on an analysis of the responses collected from 118 German expatriate managers, expatriate abilities and perceived job requirements are compared and the needs and perceived reinforcements of transferred managers are identified. Based on the findings made, it is proposed to pay closer attention to expatriate–assignment fit and to turn to task satisfaction levels and emotional satisfaction levels as antecedents of expatriate work adjustment.

## The manager's job: a review of work activity research

For more than 50 years, much research has been undertaken to study the jobs and activities of managers in a broad range of firms, industries and countries. In their investigations, researchers have examined the workplace demands as well as the behaviour and interaction of different types of managers, including executives (Kotter, 1982; Carlson, 1991), division presidents (Gabarro, 1987), middle managers (Horne and Lupton, 1965; Stewart, 1976; Stewart, 1988; Watson, 1994) and school and government administrators (Mintzberg, 1980; Allan, 1981; Kurke and Aldrich, 1983). The findings made have provided detailed accounts of the job characteristics, work routines and habits, social networks and patterns of interaction and exchange of a broad range of managers. Based on the insights gained, an understanding of managerial jobs and activities has emerged which largely stands at odds with earlier descriptions of managerial activities and duties.

First conceptualizations of managerial work can be found in the works of Fayol (1988), who, at the beginning of the 20th century, characterized and described management as an orderly process consisting of distinct tasks and activities. To this effect, Fayol (1988) came to conclude that 'to manage is to plan, organize, coordinate, command, and control' (p. 13). During the 1930s and 1940s, Urwick (1944) and Gulick and Urwick (1937) developed the notion of an administrative science and identified seven distinct managerial activities: planning, organizing, staffing, directing, coordinating, reporting and budgeting. Yet, the results obtained in different investigations on executive behaviour and managerial work that have been conducted since the early 1950s have revealed that the jobs and duties performed by managers and executives frequently consist of fragmented and disjoint activities which are inconsistent with the categories proposed by Fayol (1988), Urwick (1944) and Gulick and Urwick (1937). In order to address this deficiency, Stewart (1976; 1988), Mintzberg (1980) and Kotter (1982; 1990) have turned to a closer analysis of the manager's job by observing managerial activity in the workplace setting.

In a more recent investigation, Luthans, Hodgetts and Rosenkrantz (1988) examined data that were obtained from 457 managers working in different organizations in the private and public sector. In addition to the records compiled from direct observation, extensive material was collected through standardized questionnaires and interviews with managers and their subordinates. An analysis of the activities performed by 248 managers revealed that participants spent approximately 30 per cent of their time on traditional management activities such as planning, controlling and decision making, whereas a similar amount of time was devoted to routine communication consisting of information exchanges and the handling of paperwork. Furthermore, the findings indicated that the remaining 40 per cent of a manager's time was equally distributed between staff related matters and networking activities.

In Table 5.2 the results obtained by Luthans, Hodgetts and Rosenkrantz (1988) have been summarized. When comparing the amount of time devoted to the four sets of activities, a number of significant differences can be identified between the activity patterns of average managers, successful managers and effective managers. As Luthans, Hodgetts and Rosenkrantz

*Table 5.2:* Relative contributions to managerial success and effectiveness

| | **Distribution of managerial activity** | | |
|---|---|---|---|
| **Managerial activities** | **Average (n = 248)** | **Effective (n = 52)** | **Successful (n = 52)** |
| Routine Communication<br>• *Exchanging information*<br>• *Handling paperwork* | 29% | 44% | 28% |
| Traditional Management<br>• *Planning*<br>• *Controlling*<br>• *Decision making* | 32% | 19% | 13% |
| Human Resource Management<br>• *Motivating/reinforcing*<br>• *Staffing*<br>• *Training/developing*<br>• *Managing conflict* | 20% | 26% | 11% |
| Networking<br>• *Interacting with outsiders*<br>• *Socializing/politicking* | 19% | 11% | 48% |

*Source:* Adapted from Luthans, Hodgetts and Rosenkrantz (1988).

(1988) point out,

> the findings of the success and effectiveness analysis seem to indicate that RMs' [author's note: RM = real manager] networking activities are a way to get ahead in an organization, to be successful, but have little to do with the contribution to effectiveness of RMs. (p. 72)

More so, the authors note that effective managers largely neglect networking activities while stressing that 'communicating and human resources management activities are an *integral part* of organizational effectiveness' (Luthans, Hodgetts and Rosenkrantz, 1988: 75). Whereas successful managers are less inclined to pursue performance enhancements and productivity increases, it is being concluded that such objectives form the central determinant for effective management practices.

## Expatriate managers and their jobs abroad: self-reports from German expatriates

Between March and September 2003, an empirical investigation among German expatriate managers was conducted in order to obtain data on employment characteristics and foreign assignment conditions. Overall, 275 transferred managers working in twenty different firms received an email invitation from their respective personnel managers to complete an online survey via the Internet. By the end of the data collection phase, 140 responses had been obtained for a total response rate of 50.9 per cent. A total of 22 response files were eliminated because the records could not be matched to one of the participating companies, due to missing information (year of birth, gender, ratings of work satisfaction, etc.) or because individuals spent only a limited amount of time on managerial activities.

Out of the 118 surveys that were examined during data analysis, the vast majority of questionnaires were completed by male expatriate employees. While the ten surveys that were submitted by female assignees correspond to 8.5 per cent of the total number of responses obtained, 108 male expatriate managers completed the instrument which, in turn, reflects a male participation of 91.5 per cent. A review of the age distribution among participants reveals that the average age of expatriate managers in the sample was approximately 40 years with a standard deviation of 8 years, whereby the ages recorded ranged from 23 to 63 years. The data obtained from participants were analysed to determine the workload demands of expatriate managers, to establish the distribution of time to different managerial activities in the foreign workplace and to examine the skill utilization as well as the perceived job requirements reported by expatriate managers. In the subsequent sections, the findings made in each area are discussed in greater detail.

### Workload demands

Having conducted an empirical investigation of the working practices of German expatriate managers, Stahl (1998) notes that excessive workload demands can create dissatisfaction and stress among transferred employees. Thus, in order to obtain appropriate data on the workload encountered by study participants, a number of questions were presented to identify the average amount of time an individual attends to business matters per week and to obtain information on the time allocated by the expatriate to a range of managerial activities.

On average, participants worked approximately 53 hours per week, whereby four out of five respondents indicated a workload between 45 and 60 hours per week. While cross-tabulations of the weekly workload versus the employing organization as well as the weekly workload versus the assignment region did not provide indications for similarities or patterns, an analysis of the weekly workload and the position assumed abroad revealed a link between the manager's position abroad and the time spent at work. Approximately two out of ten managing directors worked in excess of 60 hours per week. In contrast, only one out of ten department heads and one out of twenty project managers reported an equally high amount of time spent at work.

When the findings obtained in this study are compared to previous studies where the timing demands expressed by senior executives working in Germany have been examined, similar results can be identified. While Reichwald and Goecke (1996) conclude that top-level managers work 9.4 hours per day (i.e. 9.4 h × 5 days = 47 hours per week), Schreyögg and Hübl (1992) note that observational data suggest a working day of approximately 10 hours (i.e. 10 h × 5 days = 50 hours per week). When self-assessments are used as the principal data sources to determine the workload of German executives, Müller-Böling, Klautke and Ramme (1989) compute a 59 hour work week while the findings made in a more recent study suggest that managers spent approximately 54 hours per week attending to their jobs (Hunziger, 2003). Thus, when comparing the workload requirements experienced by managers who operate in a national environment to those individuals who are exposed to a foreign workplace, similar timing demands can be identified. Thus, it can be suggested that managers are generally confronted with the demand to allocate a considerable part of their time to business matters, irrespective of national or international job considerations.

## The distribution of time to managerial activities in the foreign workplace

In addition to collecting data on the weekly hourly workload, expatriate employees were also requested to allocate the time spent at work to different categories of managerial activity. Luthans and colleagues (1985; 1985; 1988) propose to examine four sets of managerial activities: (1) routine communication, (2) traditional management, (3) human resource management and (4) networking. An analysis of the activities performed by 248 American managers revealed that participants spent over 30 per cent of their time on traditional management tasks such as planning, controlling and decision making, whereas a similar amount of time was absorbed by routine communication consisting of information exchanges and the handling of paperwork. Furthermore, the findings indicated that the remaining 40 per cent of a manager's time is equally distributed between staff related matters and networking activities (Luthans, Hodgetts and Rosenkrantz, 1988).

In Table 5.3 a comparison of the results obtained by Luthans, Hodgetts and Rosenkrantz (1988) and the findings made in this study is presented. While the proportions of time spent on traditional management duties and networking activities are similar between the two groups of study participants, expatriate managers who participated in this research allocated more time to routine communication while, at the same time, they were less inclined to attend to staffing matters and personnel management issues.

In the previous two sections, the workload demands of German expatriate managers have been examined and the allocation of time to various managerial activities has been identified. Though considerable variation has been observed between respondents in the sample, the findings made are comparable to the experiences reported by various groups of managers operating in a domestic work environment, thus suggesting that there are some commonalities that could be attributed to the general nature of managerial work and managerial jobs. In the subsequent discussion, emphasis is placed on the managerial abilities of transferred employees as well as the perceived ability requirements that are needed to perform the job abroad.

## Expatriate abilities and job requirements

Based on the four categories of managerial activity identified by Luthans, Hodgetts and Rosenkrantz (1988), study participants were asked to provide a skill rating with respect to various managerial activities and to indicate the extent to which these particular activities formed part of the requirements of their jobs abroad. In the following discussion, an assessment of the findings is presented. Particular emphasis is placed on

*Table 5.3:* Comparing the distribution of managerial activity

| **Managerial activities** | **Distribution of managerial activity**<br>**Luthans, Hodgetts and Rosenkrantz (1988) (n = 248)** | **This study* (n = 118)** |
|---|---|---|
| Routine Communication<br>• *Exchanging information*<br>• *Handling paperwork* | 29% | 39% |
| Traditional Management<br>• *Planning*<br>• *Controlling*<br>• *Decision making* | 32% | 33% |
| Human Resource Management<br>• *Motivating/reinforcing*<br>• *Staffing*<br>• *Training/developing*<br>• *Managing conflict* | 20% | 11% |
| Networking<br>• *Interacting with outsiders*<br>• *Socializing/politicking* | 19% | 17% |

* Based on an average of 53 hours worked per week; 45 hours distributed across activity categories and 8 hours unexplained (not considered for the calculation of percentages).
*Source:* Based on Luthans, Hodgetts and Rosenkrantz (1988).

the four categories of managerial activity that have previously been identified: (1) routine communication, (2) traditional management, (3) human resource management and (4) networking.

### *Routine communication*

When engaging in routine communication, managers frequently conduct meetings or they rely on mail, fax or email correspondence to exchange information with their business partners. Consequently, expatriate managers were asked to assess their abilities as well as the perceived requirements of their jobs abroad with respect to: (1) conducting staff meetings to discuss routine matters and organizational issues and (2) processing correspondence and handling internal reports.

In Figure 5.1 the ratings for conducting staff meetings have been illustrated. While a low score either reflects a low desire to perform the activity or it indicates that a particular task is rarely required in the job abroad, a high score demonstrates a high capacity to engage in the particular activity or it can be associated with a strong need for the task to

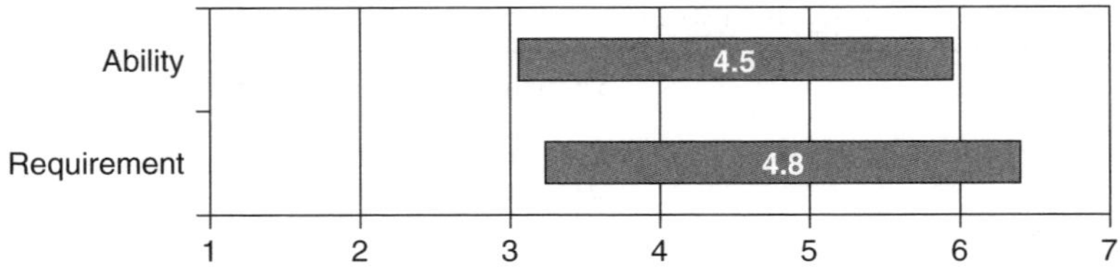


*Figure 5.1:* Ability vs. requirement rating for conducting staff meetings

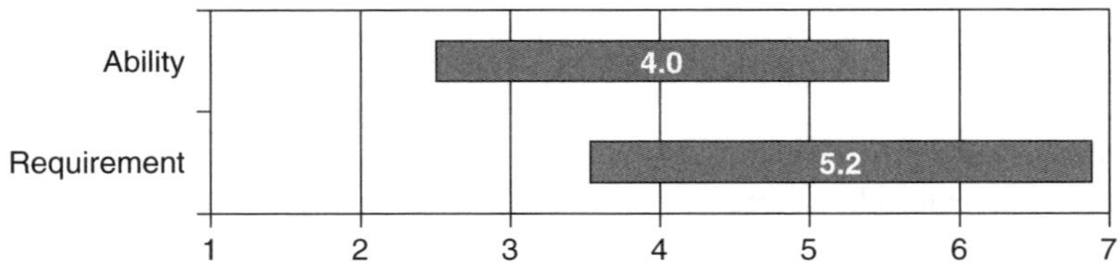


*Figure 5.2:* Ability vs. requirement rating for processing correspondence

be performed during the foreign assignment. In the diagram, the mean scores are presented whereby the bars represent one standard deviation to either side of the mean score. Thus, while respondents indicated a mean capacity of 4.5 with respect to conducting staff meetings, the perceived requirement for meetings to be held was considered to be slightly higher as expressed by a mean score of 4.8 on a 7-point scale.

Likewise, a similar discrepancy can be identified with respect to processing mail, fax and email correspondence. In Figure 5.2 a summary of the calculated mean scores has been presented. Overall, it can be noted that respondents recognized a high need to engage in routine communication during their foreign assignments. At the same time, the desire to exercise their abilities in the workplace was rated lower than the perceived need to attend to routine communication matters, thus indicating that there could be a possible mismatch between employee characteristics and job requirements.

### *Traditional management*

In their work, Luthans, Hodgetts and Rosenkrantz (1988) identify three types of managerial tasks which are subsequently classified as traditional management activities: (1) planning, (2) controlling and (3) decision making. For each particular task, expatriate managers participating in this research were asked to assess their work-related abilities and the perceived requirements to perform each of the three specific activities during the time spent abroad.

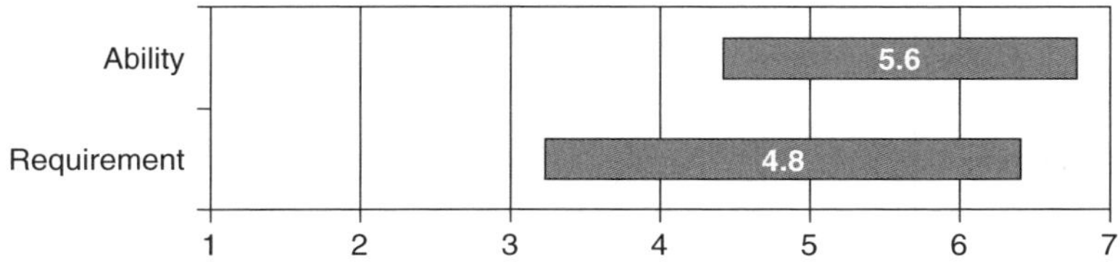


*Figure 5.3:* Ability vs. requirement rating for planning activities

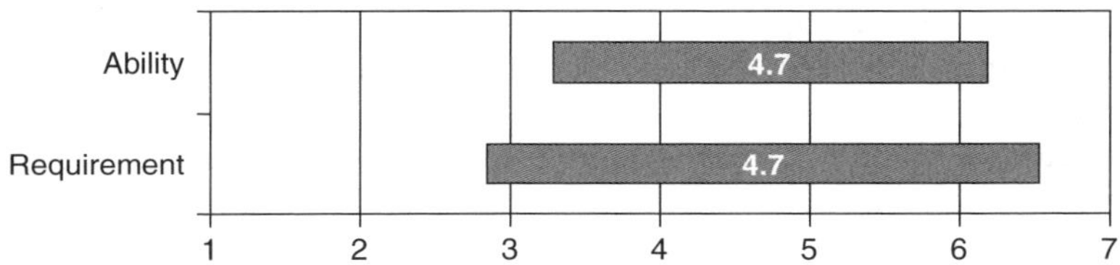


*Figure 5.4:* Ability vs. requirement rating for controlling activities

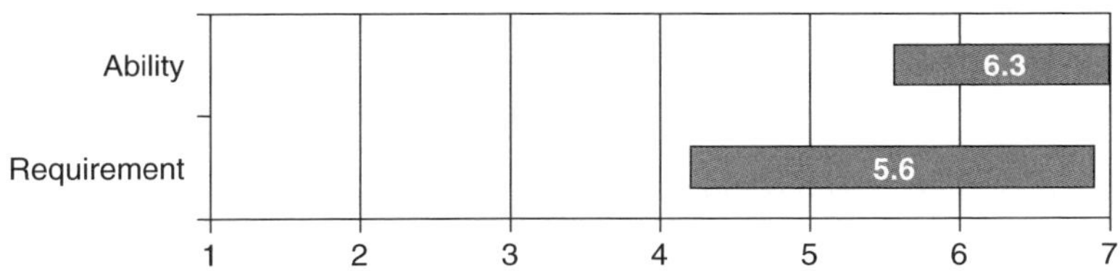


*Figure 5.5:* Ability vs. requirement rating for decision making

In Figure 5.3 the mean scores for planning activities have been summarized. When asked to rate their preferences and perceptions regarding goal setting and scheduling activities, participants indicated that their capacity to perform this particular task exceeded the requirements of their jobs abroad.

Moreover, the need to control and review the results of other members of the organization was examined. As indicated in Figure 5.4 on average, the capacity of assignees to perform this particular task was found to correspond to the requirements encountered during foreign assignments.

Lastly, when asked to consider their abilities to assess trade-offs between different solutions and to take and communicate decisions, participants expressed considerable interests while, at the same time, recognizing a great need to engage in such activities during their international assignments (see Figure 5.5).

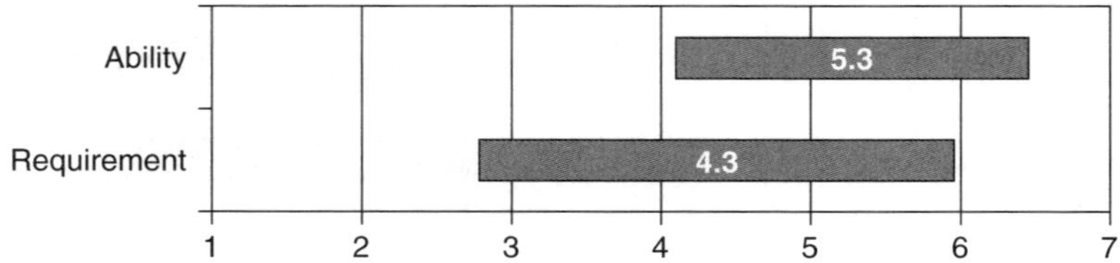


*Figure 5.6:* Ability vs. requirement rating for feedback activity

Thus, in contrast to the area of routine communication where study participants indicated that the perceived requirements of their jobs abroad exceeded their interests to apply matching abilities to the job, in the case of traditional management activities a different perspective emerged. Yet, while an employee's desire to apply work-related abilities that exceed the particular requirements of the respective job could generally be considered as beneficial for an organization, a lack of correspondence – particularly in planning and decision making – could also result in low task satisfaction ratings. In cases where expatriate managers feel that their abilities are not sufficiently used by their employers, a feeling of underutilization and frustration could ultimately be expected to emerge.

### *Human resource management*

In order to permit an assessment of the expatriate manager's exposure to staff management issues, data were collected on three sets of activities relating to human resource management: (1) conducting feedback meetings with subordinates or team members, (2) reviewing staffing requirements as well as handling hiring and dismissal decisions and (3) mediating between members of the organization in cases where conflict emerged.

In Figure 5.6 a comparison of the mean scores calculated for handling feedback is presented. Overall, based on an analysis of the data it appears that the self-reported abilities of transferred managers to hold such staff review meetings within the organization exceed the requirements of the job abroad.

Similar results are obtained when the participation of expatriate managers in hiring and dismissal decisions is analysed. As illustrated in Figure 5.7 the majority of expatriates perceived their abilities in this domain to exceed the demands of the job abroad.

Lastly, when asked to state their perceptions concerning the need to clear up conflict between subordinates or team members, participants in this study expressed moderate competencies while, at the same time,

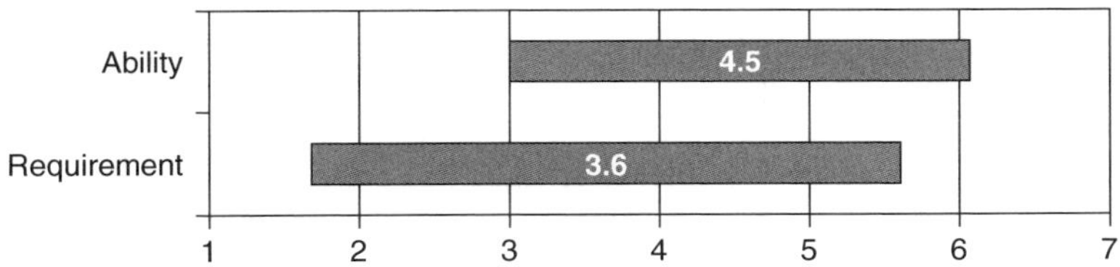


*Figure 5.7:* Ability vs. requirement rating for hiring and firing

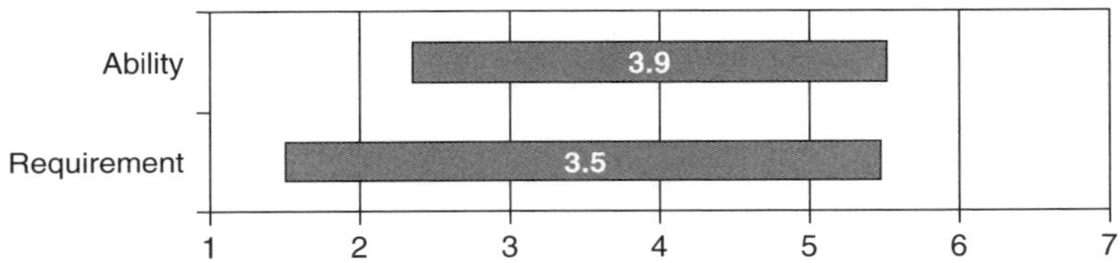


*Figure 5.8:* Ability vs. requirement rating for resolving conflict

recognizing only a reduced need to perform such activities during the time spent in the host-country organization (see Figure 5.8).

Similar to the area of traditional management, in human resources management activities, expatriate managers generally perceived their abilities to exceed the requirements encountered in their respective jobs abroad. Consequently, it could be anticipated that a lack of ability utilization on behalf of the host-country firm could result in low satisfaction levels relating to the tasks presented to the expatriate manager during the international assignment.

### *Networking*

The fourth and final category of managerial tasks established by Luthans, Hodgetts and Rosenkrantz (1988) contains networking activities whereby a distinction is made between: (1) establishing and maintaining external contacts and (2) developing and fostering contacts within the organization.

As illustrated in Figure 5.9 transferred managers expressed strong interests to develop and utilize external contacts. However, the perceived need to establish such relationships through meetings with external business partners, conference participations or tradeshow visits was considered to be less of a requirement during foreign assignments.

A similar assessment can be made with respect to the individual's abilities and perceived requirements to develop and maintain internal contacts

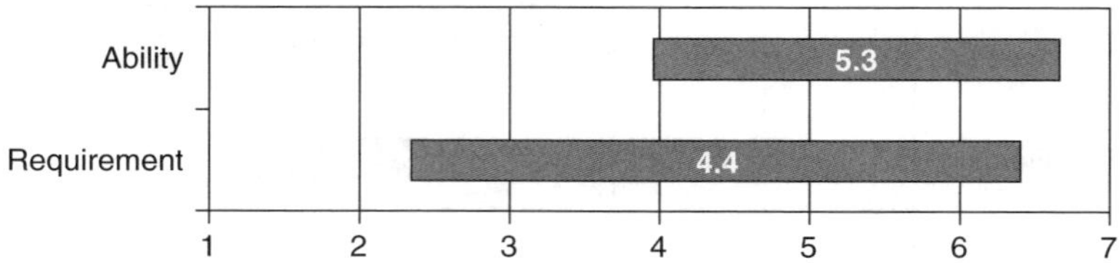


*Figure 5.9:* Ability vs. requirement rating for developing external contacts

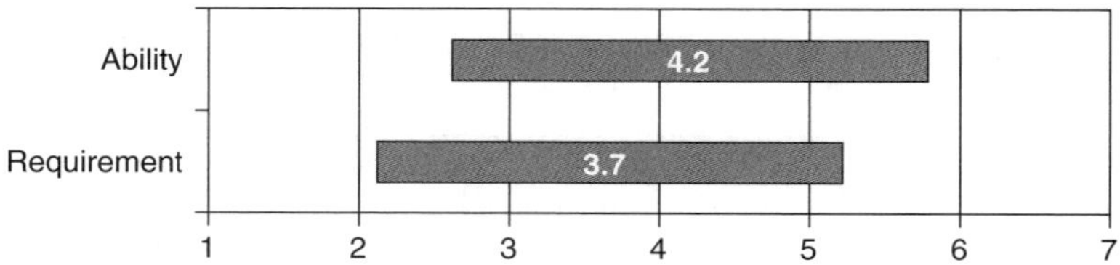


*Figure 5.10:* Ability vs. requirement rating for developing internal contacts

within the host-country organization. While expatriates acknowledged their general interest and desire to establish social ties with other members of the organization, the perceived requirement to establish such contacts was considered to be less important (see Figure 5.10).

Much to the same extent that study participants saw their abilities to attend to traditional management activities and human resources management activities exceed the requirements of their jobs abroad, on average, German expatriate managers who participated in the survey regarded their abilities to establish external as well as internal contacts to be more developed than it was perceived to be required to complete the job abroad. Again, for the expatriate manager, the identified mismatch could potentially result in a lack of satisfaction with the tasks presented abroad.

## Expatriate needs and reinforcements during the assignment

While the focus of the previous sections has been on the managerial abilities of expatriate managers as well as the perceived job requirements in the host-country organizations, in the following section an assessment of the work-related needs and perceived reinforcements available during the assignment is presented. More specifically, five distinct areas that are relevant to assess the emotional satisfaction of managers and executives (Cellucci and DeVries, 1978) are examined in greater detail: (1) work itself, (2) exchanges with colleagues and peers, (3) exchanges with superiors, (4) opportunities to advance in the company and

*Figure 5.11:* Expatriate need vs. reinforcement for work itself

(5) compensation. Much to the same extent that a mismatch between work-related abilities and job requirements is expected to result in low levels of task satisfaction, it is anticipated that a gap between the vocational needs of the expatriate manager and the reinforcements and benefits provided during the foreign assignment could yield low levels of emotional satisfaction. Consequently, it is important to establish the degree of fit between the expatriate employee's work-related needs and the perceived level of fulfilment in the five areas previously identified.

### *Work itself*

Cellucci and DeVries (1978) note that there is a link between an employee's interest in the work being performed and the individual's job satisfaction. In order to identify if expatriate employees recognize the need for an interesting work environment and to determine if they perceive their jobs abroad to cater to their needs, participants were asked to state if they felt that performing an interesting job is important and to rate the extent to which their jobs abroad fulfilled this particular requirement. While high ratings correspond to great importance or fulfilment, a low rating can be associated with a low need for an interesting job or a lack of reinforcement provided by the job abroad.

As illustrated in Figure 5.11 German expatriate employees participating in this study perceived a considerable need to perform an interesting job. At the same time, assignees also noted that the work they completed during their foreign assignments provided high levels of reinforcement.

### *Exchanges with colleagues*

A second area of interest with respect to the needs of expatriate managers and the perceived reinforcements provided by the job abroad relates to the exchanges with colleagues and the relationships developed with staff in the host-country organization.

When asked to examine the need to develop rapport with other members of the organization, respondents confirmed the importance of developing and maintaining good relations with colleagues. Yet, when asked if their needs were fulfilled while working abroad, expatriate managers provided slightly lower ratings. A summary of the results obtained has been presented in Figure 5.12.

### *Exchanges with superiors*

In addition to asking transferred managers about contacts and exchanges with co-workers in the host-country organization, study participants were also requested to assess their relationships with superiors in the company.

As illustrated in Figure 5.13, respondents reported a great need for developing and maintaining good exchanges with superiors. However, in comparison to their expectations, on average, expatriate managers who participated in this study perceived a somewhat lower presence of such close exchanges during their foreign assignments.

### *Opportunities to advance in the company*

Frequently, it has been argued that individuals who accept international assignments are particularly motivated by perceived opportunities to advance in the company (Gomez-Mejía and Balkin, 1987; Harvey, 1989; Aryee, Chay and Chew, 1996; Hirsch, 1996; Winter, 1996; Suutari and Brewster, 2001). Consequently, participants were asked to state their desire to advance to more senior positions within the company and to

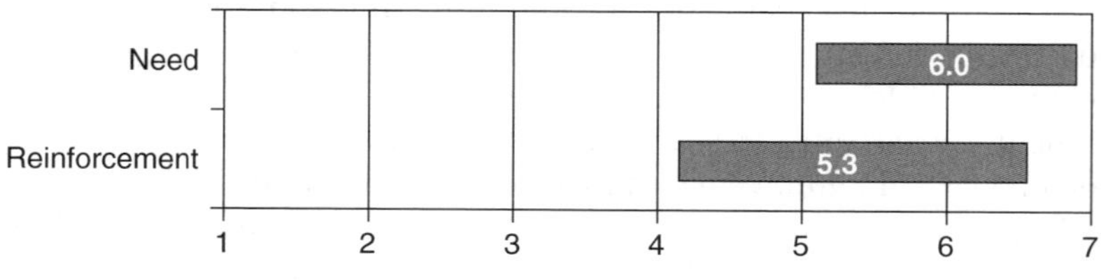


*Figure 5.12:* Expatriate need vs. reinforcement for exchanges with colleagues

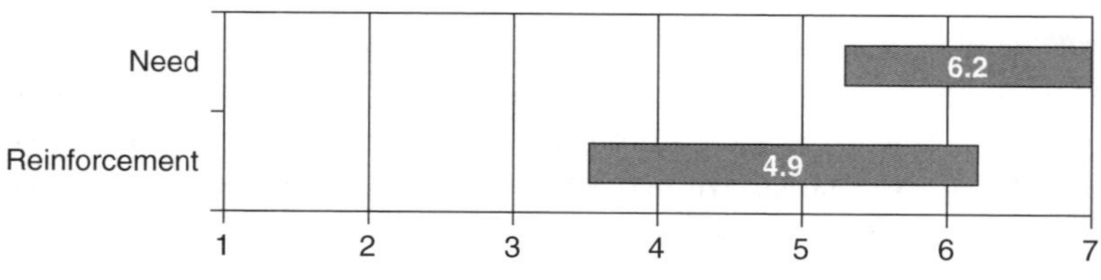


*Figure 5.13:* Expatriate need vs. reinforcement for exchanges with superiors

indicate if they recognized opportunities to be promoted during their time spent abroad or following the assignment.

In Figure 5.14 the findings made during this investigation are summarized. Overall, respondents indicated a great need to be given the possibility to advance in the company. However, when the average score relating to the expected opportunities for career advancement is calculated, a markedly lower rating is obtained, thus, suggesting that expatriate managers are hesitant to believe that their international postings will immediately lead to a promotion during the assignment or following their return to the home-country organization.

*Compensation*

Lastly, data were collected on compensation issues. In addition to rating the importance they place on salary and expatriate benefits, participants were asked to indicate the extent to which their needs were met by the remuneration package provided abroad.

While participants generally expressed a desire to receive good pay and compensation packages when transferring to a foreign subsidiary, some discrepancy could be noted with respect to conditions actually encountered in the foreign workplace. A comparison of the expatriates' needs as well as the perceived reinforcements relating to compensation issues is presented in Figure 5.15.

In summary, respondents frequently recognized a mismatch between their requirements and the conditions and benefits encountered in the

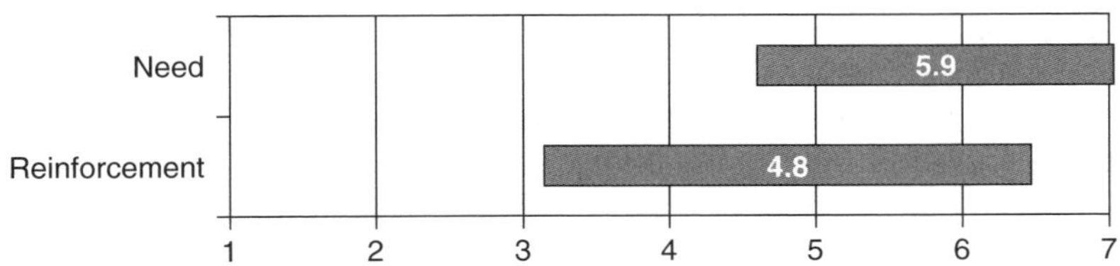


*Figure 5.14:* Expatriate need vs. reinforcement for getting promoted

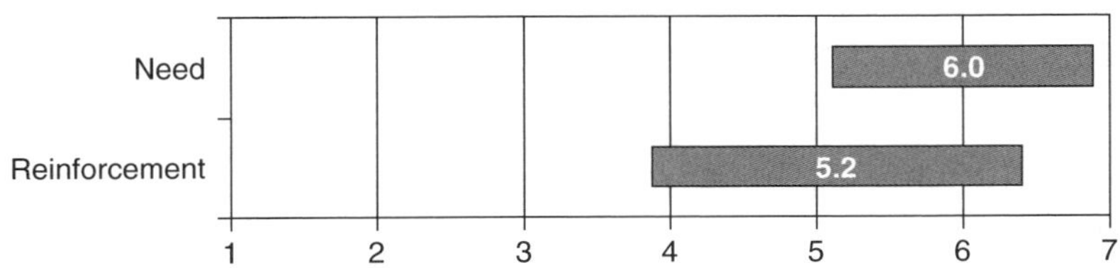


*Figure 5.15:* Expatriate need vs. reinforcement for financial compensation

workplace. Though a majority of individuals saw the need for an interesting and challenging job to be satisfied, particularly large discrepancies were apparent in the perceived opportunities to advance in the company and the contacts and exchanges developed with superiors in the host-country organization.

## Adjustment during international assignments: a three factor solution

In the previous sections, a comparison of German expatriate managers' abilities and the job requirements encountered in the foreign workplace as well as a review of the transferred employees' needs and the perceived reinforcements provided abroad have been presented. More specifically, managers were asked if they could perform certain activities in the workplace and to state if they recognized a need to complete various managerial activities during the course of the international assignment. Various researchers have suggested that there is a link between the fit of a transferred employee and the job encountered abroad and the expatriate manager's degree of adjustment (Brewster, 1993; Parker and McEvoy, 1993; Mendenhall and Wiley, 1994; Harrison, Chadwick and Scales, 1996; Aycan, 1997).

When determining the degree of adjustment achieved by an expatriate manager during the course of an international assignment, the findings made in a number of empirical investigations suggest that three specific facets of adjustment can be identified (Black, 1988; Black and Stephens, 1989): (1) work adjustment, (2) general adjustment and (3) interaction adjustment (see Figure 5.16).

While a number of domestic investigations have been undertaken to study work role transitions among job changers and employees who have been transferred or promoted within their respective organizations, more recently, the rise in international business has also led to a growing interest in the work adjustment of expatriate employees. As Black (1988) points out, in a number of studies on international personnel transfers, particular emphasis has been placed on the work-related facet of expatriate adjustment. Offering a general definition, Palthe (2001) suggests to regard work adjustment as a person's 'adaptation to new job tasks, work roles, and the new work environment' (p. 10). Similarly, Black and Stephens (1989) note that an expatriate's work adjustment is linked to the content of the job abroad, the supervisory responsibilities granted to the individual and the person's ability to cope with the performance standards encountered in the host-country organization. In a number of

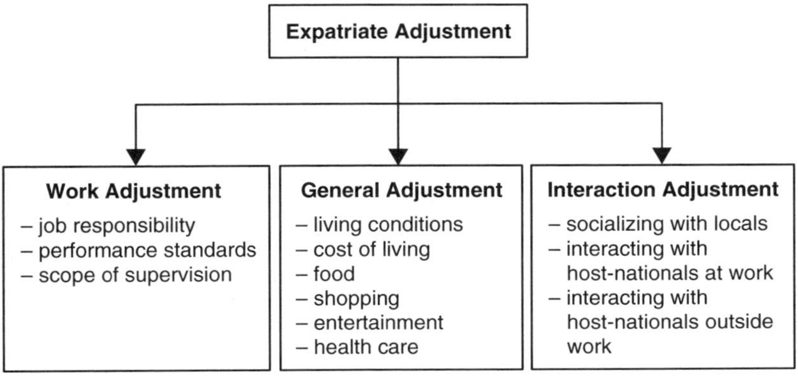


*Figure 5.16:* Three facets of expatriate adjustment
*Source:* Adapted from Black and Stephens (1989).

subsequent studies in which the work adjustment of expatriate employees has been investigated, it has been demonstrated that some individuals are challenged to cope with their new job-related roles while working abroad (Shaffer and Harrison, 1998; Shaffer, Harrison and Gilley, 1999). Shaffer and colleagues (1999) note that support provided by the organization as well as help received from colleagues can serve as predictors of a person's adjustment to the workplace. Thus, it is held that work adjustment can be regarded as a distinct facet of an expatriate's overall adjustment to the demands of an international assignment.

## Expatriate–assignment fit and its consequences for work adjustment

As illustrated in the previous section, in order to achieve work adjustment abroad, it is expected that there has to be an adequate level of fit between the expatriate employee's work-related capabilities and expectations and the characteristics of the job abroad. Building on the work of Dawis and Lofquist (1984) who advanced and tested a general Theory of Work Adjustment, a model of expatriate work adjustment is subsequently presented which is based on the understanding that the work-related abilities and demands of expatriate employees need to be compared to the requirements and reinforcements encountered during foreign assignments. Furthermore, it is suggested that the achievement of work adjustment reflects a consequence of an appropriate level of fit between the expatriate manager's abilities and expectations and the job conditions encountered abroad.

Similar to other models in which relationships between individuals and various types of settings have been identified (Feldman, 1976; Caplan, 1987; Chatman, 1989; Aycan, 1997; Lance, Vandenberg and Self, 2000), the model of expatriate work adjustment rests on the assessment of correspondence between individuals and their respective environments. In general, it is held that correspondence reflects a match between an individual's abilities and needs and the requirements and provisions encountered in a particular environment. Furthermore, the model is based on the assumption that employees in any organization aim to reach and maintain correspondence in order to achieve satisfaction and that such attempts form part of the 'basic motives of human behaviour' (Dawis and Lofquist, 1984: 54). In order to meet the requirements of the job, individuals make use of their unique abilities and skills and, in turn, they receive rewards and recognition which cater to their particular needs and demands. Thus, correspondence reflects a state where '*the individual [is] fulfilling the requirements of the work environment and the work environment [is] fulfilling the requirements of the individual*' (Dawis and Lofquist, 1984: 54).

According to Dawis and Lofquist (1984), correspondence leads to job satisfaction which, in turn, results in high levels of work adjustment and a desire on the part of the employee to stay in the job and extend organizational membership. When correspondence has been achieved in a work relationship, the firm may consider the amount of pay and the benefits provided to the jobholder appropriate in view of the individual's performance in the workplace while, at the same time, the employee is satisfied with the assigned tasks and duties and expresses emotional satisfaction with the conditions encountered in the work environment.

In Figure 5.17, the principal relationships of interest incorporated in the model have been illustrated. It is anticipated that expatriate work adjustment is the result of the levels of task satisfaction and emotional satisfaction achieved by expatriate employees during the time spent living and working abroad. While an expatriate manager's task satisfaction is expected to be the result of the fit between work-related abilities and the requirements of the job abroad, it is anticipated that emotional satisfaction is the result of an appropriate fit between the reinforcements and rewards available in the workplace and the demands and needs of the expatriate employee. In the subsequent two sections, both task satisfaction and emotional satisfaction are examined in greater detail.

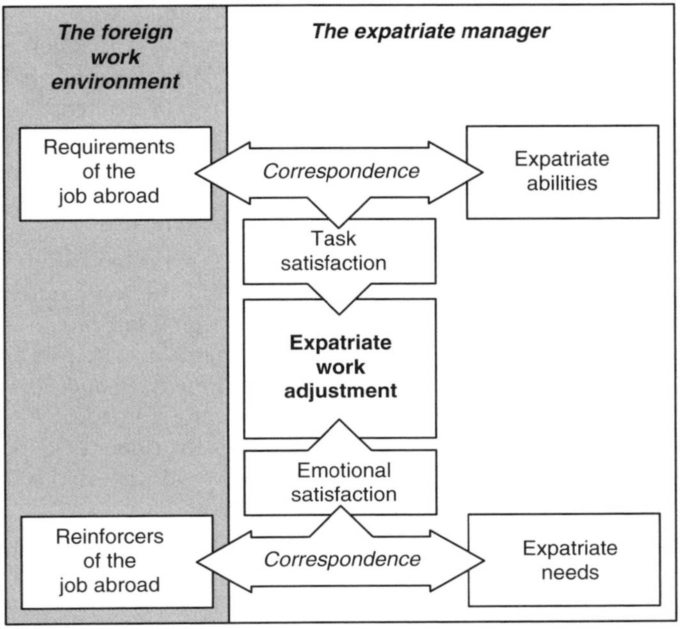


*Figure 5.17:* A model of expatriate work adjustment

### *Task satisfaction: ability–requirement correspondence*

The results obtained in previous investigations suggest that there is a prominent risk that managers who embark on foreign assignments may initially not possess the necessary competence and all the skills which are needed to fulfil the requirements of their new jobs abroad. In particular, it has been noted that a lack of cross-cultural abilities on the part of the transferred employee can be associated with low levels of adjustment to the foreign work environment (Tung, 1981; Mendenhall and Oddou, 1986; Zakaria, 2000). Consequently, when determining the degree of correspondence between the requirements of a job abroad and the abilities of an expatriate manager, it is critical to review the employee's managerial abilities as well as cross-cultural abilities with regard to the demands of the particular assignment.

In the model of expatriate work adjustment, it is held that an expatriate's *task satisfaction* relates to the person's satisfaction derived from meeting the work-related demands of the job abroad. Therefore, whenever the perceived ability requirements of an assignment match the employee's job-related abilities, it is expected that the individual will report high levels of task satisfaction. Likewise, low levels of task satisfaction among expatriates are anticipated whenever a lack of correspondence is identified. More specifically, a lack of correspondence is expected to be linked to one of the following two conditions: (1) a lack of ability requirements of the job abroad or (2) a lack of ability on the part of the expatriate manager.

### *Emotional satisfaction: need–reinforcement correspondence*

While an expatriate's level of task satisfaction is expected to depend on the match between the individual's abilities and the job requirements encountered abroad, it is anticipated that emotional satisfaction can be linked to the demands and expectations of expatriate managers and the rewards and benefits available during the assignment. In addition to the financial rewards available to employees working abroad, it has been stressed that social contacts and opportunities for career development need to be examined in order to assess the emotional satisfaction of expatriate employees in their foreign workplaces.

It is held that *expatriate needs* are characterized by a person's financial, intellectual and emotional aspirations as they pertain to the workplace setting, whereas the *reinforcers of the job abroad* consist of financial rewards and incentives, contacts and exchanges with other members of the organization, the potential for achieving recognition and praise for the work accomplished abroad and opportunities for subsequent career advancement. It is anticipated that high levels of *emotional satisfaction* are the result of a close fit between the needs and aspirations of an individual and the tangible and intangible rewards available in the workplace. Likewise, lower levels of *emotional satisfaction* are expected to be caused by a lack of correspondence between the expatriate's work-related needs and the reinforcements and rewards offered during the international posting.

Two principal reasons can be associated with a lack of correspondence between expatriate needs and the reinforcements available during the foreign assignment: (1) a lack of rewards and reinforcements available in the workplace and (2) excessive expectations, demands or needs on the part of the international sojourner. The findings made in previous investigations in which expatriate practices have been examined suggest that the financial rewards as well as the types of jobs being offered to candidates selected for international transfers are rarely regarded as a source of apprehension or dissatisfaction (Wirth, 1992; Horsch, 1995; Stahl, 1998; Suutari and Tornikoski, 2001; Boies and Rothstein, 2002). Yet, it has been demonstrated that uncertainty as well as excessive or unrealistic expectations regarding the foreign assignment can cause managers to experience difficulties in adjusting to the new cultural setting (Harrison, Chadwick and Scales, 1996; Caligiuri, Phillips, Lazarova, Tarique et al., 2001). Therefore, when an expatriate's level of work adjustment is examined, it is not only important to consider the requirements of the job and the work-related abilities of the individual, but it is also critical to identify the level of correspondence between the individual's specific needs and the emotional, intellectual and financial incentives available in the foreign work environment.

## Conclusion

In order to minimize the risk of assignment failure, it has been suggested that it is in the interest of the organization as well as the expatriate manager to achieve high levels of satisfaction and work adjustment. Shaffer and Harrison (1998) conclude that insufficient job satisfaction has strong predictive power to explain low levels of organizational commitment among expatriate employees. Likewise, Naumann (1993) suggests that an employee's ability to cope with issues of 'role ambiguity, participation in decision making, perceived value of the international assignment to career advancement, and tenure' (p. 180) has considerable implications for the outcome of an international assignment and has an impact on the level of expatriate turnover.

In order to recognize frustration and dissatisfaction at an early stage, it appears feasible to compare the expatriate manager's abilities and needs to the requirements and reinforcements that can be associated with the job abroad. While the 118 German expatriate managers who participated in this study generally regarded the requirements for routine communication to exceed their particular interests, their abilities were frequently underutilized with respect to traditional management activities, human resources management issues and social networking. Turning to the work-related needs and the reinforcements provided by the job abroad, respondents frequently recognized a mismatch between their requirements and the conditions and benefits encountered in the workplace. Though a majority of individuals saw the need for an interesting and challenging job to be satisfied, particularly large discrepancies were apparent in the perceived opportunities to advance in the company and the contacts and exchanges developed with superiors in the host-country organization.

Based on the understanding that a comparison between expatriate characteristics and assignment characteristics can help to predict satisfaction and work adjustment among expatriate managers, a model of expatriate work adjustment has been presented. The principal concepts and mechanisms incorporated in the model have been formulated in line with the general Theory of Work Adjustment proposed by Dawis and Lofquist (1984). Based on the theory, it is held that an expatriate manager's work adjustment during an international assignment is related to two distinct facets of satisfaction: (1) task satisfaction and (2) emotional satisfaction. While the degree of task satisfaction is linked to the level of correspondence between the job requirements and an individual's work-related abilities, emotional satisfaction is regarded as the outcome of an appropriate fit between the reinforcements available in the foreign work environment and the expatriate's expectations and needs. Lastly, in line with the general Theory of Work Adjustment, it is expected that the work adjustment achieved by an expatriate manager can be derived from the levels of task satisfaction and emotional satisfaction reported by the individual. Thus, by assessing the fit between the characteristics of an expatriate manager and the specificities of a foreign assignment, it appears possible to make more accurate predictions regarding the level of work adjustment achieved by an expatriate manager sent abroad to complete an international assignment.

## References

Allan, P. (1981) Managers at work: a large-scale study of the managerial job in New York City government, *Academy of Management Journal*, 24, 3: 613–19.

Aryee, S., Chay, Y. W. and Chew, J. (1996) An investigation of the willingness of managerial employees to accept an expatriate assignment, *Journal of Organizational Behavior*, 17, 3: 267–83.

Aycan, Z. (1997) Acculturation of expatriate managers: a process model of adjustment and performance, in Aycan, Z. (ed.) *New Approaches to Employee Management – Expatriate Management: Theory and Research*, vol. 4 (Greenwich, CT: JAI Press).

Black, J. S. (1988) Work role transitions: a study of American expatriate managers in Japan, *Journal of International Business Studies*, 19, 2: 277–94.

Black, J. S. and Gregersen, H. B. (1999) The right way to manage expats, *Harvard Business Review*, 77, 2: 52–62.

Black, J. S. and Stephens, G. K. (1989) The influence of the spouse on American expatriate adjustment and intent to stay in Pacific Rim overseas assignments, *Journal of Management*, 15, 4: 529–44.

Boies, K. and Rothstein, M. G. (2002) Managers' interest in international assignments: the role of work and career satisfaction, *International Journal of Intercultural Relations*, 26, 3: 233–53.

Brewster, C. (1993) The paradox of adjustment: UK and Swedish expatriates in Sweden and the UK, *Human Resource Management Journal*, 4, 1: 49–62.

Caligiuri, P. M., Phillips, J., and Lazarova, M., et al. (2001) The theory of met expectations applied to expatriate adjustment: the role of cross-cultural training, *International Journal of Human Resource Management*, 12, 3: 357–72.

Caplan, R. D. (1987) Person-environment fit theory and organizations: commensurate dimensions, time perspectives, and mechanisms, *Journal of Vocational Behavior*, 31: 248–67.

Carlson, S. (1991) *Executive Behaviour: Reprinted with Contributions by Henry Mintzberg and Rosemary Stewart* (Uppsala, Sweden: Acta Universitatis Upsaliensis).

Cellucci, A. J. and DeVries, D. L. (1978) *Measuring Managerial Satisfaction: A Manual For The MJSQ*, Technical Report, No. 11 (Greensboro, NC: Center for Creative Leadership).

Chatman, J. A. (1989) Improving interactional organizational research: a model of person-organization fit, *Academy of Management Review*, 14, 3: 333–49.

Dawis, R. V. and Lofquist, L. H. (1984) *A Psychological Theory of Work Adjustment: An Individual-Differences Model and Its Applications* (Minneapolis, MN: University of Minnesota Press).

Fayol, H. (1988) *General and Industrial Management*, rev. edn by Gray, I. (London: Pitman).

Feldman, D. C. (1976) A contingency theory of socialization, *Administrative Science Quarterly*, 21, 3: 433–52.

Gabarro, J. J. (1987) *The Dynamics of Taking Charge* (Boston, MA: Harvard Business School Press).

Gomez-Mejía, L. and Balkin, D. B. (1987) The determinants of managerial satisfaction with the expatriation and repatriation process, *Journal of Management Development*, 6, 1: 7–17.

Gulick, L. H. and Urwick, L. F., eds (1937) *Papers on the Science of Administration* (New York: Institute of Public Administration, Columbia University).

Harrison, J. K., Chadwick, M. and Scales, M. (1996) The relationship between cross-cultural adjustment and the personality variables of self-efficacy and self-monitoring, *International Journal of Intercultural Relations*, 20, 2: 167–88.

Harvey, M. G. (1989) Repatriation of corporate executives: an empirical study, *Journal of International Business Studies*, 20, 1: 131–44.

Hirsch, K. (1996) Reintegration von Auslandsmitarbeitern, in Bergemann, N. and Sourisseaux, A. L. J. (eds). *Interkulturelles Management*, 2nd edn. (Heidelberg, Germany: Physica-Verlag).

Horne, J. H. and Lupton, T. (1965) The work activities of 'middle' managers – an exploratory study, *Journal of Management Studies*, 2, 1: 14–33.

Horsch, J. (1995) *Auslandseinsatz von Stammhaus-Mitarbeitern: Eine Analyse ausgewählter personalwirtschaftlicher Problemfelder multinationaler Unternehmen mit Stammsitz in der Bundesrepublik Deutschland* (Frankfurt am Main, Germany: Europäischer Verlag der Wissenschaften).

Hunziger, A. (2003) *Zeitmanagement und Worklife-Balance internationaler Top-Manager*, Consultant Report (Gummersbach, Germany: Kienbaum Management Consultants).

Kotter, J. P. (1982) What effective general managers really do, *Harvard Business Review*, 60, 6: 156–67.

Kotter, J. P. (1990) What leaders really do, *Harvard Business Review*, 68, 3: 103–11.

Kurke, L. B. and Aldrich, H. E. (1983) Mintzberg was right!: A replication and extension of the nature of managerial work, *Management Science*, 29, 8: 975–84.

Lance, C. E., Vandenberg, R. J. and Self, R. M. (2000) Latent growth models of individual change: the case of newcomer adjustment, *Organizational Behavior and Human Decision Processes*, 83, 1: 107–40.

Light, D. A. (1997) Expatriate employees – getting the most out of their experience, *Harvard Business Review*, 75, 6: 20.

Luthans, F., Hodgetts, R. M. and Rosenkrantz, S. A. (1988) *Real Managers* (Cambridge, MA: Ballinger).

Luthans, F. and Lockwood, D. L. (1985) Toward an observation system for measuring leader behavior in natural settings, in Hunt, J. G., Hosking, D.-M., Schriesheim, C. A. and Stewart, R. (eds). *Leaders and Managers: International Perspectives on Managerial Behavior and Leadership*, 2nd printing (Elmsford, NY: Pergamon Press).

Luthans, F., Rosenkrantz, S. A. and Hennessey, H. W. (1985) What do successful managers really do? An observation study of managerial activities, *Journal of Applied Behavioral Science*, 21, 3: 255–70.

Mendenhall, M. E. and Oddou, G. (1986) Accultation profiles of expatriate managers: implications for cross-cultural training programs, *Columbia Journal of World Business*, 21, 4: 73–9.

Mendenhall, M. E. and Wiley, C. (1994) Strangers in a strange land: the relationship between expatriate adjustment and impression management, *American Behavioral Scientist*, 37, 5: 605–20.

Mintzberg, H. (1980) *The Nature of Managerial Work*, 2nd edn. (Englewood Cliffs, NJ: Prentice Hall).

Morley, M. J., Burke, C. and O'Regan, T. (1997) The Irish in Moscow – a question of adjustment, *Human Resource Management Journal*, 7, 3: 53–66.

Müller-Böling, D., Klautke, E. and Ramme, I. (1989) Manager-Alltag, *Bild der Wissenschaft*, 26, 1: 104–9.

Naumann, E. (1993) Antecedents and consequences of satisfaction and commitment among expatriate managers, *Group & Organization Management*, 18, 2: 153–87.

Osland, J. S. (2000) The journey inward: expatriate hero tales and paradoxes, *Human Resource Management*, 39, 2&3: 227–38.

Palthe, J. (2001) *Toward an Integrative Model of Cross-Cultural Adjustment: Implications for Managing a Global Workforce*, PhD Dissertation (East Lansing, MI: Michigan State University, School of Labor and Industrial Relations).

Parker, B. and McEvoy, G. M. (1993) Initial examination of a model of intercultural adjustment, *International Journal of Intercultural Relations*, 17, 3: 355–79.

Reichwald, R. and Goecke, R. (1996) Was tut ein Top-Manager an einem durchschnittlichen Arbeitstag? *gdi impuls*, 1: 32–45.

Schreyögg, G. and Hübl, G. (1992) Manager in Aktion: Ergebnisse einer Beobachtungsstudie in mittelständischen Unternehmen, *Zeitschrift Führung und Organisation (zfo)*, 61, 2: 82–9.

Shaffer, M. A. and Harrison, D. A. (1998) Expatriates' psychological withdrawal from international assignments: Work, nonwork, and family influences, *Personnel Psychology*, 51, 1: 87–118.

Shaffer, M. A., Harrison, D. A. and Gilley, K. M. (1999) Dimensions, determinants, and differences in the expatriate adjustment process, *Journal of International Business Studies*, 30, 3: 557–81.

Stahl, G. K. (1998) *Internationaler Einsatz von Führungskräften* (Munich and Vienna: Oldenbourg).
Stewart, R. (1976) *Contrasts in Management: A Study of Different Types of Managers' Jobs – Their Demands and Choices* (Maidenhead, England: McGraw-Hill).
Stewart, R. (1988) *Managers and their Jobs: A Study of the Similarities and Differences in the Ways Managers Spend their Time*, 2nd edn (Basingstoke Macmillan – now Palgrave Macmillan).
Suutari, V. and Brewster, C. (2001) Expatriate management practices and perceived relevance: Evidence from Finnish expatriates, *Personnel Review*, 30, 5: 554–77.
Suutari, V. and Tornikoski, C. (2001) The challenge of expatriate compensation: the sources of satisfaction and dissatisfaction among expatriates, *International Journal of Human Resource Management*, 12, 3: 389–404.
Tung, R. L. (1981) Selection and training of personnel for overseas assignments, *Columbia Journal of World Business*, 16, 1: 68–78.
Urwick, L. F. (1944) *The Elements of Administration* (New York: Harper & Row).
Watson, T. J. (1994) *In Search of Management: Culture, chaos and control in managerial work* (London and New York: Routledge).
Winter, G. (1996) Reintegrationsproblematik: Vom Heimkehren in die Fremde und vom Wiedererlernen des Vertrauten, in Thomas, A. (ed.). *Psychologie interkulturellen Handelns* (Göttingen, Bern, Toronto and Seattle: Hogrefe-Verlag).
Wirth, E. (1992) *Mitarbeiter im Auslandseinsatz: Planung und Gestaltung* (Wiesbaden, Germany: Gabler).
Zakaria, N. (2000) The effects of cross-cultural training on the acculturation process of the global workforce, *International Journal of Manpower*, 21, 6: 492–510.

# 6
# The Effect of Culture of Origin on the Adjustment Process

*Marie-France Waxin*

## Introduction

Expatriates' adjustment to their new role and environment is of great significance, both to the organization and to the managers themselves. From the organization's perspective, expatriates' degree of adjustment partially predicts performance and completion of the mission (Parker and McEvoy, 1993). From the managers' perspective, adjustment is a factor of job satisfaction and psychological well being (Aryee and Stone, 1996). As a result, there has been a burgeoning academic and practical interest in understanding and measuring the adjustment process and its antecedents. Black (1988) defined intercultural adjustment (IA) as 'the degree of an individual's psychological comfort with various aspects of a host country'.

Black (1988) conceptualized and demonstrated that intercultural adjustment contains three related but conceptually distinct facets: adjustment to work in regard to setting, responsibilities and performance, relational adjustment in regard to interaction with members of the host community and general adjustment in regard to living conditions in the foreign country. Although these three facets have a strong correlation, each has its own distinct antecedents. Many authors have utilized this typology (Black and Gregersen, 1991; Parker and McEvoy, 1993; Cerdin, 1999). In this research, we will study these three facets of adjustment.

Much of the research on expatriates has focused on adding to the list of antecedents, which influence cross-cultural adjustment. However, the theoretical development for understanding *how* these antecedents impact on cross-cultural adjustment has not advanced much since the initial work of Black and his colleagues (Caligiuri, 2000). In particular, there has been a paucity of research on the effect of culture of origin (CO) on expatriates' adjustment. Parker and McEvoy (1993) reported that culture novelty (Hofstede's cultural distance) explains as much variance in interaction and general living adjustment as the other organizational and individual variables, but that additional research is needed to truly understand its impact on the adjustment process. Redmond (2000) showed that cultural distance was a mediating factor between stress and intercultural communication competence. Black and Gregersen (1991) and Gregersen and Stroh (1997) found contradictory effects of subjective cultural distance on interaction adjustment. One possible explanation could be the impact of cultural differences among the respondents. The cultural differences might modulate the effects of the classical antecedents of adjustment. Surprisingly, existing models have not considered how expatriate's culture of origin interacts with the classical antecedents to predict adjustment. No research has been organized to control systematically for culture of origin in order to examine its effects on expatriates' adjustment.

This research seeks to contribute to our understanding of the expatriate experience by first, partially replicating previous research on expatriates' adjustment, and, second, by examining the effect of culture of origin on adjustment and its antecedents. The research questions are the following: What is the relative importance of the antecedents of each adjustment facet? What is the direct effect of culture of origin on each adjustment facet? What is the moderator effect of culture of origin on the antecedents of each adjustment facet? The chapter examines these issues in the literature; develops a model of the antecedents of the adjustment process as moderated by culture of origins effects; discusses the methodology and the findings; and finally draws out the implications of this research.

## Literature review and hypotheses

A review of the literature (summarized in Figure 6.1 and explained below) suggests that there are three major categories of factors influencing expatriates' adjustment following expatriation: organizational, individual and contextual factors. Our contribution to this field of research consists in introducing the country of origin as a moderator variable of the relations between adjustment and its antecedents.

### Organizational antecedents

Organizational variables comprise two job-related variables (role clarity and role discretion), three social support factors (supervisory, coworker(s), home-country organizational support), logistical support, expatriation

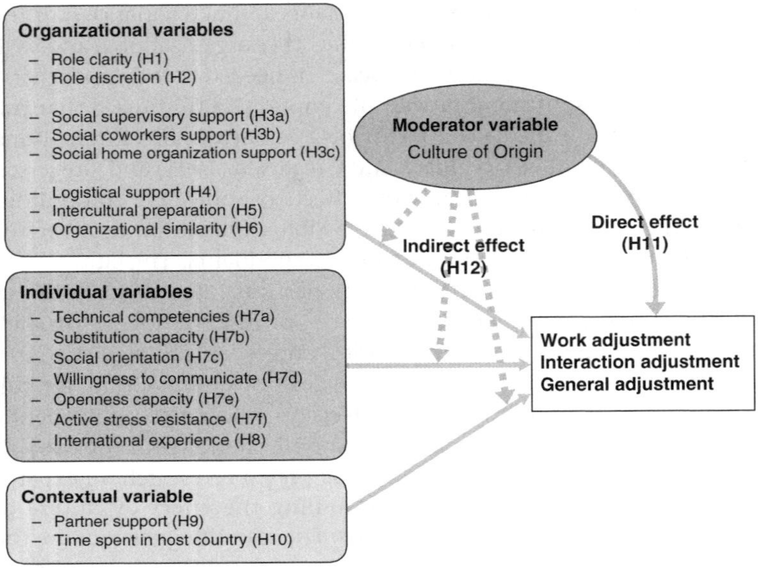


*Figure 6.1* Conceptual frame
*Source:* based on Black, Mendenhall and Oddou (1991).

training, and organizational culture similarity. In the adjustment literature, work-related variables are only related to work adjustment.

### *Role clarity*

The lack of clarity or the level of uncertainty surrounding expectations about a single role has been generally treated as a source of stress in the organizational literature (Ilgen and Hollenbeck, 1991); and role clarity as leading to a faster time to proficiency (Pinder and Schroeder, 1987) and to be positively related to work adjustment (Black and Gregersen, 1991).

*(H1) Role clarity is positively related to work adjustment.*

### *Role discretion*

Role discretion (Karasek, 1979) reduces uncertainty in a new situation, because it enables individuals to adapt their work role and setting by themselves rather than adapting themselves to the work setting (Black and Gregersen, 1991). Aryee and Stone (1996), Black (1988), Black and Gregersen (1991) and Cerdin (1999) have shown that role discretion is positively related to work adjustment.

*(H2) Role discretion is positively related to work adjustment.*

### *Organizational social support*

Organizational social support encompasses supervisory, co-workers and home-country organization social support. Black et al. (1991) suggested that social support provide expatriates with information about what is acceptable and unacceptable in the new work context. Organizational social support has been shown to reduce the time to proficiency of French expatriates in Norway (Waxin, Roger and Chandon, 1997) and to be positively related to the three facets of adjustment (Cerdin, 1999). We hypothesize that *supervisory (H3a), coworkers (H3b) and home-country organization (H3c) social support are positively related to the work, interaction and general adjustment.*

### *Logistical support*

Organizational logistical support can include a career assistance service for the spouse or a relocation service, which helps to reinstall the transferee's family. If these services do not directly help the individual adapt to his new post, they at least help to diminish fear of the unknown. Black et al.'s (1991) model of adjustment associates logistical support for interaction integration with general adjustment, but not with work adjustment. Cerdin (1999) confirms these results. However, for interaction adjustment to occur, the help given by the organization must not isolate the expatriate manager from his environment, or the acculturation process might be inhibited (Tung, 1993).

*(H4) Logistical support is positively related to I and G adjustment.*

### *Intercultural training*

Much of the literature suggests that training enhances expatriates adjustment (Black and Mendenhall, 1990; Black et al., 1991; Deshpande and Vivwesvaran, 1992; Eschbach et al., 2001; Waxin and Panaccio, 2005).

*(H5) Expatriation training is positively related to W, I, G adjustment.*

### *Organizational dissimilarity*

Perceived dissimilarity between home-country and host-country organizations is a source of uncertainty and stress (Parker and McEvoy, 1993) and thus is expected to relate negatively to expats adjustment.

*(H6) Organizational similarity is negatively positively related to W, I, G adjustment.*

## Individual antecedents

Individual antecedents of expatriates' interaction adjustment are the six dimensions of expatriates' adjustability and prior international experience.

### *Adjustability*

Based on the works of Mendenhall and Oddou (1985), and Black (1990), recent studies (Cerdin, Chandon and Waxin, 1999; Waxin, 2000; Waxin, 2004) have identified six dimensions of the expatriate's adjustability, each one being measured by a battery of items. The dimensions are confidence in their own technical competencies (H7a), social orientation (H7b), willingness to communicate (H7c), substitution capacity (H7d), cultural openness (H7e) and stress resistance (H7f).

*(H7a–f). The six dimensions of adjustability are positively related to W, I, G adjustment.*

### *Prior international experience*

Theoretical discussions have, for a long time, included previous international experience as relevant for the adjustment process (Church, 1982; Black, 1988). However, empirical evidence, particularly when focused on the length of exposure, has been weak (Haslberger, 1999). Black (1988) finds that prior international experience facilitates general adjustment, but not interaction and work adjustment. Parker and McEvoy (1993) found that it correlates significantly only with general adjustment. Black and Gregersen (1991) point out that the problem may lie in the quantitative measurement of the variable rather than its lack of relevance. Theoretically and intuitively, it makes sense to assume that international experience allows a quicker and more complete adjustment.

*(H8) Prior international experience is positively related to W, I, G adjustment.*

## Contextual antecedents

Finally, contextual antecedents encompass partner social support, time spent in the host country and culture of origin.

### *Partner social support*

Partner social support is viewed in the literature as an important influence on the worker abroad. According to Fenlason and Beer (1994), partner social support reduces the stress generated by the new work environment and thus facilitates expatriates' adjustment.

*(H9) Partner social support is positively related to W, I, G adjustment.*

### *Length of time spent in host country*

Adjustment is a time related process. Individuals need time to get accustomed to their new environment and learn the host country culture and appropriate and acceptable behaviours. Whereas Janssens (1995) did not find any significant relationship between time spent in the host country and adjustment, in a sample of Belgian and British expatriates, Cerdin (1999) obtained the opposite results for French expatriates.

*(H10) Time spent in the host country will be positively related to W, I, G adjustment.*

### *Culture of origin*

Previous research suggests that the more different the host culture is from the home culture, the more demanding the adjustment will be (Black et al., 1991; Gao and Gudykunst, 1990). Although it may also be difficult to adjust to a similar culture (Brewster, 1995; O'Grady and Lane, 1996; Selmer, 2005), the balance of the literature is clearly that cultural distance makes adjustment harder. This phenomenon is known variously as the effect of cultural distance (Church, 1982) or culture toughness (Mendenhall and Oddou, 1985). Furnham and Bochner (1982) identified cultural differences as one of the primary factors contributing to culture shock. In their study, they found general support for a relationship between the level of social difficulty and cultural distance. Gudykunst and Hammer (1984) posited that cultural similarity (short cultural distance) produces more accuracy in a sojourner's ability to predict and explain host behaviour. In the international adjustment literature, Parker and McEvoy (1993) and Gregersen and Stroh (1997) show that host culture novelty is negatively associated to expatriates' adjustment. We term this the direct effect of culture of origin. We hypothesize that expatriates' adjustment degree will vary significantly according to their culture of origin.

*(H11) Culture of origin has a direct effect on W, I, G adjustment.*

There is a further point arising out of the cultural differences literature. Different cultures may be more or less effective as expatriates in certain countries. It may be the case, for example, that countries with low uncertainty avoidance have less trouble finding individuals who make successful expatriates. One the other hand, it may be that some cultures will have problems finding people who are less modest (the Swedish *lagom*) and who therefore rate their success more highly. Furthermore, it is anticipated that the antecedents of TTP will vary according to the specificities of expatriates' culture of origin. We term this the moderator effect of culture of origin. Redmond (2000) notes that Hofstede (1991) does not discuss the impact of cultural dimensions on intercultural interactions.

*(H12) Country of origin has a moderator effect on the antecedents of adjustment.*

## Methodology

### Sample and data collection

Our sample consisted of 224 managers, of which 56 were French, 53 German, 60 Korean and 57 Scandinavian,[1] who were expatriated in New Delhi, India. Respondents were working in multinational companies from their home culture, assigned to general management or high technical positions, for a maximum period of four years there. There was no relationship between gender, time, and seniority and scores on the dependent variables. The response rate was above 75%.

## Measures and questionnaire

### Adjustment

There is an ongoing debate about the way to measure adjustment. The three facets of adjustment identified by Black and Stephens (1989) are in fact strongly correlated with each other. Some authors therefore prefer to measure the degree of overall adjustment (Caligiuri, 2000). Others prefer to measure the time required for the expatriate to reach an equilibrium between contribution and retribution while taking into account integration time or 'time to proficiency' (Pinder and Schroeder, 1987; Waxin, Roger, and Chandon, 1997; Waxin and Brewster, 2005). In this research, we reuse the scale created by Black and Stephens (1989), measuring all three adjustment facets with 14 statements. The scale goes from (1) not at all adjusted to (7) completely adjusted.

Role clarity and discretion were averaged respectively from eight items created by Breaugh and Colihan (1994) and nine items created by Black and Gregersen (1991). Supervisory and co-workers social support were averaged from four-item scales adapted from Pinder and Schroeder (1987). Home-country social organization and logistical support were averaged from the respectively four-and three-items scales adapted from Cerdin (1999). Organizational similarity was averaged from an adjustment of the six-item scale created by Cerdin (1999). To measure the first five dimensions of expatriate's adjustability, we used Waxin (2000) scales, adapted from Cerdin (1999): willingness to communicate (4 items), substitution capacity (3 items), social orientation (3 items), confidence in one's technical competencies (3 items) openness capacity (3 items), and active stress resistance

(8-item index based on the work of Folkman et al. 1986). Partner social support was measured adapting Roques' four-item scale (1999). For all these quantitative variables, we used seven-point Likert scales, ranking from totally agree to totally disagree. International experience was assessed by collating the duration in months of expatriate's international experiences (studies, internships and expatriations). Respondents were also asked to indicate if they had received any kind of intercultural training (later scored on a yes (1)/no (0) basis) and to describe it, the time they had already spent in the host country, their position's level (top or middle management), their company's branch activity (production, services, transport and telecommunication, public sector, other), their gender, age and marital status.

All the multi-item scales used in this research are one-dimensional with a percentage of variance accounted for by PCA's first axis greater than 66%. All the scales show good reliability, with Cronbach's alpha greater than 0.83.

To conduct the empirical part of this study, we wanted to control the cultural factors, i.e. the host country and expatriates' culture of origin. To meet the statistical requirements, we needed to get at least 4 'culture-of-origin samples', containing each at least 50 expatriates, all located in the same area of the same host country. India has been chosen as host country for the following reasons. First, we wanted a host country which presents some difficulties for westerners. Second, very few studies on expatriates' adjustment have focused on India. Third, India attracts a lot of foreign firms, and so has many expatriates. To counteract the fact that India has considerable cultural variability, we focused on the New Delhi area. Korea, France, Germany and Scandinavia have been chosen as country/culture of origin for the following reasons. First, these countries are relatively culturally homogeneous. Second, there were more than 50 expatriates coming from these countries in the region of New Delhi. We wanted to include a Scandinavian culture. However, no Scandinavian country alone could offer 50 expatriates in the region of New Delhi. As Denmark, Norway and Sweden are relatively culturally close, and very different from the other countries in this study (Hofstede, 1991), we decided to form a Scandinavian sample. Our discussion below uses the terms 'country' or 'national sample' rather than culture, in order a) to reflect our data more accurately (we identified country of origin but did not test for culture) and b) not to confuse the discussion of cultural difference. With apologies we use these terms to include the three Scandinavian samples in the one category.

### Statistical analysis

In a preliminary step, we verified that we would indeed find all three distinct facets of adjustment and that the averages for each of the facets varied in accordance with the country samples. We then examine each adjustment facet individually, so the following analyses are run for W, I and G adjustment The analysis of the data consists of three major parts. First, we test the classical model of adjustment (H1 to H10), using multiple regression analysis on the global sample. Second, to test the direct effect of culture of origin on adjustment (H11), we introduce culture of origin indicator variables in the regression of adjustment and we use a Chow test (note 2). Third, to test the moderator effect of culture of origin on adjustment antecedents (H12), we use multiple regressions with moderator variable and a Chow test. This allows us to propose simplified models of adjustment per culture of origin.

## Results

The three facets of adjustment: the analyses of the main components of Black and Stephens (1989) 14 statements, taking the *global sample* and then the four *country samples*, showed that adjustment is in fact tri-dimensional. The statements of general adjustment, interaction adjustment and work adjustment were all grouped according to the three expected factors. For each dimension, the percentage of variance explained by the first axis varied according to the facet and the sample between 64 and 91%. The Cronbach alpha coefficient oscillates between 0.89 and 0.94. These results are comparable to the previous studies carried out on different samples (0.88, 0.92 and 0.87 for Black and Gregersen, 1991; 0.83, 0.91 and 0.86 for Cerdin, 1999).

One way analyses of variance show that the mean degrees of adjustment vary significantly among the four cultures of origin (Table 6.1). The $eta^2$ coefficients indicate that culture of origin explains respectively 5.4, 12.6 and 27.2% of the total variance in W,I, G adjustment.

*For all samples*, the averages for work and general adjustment were significantly higher than for interaction adjustment (with the 5% threshold). Among Koreans, the average of general adjustment was also significantly superior to interaction adjustment (with the 5% threshold).

### Testing the classical model of adjustment on the global sample (H1 to H10)

The test of the classical model is necessary because it gives us a comparative basis on which to evaluate the effect of culture of origin on the three facets of adjustment.

*Table 6.1:* Analyse of variance: mean degree of adjustment according to culture of origin

| **Country of origin** | **N** | **Work** | **Interaction** | **General** | **Comparison Bonferroni F test** |
|---|---|---|---|---|---|
| **Global** | **224** | **5.16** | **4.42** | **4.77** | **I < G < T** |
| France | 54 | 5.68 | 4.89 | 5.44 | I < G, T |
| Germany | 53 | 5.13 | 4.67 | 4.98 | I < G, T |
| Scandinavia | 57 | 5.03 | 4.56 | 4.87 | I < G, T |
| Korea | 60 | 4.83 | 3.67 | 3.87 | I, G < T |
| Bonferroni | | F > K, S | F, G, S > K | F > S > K, G > K | |
| F test | | 4.22, $p < 0.01$ | 10.60, $p < 0.001$ | 27.79, $p < 0.000$, | |
| $eta^2$= | | 0.054, $p < 0.06$ | 0.126, $p < 0.001$ | 0.272, $p < 0.000$ | |

*Note:* Only significant differences in accordance with the Bonferroni test with a 5% threshold are indicated.

We conducted the regressions of W, I and G adjustment separately on the 17 classic antecedents, on the global sample. In Table 6.2, we present the antecedents retained with a risk factor of less than 5%. The antecedents are classified in order of significance (decreasing t test). The different facets of adjustment are explained by different antecedents. These antecedents explain 50 to 52% of the variance in each adjustment facet. However, all the classical antecedents globally produce a high multicollinearity (CI ranging from 49 to 68). The next step therefore is to examine the direct effect of the culture of origin on the model of adjustment.

## Testing the direct effect of culture of origin on adjustment (H11)

To test the direct effect of culture of origin on adjustment, we introduce indicator variables of the culture of origin in the regression of each facet of adjustment. The results show a substantial increase in the model's quality (Table 6.3). For each facet, we observe three arguments. First, the percentages of explained variance increase and F tests increase clearly. Second, the standard errors diminish clearly. Third, the high values of the Chow tests ($p < 0.001$) indicate that the direct effect of culture of origin on adjustment is significant. We conclude that H11 is validated, and that culture of origin has a significant direct effect on expatriates' adjustment.

*Table 6.2:* Summary of the results: regression of W, I, G adjustment on all the classical antecedents, on the different samples: global (N = 224), France (N = 54), Germany (N = 53), Korea (N = 60), Scandinavia (N = 57); the antecedents are classified in order of significance in the regression (decreasing T test)

| Antecedents/ | Work | | | | | Interaction | | | | | General | | | | |
|---|---|---|---|---|---|---|---|---|---|---|---|---|---|---|---|
| samples | Global | F | G | S | K | Global | F | G | S | K | Global | F | G | S | K |
| Role clarity (H1) | 4 | 2 | 5 | | 3 | | | | | | | | | | |
| Role discretion (H2) | 1 | 3 | 1 | 1 | | | | | | | | | | | |
| Supervisory social support (H3a) | 2 | 4 | | | 2 | 5 | 1 | | 6 | 6 | 3 | 5 | | | 1 |
| Co-workers social support (H3b) | | | 3 | | 5 | | | 5 | | 1 | | | 4 | 3 | 9 |
| Home org. social support (H3c) | 8 | | | 2 | | | | | 5 | | | | | 6 | |
| Logistical support (H4) | | | | | | | | | | | 6 | 2 | 7 | 7 | 2 |
| Intercultural training (H5) | | | 6 | | | 6 | 4 | 3 | | | | | 3 | 5 | 7 |
| Organizational similarity (H6) | | 6 | | 4 | | | | | | | | | | | |
| Technical competencies (H7a) | 6 | | 4 | | 4 | | | | | | | | | | |

| | | | | | | | | | | | | | | | |
|---|---|---|---|---|---|---|---|---|---|---|---|---|---|---|---|
| Substitution capacity (H7b) | | | | | | | | | | | 2 | 1 | 2 | 2 | 3 |
| Social orientation (H7c) | 7 | | | 3 | | 2 | 3 | | 2 | | 5 | | | | |
| Willingness to communicate (H7d) | | | 2 | | | 3 | | 1 | 1 | 4 | | | | | |
| Openness capacity (H7e) | | | | | | 4 | 2 | 4 | 3 | 3 | | | 6 | 4 | |
| Active stress resistance (H7f) | 5 | 5 | | 5 | | | 7 | | | 2 | | 3 | | | 5 |
| International experience (H8) | | | | | 6 | | | | | 5 | | | | | 6 |
| Partner social support (H9) | | | | 6 | | 1 | 5 | 2 | 4 | | 1 | 4 | 1 | 1 | 8 |
| Time spent in India (H10) | 3 | 1 | | | 1 | | 6 | | | | 4 | | 5 | | 4 |
| **$R^2$ adjusted** | 0.51 | 0.70 | 0.66 | 0.86 | 0.72 | 0.50 | 0.55 | 0.69 | 0.71 | 0.60 | 0.52 | 0.58 | 0.70 | 0.69 | 0.765 |
| **F** | 12.41 | 22.16 | 17.56 | 59.51 | 23.04 | 13.59 | 10.38 | 26.36 | 25.42 | 15.78 | 13.09 | 15.45 | 18.43 | 18.85 | 22.38 |
| **CI** | 59.6 | 15.6 | 19.9 | 21.3 | 18.4 | 48.8 | 27.34 | 25.85 | 29.94 | 19.69 | 67.71 | 15.67 | 26.85 | 32.06 | 21.71 |
| **Standard error** | 0.95 | 0.61 | 0.64 | 0.563 | 0.78 | 0.94 | 0.94 | 0.145 | 0.56 | 0.73 | 0.764 | 0.566 | 0.39 | 0.59 | 0.51 |

*Note:* F = France, G = Germany, C = Korea, S = Scandinavia.

*Table 6.3:* The direct effect of culture of origin (CO) on W, I, G adjustment, on the global sample

| | Work | | Interaction | | General | |
|---|---|---|---|---|---|---|
| | Without CO | With CO | Without CO | With CO | Without CO | With CO |
| Adjusted $R^2$ | 0.50 | 0.59 | 0.50 | 0.59 | 0.52 | 0.74 |
| F test | 12.1 | 15.27 | 13.59 | 17.89 | 13.09 | 28.11 |
| Standard error | 0.95 | 0.86 | 0.94 | 0.85 | 0.764 | 0.566 |
| Chow test | 16.1, $p < 0.001$ | | 17.58, $p < 0.000$ | | 62.5, $p < 0.000$ | |

## Testing the moderator effect of culture of origin on adjustment's antecedents (H12)

To test the moderator effect of culture of origin on each adjustment facet's antecedents, we will proceed in two steps. First, we examine whether the quality of the model increases significantly when the global regression is replaced by four separated regressions per culture. Second, we test the possibility to propose culture-specific models of adjustment.

First, we run a regression of each adjustment facet on the 17 classical antecedents, in the four cultural samples. The results indicate that regressions per culture elicit several improvements: adjusted $R^2$ and standard error in culture-specific samples are respectively higher and weaker than in the global sample, and the high values of the Chow tests indicate that the moderator effect of culture of origin on each adjustment facet is significant. We conclude that H12 is validated and that there is a significant and strong moderation effect between culture of origin and the classical antecedents of each adjustment facet.

The purpose of the second step is to reinforce the validation of H12 and to propose specific, simplified models of adjustment per facet and culture of origin, which would retain only significant antecedents. We perform hierarchical regressions of each adjustment facet on the 17 classical antecedents, in using the backward regression method, on each culture-sample. Results show that the optimal models contain five to seven variables, depending on the adjustment facet and culture of origin. The moderator effect of culture of origin appears very clearly since, for the same facet, the significant variables retained in the regressions diverge from one culture to another.

For example, let us focus on interaction adjustment. The unique common antecedent of interaction adjustment in the four culture samples is openness capacity. The others antecedents are culture-specific (Table 6.2). The results concerning social support related antecedents are clearly distinct. Whereas supervisory support is significantly predictive of interaction adjustment in the French, Korean and Scandinavian samples, co-workers support is significant in the German and Korean samples, home country organization support is significant in the Scandinavian sample and partner support is significant in all the samples except the Korean one. Intercultural training is significant in the German and French ones. The results regarding individual antecedents are equally contrasted. Openness capacity is significant in all national samples. Whereas social orientation is significant in the French and Scandinavian samples, willingness to communicate is significant in the German, Scandinavian and Korean samples, and active stress resistance is significant in the French and Korean ones. Previous international experience facilitates the interaction adjustment of Koreans. Finally, time spent in India is only significant in the French sample.

The culture specific models present a much better statistical fit than the classical one. The adjusted $R^2$ increases substantially when passing from the global to the specific model. For example, adjusted $R^2$ for interaction adjustment increases from 0.50 in the global to 0.71 in the Scandinavian one. As shown in Table 6.2, culture-specific models present higher F tests and weaker standard errors. In all culture specific models, all antecedent present t tests with absolute values larger than 2, indicating a significant effect on adjustment.

## Discussion

### Limitations of the research

A number of features of the design of the research should be acknowledged and addressed before discussing the results. The first limitations of the research concern the sample. Only four countries of origin and one host country are examined. Due to sample size limitation, Danish, Norwegian and Swedish expatriates had to be bundled together within one sample called Scandinavia. Future studies should include more countries of origin, more respondents per culture and more host countries. Moreover, the samples excluded *de facto* those who had left for any reason after the expatriation. There are also limitations concerning the data collection. First, the questionnaire was written in English, which is a foreign language for all the respondents (although pre-test showed that the expatriates did not have any comprehension problems). English is the working language of expatriates in India. Second, the dependent and independent variables were collected simultaneously via a single questionnaire from individual respondents, at a single point in time. To check that retrospective rationality was not responsible for the results of this study: we verified that the W,I,G adjustment means were not significantly different for expatriates who had requested the expatriation and those who had not, and for expatriates who had been promoted and those who had not. A third limitation concerns the focus of this research on the perception of expatriates themselves. However, Nicholson (1984) notes in his person-centered theory of work role transitions, that what is operationally important is a person's subjective perceptions of the reality at work, following the reasoning that what is perceived as real is real in its consequences. The model also presents several limitations. First, we used the classical adjustment facets. Further studies should concentrate on managerial oriented measures, like time to proficiency. Second, further research is needed to investigate the impact of culture on the other factors of expatriates' adjustment. Organizational factors, such as compensation and benefits policies, individual factors, such as motivation to go abroad, and contextual factors such as family/spouse adjustment should also be taken into consideration. Finally, this research presents methodological limits. It would be useful in future to use more sophisticated data analysis methods, like structural equation modeling, allowing simultaneous analysis of several facets of adjustment. The size of our sample did not allow us to use this method. Qualitative methods could also bring complementary information. Given the temporal aspect of adjustment, longitudinal studies would also be very useful. Finally, future research could include several host countries and more countries of origin, and study more precisely the relationships between adjustment and culture of origin's characteristics, like Hofstede's (1991) cultural factors.

## Discussion of the results

Despite these considerations, the results are instructive. This research aimed to increase understanding of the intercultural adjustment process first by replicating previous research (H1 to H10) and second by examining the direct (H11) and moderating (H12) effects of culture of origin on the interaction adjustment process.

Our preliminary results confirm the existence of three dimensions of adjustment, in our global sample as well as in our national samples. Our research therefore confirms the findings of previous works. However, the three facets of adjustment are strongly correlated with each other. The strongest correlation exists between general adjustment and interaction adjustment. Cerdin (1999) remarks that future research might take an interest in the meaning of the relationships between the different facets of adjustment. Our results also show that expatriate managers adjust better to work than to living conditions or interaction, confirming the findings of Cerdin (1999). The author suggests that the level of uncertainty in relation to the sphere of work is weaker than the levels of uncertainty related to general living conditions and relations with members of the host country. However, the three facets are explained by different factors in each sample.

First, we will discuss the results related to the classical antecedents. The variables related to work are not significantly related only to work adjustment. The social and organizational support variables have a beneficial effect on all three facets. On the global sample, *supervisory support* facilitates the three facets of adjustment. The culture-specific samples allow us to be more specific. It was noted that supervisory support remains significant specifically for the expatriates whose culture is characterized by a large power distance (French and Koreans). Not surprisingly, *co-workers* support turns out to be the most significant factor of I adjustment for the Korean managers, characterized by Hofstede as collectivist. Co-workers support is also significant of W, I and G adjustment for the German managers. Future studies may need to examine whether the co-workers are locals or fellow expatriates and the role of the expatriate community in assisting expatriates to adjust (Brewster and Pickard, 1994). *Home country organization support* facilitates W adjustment. This antecedent is significant of the three facets of adjustment in the Scandinavian sample. Finally, *partner support* is a very significant predictor of I and G adjustment in all the samples. There are however two exceptions: partner support is not significant of IA for Korean managers, but is also significant of WA for Scandinavian ones. *Logistical support* contributes to all the regression equations of GA. *Organizational dissimilarity* only has a significant effect on work adjustment for the French and Koreans.

Analyses of variance revealed that expatriates who received any kind of *intercultural training* reported a higher interaction adjustment mean than those who did not receive any training. Intercultural training contributed to the I adjustment regression equations in the global sample, and in some other regressions in the country samples. In this article, the type of intercultural training was not taken into consideration. However, Waxin and Panaccio (2005) demonstrate that that the three facets of intercultural adjustment vary significantly according to the type of cross-cultural training received, that experimental methods of training that focus on the host country are the most effective ones, that the positive effects of cross-cultural training are even more noticeable for managers who have little or no prior international experience and finally, that the larger the cultural distance between the country of origin and the host country, the more pronounced are the effects of cross-cultural training.

Among the *six facets of expatriates' adjustability*, technical competencies facilitate W adjustment in the global and in two country samples. Social orientation appears to be a very important facet since it facilitates the three facets of adjustment significantly. The results in the culture-specific samples are more contrasted. Willingness to communicate and openness capacity were found to be very significantly predictive of interaction adjustment. Stress resistance facilitates W adjustment in the global sample and appears also in the French and Korean country samples regressions of W, I, and G adjustment. Openness capacity contributes to all the regression equations of GA.

Our data on the global samples did not support the hypothesis that *international experience* would be a factor of adjustment, although it correlated clearly. In the Korean sample, though, international experience predicts adjustment. This may be explained by the fact that the international exposure of Korean managers is relatively recent in comparison to the European ones.

*Length of time spent in India* had a significant relation with W and G adjustment on the global samples. Time spent in the host country is a significant factor of work and general living adjustment, allowing routine to take place and then reducing uncertainty. Cerdin (1999) notes that interaction adjustment implies other intermediary processes, like personal motivation to adjust and willingness to make efforts to 'move towards' locals, and that these processes are not linked with the length of time spent in the host country. Nevertheless, the results in the culture-specific samples are more contrasted. That may be explained by the fact that perception and apprehension of time and its consequences are culture bound.

Then we discuss our results related to the direct and moderator effects of *country of origin* on expatriates' adjustment. First, our research demonstrates that culture of origin has a direct effect on the three adjustment facet, accounting for respectively 9, 9 and 22% of the explained variance of W, I and G adjustment. So, our research shows that adjustment will be more or less difficult according to the expatriate's country of origin. For example, in our sample, the Koreans all together report a lesser degree of W, I and G adjustment than the French. Our results are consistent with

Hofstede's (1991) work: French, German and Scandinavian managers report decreasing degrees of W, I and G adjustment and increasing Hofstede's cultural distance to India (respectively 91, 96 and 125–142). So, the bigger the cultural distance, the lesser the adjustment degree. Koreans are the exception: they report a lesser degree of adjustment than Scandinavians (3.67), but their cultural distance to India is larger (109) (see Table 6.1 and Annex 6.1). This exception could be explained by the fact that the international exposure of Koreans is relatively recent in comparison to the Europeans one.

Second, our research demonstrates that culture of origin effects what antecedents, and to which degree, play a role in the explanation of expatriates' adjustment. The antecedents that significantly contributed to the regression equations of each facet of adjustment varied in nature and strength according to the country of origin. For example, supervisory social support is a very important antecedent of adjustment for French and Korean expatriates, but less so for the Scandinavians, who rely more on partner support and on home organization support. These country-of-origin-effects are consistent with Hofstede's (1991) work, at least on two points. First, for French and Korean expatriates, whose cultures are characterized by a high score on power distance factors, it seems logical that supervisory support is an important factor of adjustment. Second, for Korean expatriates, whose culture is characterized by strong collectivism, it seems also logical that co-workers support should be helpful in facilitating adjustment.

Further research is needed to examine the effects of culture of origin and its characteristics on expatriates' adjustment. What hides behind the culture of origin effect? Which cultural characteristics are mostly affecting the adjustment process? What are the effects of Hofstede's cultural factors on the adjustment process? How do they impact on the different facets of cross-cultural adjustment?

### Practical implications

The results of this research have important implications for the management of expatriates, especially in the fields of recruitment, intercultural training and support management policies. As far as expatriate recruitment is concerned, technical expertise and domestic track record are by far the dominant selection criteria (Scullion and Brewster, 2002). Factors like language skills, relational and perceptual adjustability are much less commonly taken into account (Stone, 1991; Barnham and Devine, 1991). Our results show that different facets of adjustability, including expatriates' willingness to communicate, social orientation, active stress resistance and openness capacity are crucial to the adjustment process. Crucially, knowledge that culture of origin/cultural distance is a significant predictor of adjustment suggests that organizations may need to revise their international staffing policies. If culture of origin is critical then selecting third country nationals for whom the country of assignment is not that different culturally from their own may be a sensible policy (Parker and McEvoy, 1993).

Cross-cultural training appears to be an important factor of adjustment, especially when it comes to interaction and general adjustment. Nevertheless, corporations often neglect to provide any kind of cross-cultural training to their international managers. The mere existence of some kind of cross-cultural training is not sufficient (Waxin and Panaccio, 2005). The training must be in accordance with the hardness of the culture of the host country. The more different that culture is from that of the country of origin, the more important and necessary is the use of cross-cultural training programmes. Furthermore, the method of training should be tailored to the cultural distance between the expatriate's country of origin and the host country, but also to the nature of his assignment, to his position and to the duration of his contract. As an alternative to pre-departure training, cross-cultural training in the host country could also be envisaged. Briody and Chrisman (1991) and Selmer (2001) report that some expatriates and their families would have preferred to receive the training in the host country. Mendenhall and Stahl (2000) mention 'in country real-time training' as one of the three new tendencies that are emerging for HR managers who work in the international HR area, alongside with global mindset training, and CD-ROM/Internet-based training. However, since culture shock manifests itself in the first few months of expatriation, pre-departure training seems indispensable. Black et al. (1992) believe that pre-departure training would be more effective if it were continued in the host country, considered as the ideal place for learning a new culture. Further, Barham and Devine (1991) mention that cross-cultural training of the accompanying family is an often-neglected aspect of the cross-cultural preparation of international managers. Harris (1989) notes that corporations would benefit from using their former expatriates as trainers for the new expatriates.

Finally, managers might use the results of this study to facilitate the adjustment of expatriates to their new position abroad. Antecedents of adjustment are not the same across the national groups of expatriates. Our results suggest that management may be well advised to implement policies and practices to provide effective support and encouragement to expatriates, which take account of cultural and personal needs.

*Annex Table 6.1:* Calculation of intercultural distance

| Country | Power distance | Uncertainty avoidance | Individualism | Masculinity | Intercultural distance to India* |
|---|---|---|---|---|---|
| France | 68 | 86 | 71 | 43 | 91 |
| Germany | 35 | 65 | 66 | 31 | 96 |
| Korea | 60 | 85 | 18 | 39 | 109 |
| India | 77 | 40 | 48 | 56 | — |
| Norway | 31 | 50 | 69 | 8 | 125 |
| Sweden | 31 | 29 | 71 | 5 | 131 |
| Denmark | 18 | 23 | 74 | 16 | 142 |

* Distances were calculated using the 'city block' method.
*Source:* Hofstede (1991).

## References

Aryee, S. & Stone, R. J. (1996). Work experiences, work adjustment and psychological well being of expatriate employees in Hong Kong. *International Journal of Human Resource Management*, 7, 1: 150–64.

Barham, K. & Devine, M. (1991). *The quest for international manager: A survey of global human resource strategies,* Special Report n° 2098. London: Ashridge Management Research Group, The Economist Intelligence Unit.

Black, J. S. (1988). Work-role transition: A study of American expatriate managers in Japan. *Journal of International Business Studies*, 19: 274–91.

Black, J. S. (1990). The relationship of personal characteristics with the adjustment of Japanese expatriate managers. *Management International Review,* 30: 119–34.

Black, J. S. & Gregersen, H. B. (1991). Antecedents to cross-cultural adjustment for expatriates in Pacific Rim assignments. *Human Relations*, 44, 5: 497–515.

Black, J. S., Gregensen, H. B. & Mendenhall, M. (1992). *Global Assignments: successfully expatriating and repatriating international managers*, San Francisco, Jossey-Bass.

Black, J. S. & Mendenhall, M. (1990). Cross-cultural training effectiveness: A review and theoretical framework. *Academy of Management Review*, 15: 113–36.

Black, J. S., Mendenhall, M. & Oddou, G. (1991). Towards a comprehensive model of international adjustment: An integration of multiple theoretical perspectives. *Academy of Management Review*, 16, 2: 291–317.

Black, J. S. & Stephens, G. K. (1989). Expatriate adjustment and intent to stay in pacific rim overseas assignments. *Journal of Management*, 15: 529–44.

Breaugh, J. A. & Colihan, J. P. (1994). Measuring facets of job ambiguity: construct validity evidence, *Journal of Applied Psychology*, 79, 2: 191–202.

Brewster, C. (1995). Effective expatriate training, in Selmer J. (ed.) *Expatriate Management: new ideas for international business,* Westport, Quorum Books.

Brewster, C. & Pickard, J. (1994). Evaluating expatriate training. *International Studies of Management and Organisation,* 24, 3: 18–35.

Scullion, H. & Brewster, C. (2002). The management of expatriates: Messages from Europe? *Journal of World Business*, 36, 4: 346–65.
Briody, E. K. & Chrisman, J. B. (1991). Cultural adaptation on overseas assignments, *Human Organisation*, 50, 3: 264–82.
Caligiuri, P. (2000). Selecting expatriates for personality characteristics: A moderating effect of personality on the relationship between host national contact and cross-cultural adjustment. *Management International Review*, 40: 61–80.
Cerdin, J-L. (1999). *La mobilité internationale: Réussir l'expatriation*. Paris: Editions d'Organisation.
Cerdin, J-L., Chandon J-L. & Waxin, M. (1999). The adaptability of French expatriates: A confirmatory analysis. Paper presented at *Workshop on Expatriation*, Madrid, Spain.
Church, A. (1982). Sojourner adjustment. *Psychological Bulletin*, 91: 540–72.
Deshpande, S. P. & Viswesvaran, C. (1992). Is cross-cultural training of expatriate managers effective: a meta analysis. *International Journal of Intercultural Relations*, 16(3): 295–310.
Eschbach, D. M., Parker, G. E. & Stoeberl, P. A. (2001). American repatriated employees' retrospective assessments of the effects of cross-cultural training on their adaptation to international assignments. *International Journal of Human Resource Management*, 12, 2: 270–87.
Fenlason, K. J. & Beehr, T. A. (1994). Social support and occupational stress: Effects of talking to others. *Journal of Organizational Behavior*, 15: 157–75.
Folkman, S., Lazarus, R. S., Dunkel-Schetter, C., Delongis, A. & Gruen, R. J. (1986). Dynamics of a stressful encounter: Cognitive appraisal, coping, and encounter outcomes. *Journal of Personality and Social Psychology*, 50: 992–1003.
Gao, G. & Gudykunst W. (1990). Uncertainty, anxiety, and adaptation, *International Journal of Intercultural Relations*, 14, 301–17.
Gregersen, H. B. & Stroh, L. (1997). Coming home to the Arctic cold: Antecedents to Finnish expatriates and spouse repatriation. *Personnel Psychology*, 50, 3: 635–54.
Gudykunst, W. B. & Hammer, M. R (1984). *Basic Training Design: approaches to intercultural training; Handbook of Intercultural Training, vol. I*, New York, Pergamon.
Haslberger, A. (1999). The measurement of cross-cultural adaptation. Unpublished Ph.D. Dissertation, Universität Linz.
Harris, J. E. (1989). Moving managers internationally: the care and feeding of expatriates, *Human Resources Planning*, 12, 49–53.
Hofstede, G. (1991). *Cultures and Organizations: Software of the mind*. London: McGraw Hill.
Furnham, A. & Bochner, S. (1982). Social difficulty in a foreign culture. In S. Bochner (ed.), *Cultures in Contact*, Elmsford, NY: Pergamon: 161–98.
Ilgen, D. R. & Hollenbeck, J. R. (1991). The structure of work: job design and roles, in Dunnette M. D. & Hough L. M. (eds*), Handbook of Industrial and Organisational Psychology*, Vol. 2., Palo Alto, CA: Consulting Psychologists Press: 165–207.
Janssens, M. (1995). Intercultural interaction: A burden on international managers? *Journal of Organisational Behavior*, 16: 155–67.
Karasek, R. A. (1979). Job demands, job decision latitude and mental strain: implications for job redesign, *Administrative Science Quarterly*, 24: 285–308.
Mendenhall, M. & Oddou, G. (1985). The dimensions of expatriate acculturation. *Academy of Management Review*, 10, 3: 39–47.

Mendenhall, M. E. & Stahl, G. (2000). Expatriate training and development: Where do we go from here?, *Human Resource Management,* 39, 2,3, 251–65.

Nicholson, N. (1984). A theory of work role transitions. *Administrative Science Quarterly,* 29: 172–91.

O'Grady, S. & Lane, H. W. (1996). The psychic distance paradox, *Journal of International Business Studies,* 27(2): 309–33.

Parker, B. & Mcevoy, G. M. (1993). Initial examination of a model of intercultural adjustment. *International Journal of Intercultural Relations,* 17: 355–79.

Pinder, C. C. & Schroeder, K. G. (1987). Time to proficiency following job transfer. *Academy of Management Journal,* 30, 2: 336–53.

Redmond, M. V. (2000). Cultural distance as a mediating factor between stress and intercultural communication competence. *International Journal of Intercultural Relations,* 24: 151–59.

Roques, O. (1999). Les réactions des salariés aux transitions de carrières: Une approche en termes de stress au travail, Unpublished Ph.D. Dissertation, IAE d'Aix en Provence.

Selmer, J. (2001). The preference for predeparture or postarrival cross-cultural training – An exploratory approach, *Journal of Managerial Psychology,* 16, 1, 50–58.

Selmer, J. (2005). Cultural novelty and adjustment: western business expatriates in China, *Asia Pacific Business Review,* 3: 122–33.

Stone, R. J. (1991). Expatriate selection and failure. *Human Resource Planning,* 14, 1: 9–18.

Tung, R. L. (1993). Managing cross-national and intra-national diversity, *Human Resource Management,* 321 (4): 461–77.

Waxin, M. F. (2000). L'adaptation des cadres expatriés en Inde: Ses déterminants et l'effet de la culture d'origine, Unpublished Ph.D. Dissertation, IAE Aix-en-Provence, France.

Waxin, M. F. (February 2004). Expatriates' interaction adjustment: the direct and moderator effects of culture of origin, *International Journal of Intercultural Relations,* 28, 1, 61–79.

Waxin, M. F. (June 2004). L'adaptabilité du cadre expatrié : proposition d'une échelle de mesure améliorée, *ASAC Conference, Quebec City,* 5–8 June 2004.

Waxin, M. F. & Brewster, C. (2005). Expatriates' time to proficiency: antecedents and country of origin effects, *8th Conference on International Human Resource Management,* 'Making a Difference in a World of Differences' Cairns, Australia, 14–17 June 2005.

Waxin, M. F. & Panaccio A. J. (2005). Cross-cultural training to facilitate expatriate adjustment: it works!, *Personnel Review,* Special Issue on global human resource management (development), 34, 1.

Waxin, M. F., Roger, A. & Chandon, J-L. (1997). L'intégration des expatriés dans leur nouveau poste, une analyse contingente et quantitative, le cas des expatriés Français en Norvège. In M. Tremblay & B. Sire, Montréal (ed.), *GRH face à la crise: GRH en crise* ? Paris: Presse HEC.

# 7

# Gender Diversity and Organizational Success: the Impact of Female Foreign Assignments

*Maike Andresen, Elena Hristozova & Uta B. Lieberum*

> An international assignment is the single most powerful experience shaping the perspectives and capabilities of effective global leaders.
>
> (Black, Gregersen, Mendenhall and Stroh, 1999)

## Introduction

According to research on diversity in organizational contexts, the mix of female and male employees in organizations and especially in management ranks is seen as an inherent source of innovation and hence as a value driver for companies. It is seen as a key factor in achieving a competitive advantage and in realizing strategic goals in a better way (Friday & Friday, 2003; Stark, 2001; Thomas & Ely, 1996). However, when analysing the proportion of women in management positions in companies it becomes obvious that they represent only a very low percentage, and that companies are still far from realizing and profiting from a gender mix in many countries. This result does not only apply to those companies which have a very low proportion of women but also to those that have an almost equal distribution of men and women in their *overall* workforce, as is the case, for example, in banks and insurance companies. One effective solution to solve this problem and to achieve a better gender mix within management is the promotion of female foreign assignments, as international experience is viewed by companies as being crucial to upward movement (Catalyst, 2001; Harris, 2004; Marmer Solomon, 1998).

On examining the situation in practice, it can be seen that the number of expatriates sent abroad by multinational corporations (MNCs) in North America and Europe is increasing steadily, according to research studies on international assignments (for example PricewaterhouseCoopers, 2002). However, regarding the distribution of employees by gender, it becomes obvious that the number of female managers pursuing international careers remains considerably lower than is the case with male managers. In addition, the percentage is disproportionately lower to the rate for women in domestic management (Caligiuri and Lazarova, 2002).

Based on the above mentioned phenomena, our study has been conducted with *a view to exploring corporate practice in Germany with respect to gender diversity in management ranks with particular focus on female foreign assignments.*

The following section provides an overview of existing research exploring the reasons for the limited use made of female expatriates. In addition, this chapter outlines the implications these barriers have for the achievement of organizational and strategic goals related to the promotion of equal opportunities and gender diversity on a national as well as on an international level. Finally, we outline the aim of our empirical study of some of the largest companies in the banking and insurance industries in Germany, and establish the research questions. In the subsequent section we present our empirical results regarding those practices aiming at the promotion of women in general and also with respect to female foreign assignments. In the last section we make recommendations for methods of calculating and quantifying the effects of the impact of gender diversity in management ranks on organizational success. We finish with a résumé and suggestions for further research.

## Female foreign assignments: status quo, motives, and barriers

### Status quo

Over the last twenty years the amount of research undertaken on women involved in global assignments has been increasing (for example Adler, 1984abc, 1993, 1994, 2002; Harris, 1993, 1995, 2004; Izraeli and Adler, 1994; Izraeli et al., 1980; Jelinek and Adler, 1988; Kirk and Maddox, 1988; Linehan and Scullion, 2001ab, 2002ab; Marmer Solomon, 1998; Selmer and Leung, 2003; Tung, 1988; Westwood and Leung, 1994). According to these studies the proportion of women as expatriates has increased from 3 per cent in the early 1980s (USA) (Adler, 1984c) to 11 per cent in 2002 (USA, Europe) (PricewaterhouseCoopers, 2002). If the proportion of female expatriates is differentiated in terms of industry sector, big variations can be identified, with (investment) banks leading the way with nearly a quarter of their expatriates being women. This may be explained by the fact that the banking industry makes greater use of younger/more junior-level managers for international assignments, whereas oil and gas, manufacturing and engineering firms have a relatively poor record in comparison (Adler, 1987; PricewaterhouseCoopers, 2002: 16f.). However, despite this increase the under-representation of women is still substantial.

A comparison of the number of female employees domestically with the number of female expatriates reveals that (even) greater barriers exist for women in international than in domestic management. This situation is alarming in that international experience is considered as a prerequisite for promotion to the top of the organizational hierarchy (Caligiuri and Tung, 1999; Stroh and Caligiuri, 1998). This is reflected in an explorative study by Bittner and Reisch (1991) showing that on average 13.7 per cent of managers and 35.9 per cent of top managers in Germany have working experience in a foreign country. This intentional or incidental practice of selecting only small numbers of women for international assignments may be contributing to the already existing workplace phenomenon known as the 'glass ceiling'. In addition to this, companies are missing an effective opportunity to achieve gender diversity (also) within the management ranks.

## Motives

The motives encouraging firms to consider sending more women on global assignments could encompass any or a combination of the following:

- *affirmative action* with respect to women. The focus of this strategy is to create an even playing field regarding their access to national as well as international management positions; this is to be achieved by a favourable treatment of women which might imply a temporary discrimination of men. Affirmative action is aimed at satisfying legal requirements and to remedy abuses (Jain, Sloane and Horwitz, 2003; Kovach, Kravitz and Hughes, 2004; Wright et al., 1995).
- *equal opportunities* for domestic as well as expatriate (management) positions. Equal opportunity activities seek to eliminate discrimination in the workplace by removing/overcoming structural and procedural barriers preventing women from taking advantage of opportunities regarding jobs, development, promotions, compensation and so on (e.g. Pérotin, Robinson and Loundes, 2003; Whitehead, 2001). This aim is consistent with the corporate values of many MNCs. The extremely

competitive economic environment forces MNCs to select the very best people available, irrespective of their gender.
- *gender (and cultural) diversity* related to the combination of female and male employees (of different nationalities) in such a way as is apt to create more value for the firm than would be the case with homogeneous groups. Well-managed diversity, including gender diversity, is seen as an inherent source of innovation which is a key factor in achieving a competitive advantage and in realizing strategic goals in a better way (for example Lepak and Snell, 1999; Richard, 2000).

Whereas affirmative action and equal opportunity initiatives shall lead to a balanced proportion of women and men on an organizational level (quantitative approach), gender diversity aims at a mixture of women and men on a team, departmental or hierarchical level in such a way as to maximize the potential advantages of diversity in the sense of, for example, innovativeness or effectiveness (qualitative approach). Hence, diversity does not necessarily lead to an equal proportion of women and men in a team or at other levels. In other words, the diversity approach shifts the focus from *eliminating* difference (due to structural and procedural barriers) to *valuing* similarities as well as differences between men and women that can be traced back to socialization. Managing diversity is strategically and not legally driven.

The investigation of the initiatives taken in order to achieve affirmative action, equal opportunities and/or gender diversity was the starting point of our empirical study. Although our focus is on gender diversity we also analyse affirmative action and equal opportunity activities; this is because the initiatives taken by companies regarding these goals are similar or even identical, to the implementation of equal opportunities in the long run as a prerequisite to achieve gender diversity.

According to, for example, Barkema, Baum and Mannix (2002), Lau and Murnighan (1998), Schuler, Jackson and Luo (2004), Wentling and Palma-Rivas (2000), and Wright et al. (1995), there are numerous positive benefits for organizations that implement diversity initiatives in order to achieve gender diversity within their workforce and especially within their management ranks. These economic benefits include the possibility for firms to recruit and capitalize on the contributions of talented human beings; lower operating costs due to lower absenteeism, turnover, and job dissatisfaction in the workforce; enhanced reputations with potential customers who also shared the value of diversity; more creativity and better problem-solving capabilities; and strong community and institutional support due to their cultivated diverse work forces. Furthermore, companies that voice their support for and run management practices that serve to achieve gender diversity experience a significant and positive improvement in their stock price. The above mentioned economic benefits can be classified into *external* and *internal* effects. The first-mentioned external effects concern the *market* and *customers, shareholders, labour market* and *community*. The internal benefits have an effect at three levels: *individual level, level of interpersonal relations* and *organizational level.*

## Barriers

In previous empirical studies the following reasons from both corporate and female expatriates' perspectives have been given for the relatively low number of female expatriates compared to male assignees (a table summarizing the main research results and a reference list is available at http://www.hsu-hh.de/domsch, Forschung, Female Foreign Assignments). An analysis of the empirical results, almost exclusively from Anglo-American researchers, shows that women are as equally *interested* as men in pursuing international careers (e.g. Harris, 2002; Stroh, Varma and Valy-Durbin, 2000). However, the empirical results regarding *willingness* are not that clear. Whereas some studies found that women are not as willing as men to go abroad (e.g. Catalyst, 2001; Yurkiewicz and Rosen, 1995), others did not detect significant differences (both from company and female expatriates' perspective) (e.g. Domsch and Lieberum, 1997; Varma and Stroh, 2001). This specific finding does not necessarily contradict the former argument, since there is a difference between expressing an interest in expatriate assignments, and in actually actively pursuing it. The argument regarding the limited *availability* of qualified women has not been investigated in depth (e.g. Adler, 1984ac). Nevertheless, when comparing the number of female and male managers (as the primary interest group) it becomes obvious that, in general, the pool of potential female candidates is significantly lower, meaning that this argument is corroborated with evidence. In addition to this argument several studies focusing on the female expatriates' perspective reveal (unintentional) *discriminatory practices* in relation to the recruitment and selection of female managers for international assignments (e.g. Izraeli and Zeira, 1993; Linehan and Scullion, 2001ab). In consequence, even female managers who are interested in an international career and who are willing to go abroad face additional barriers within the parent company that hinder their career. When asking companies about their belief as to whether women may be more *vulnerable to harassment and other dangers* than men, they unambiguously confirmed this to be a matter of concern, and indicated it as a reason for not sending women to insecure foreign countries (e.g. Izraeli and Zeira, 1993; Napier and Taylor, 2002). Interestingly, the argument that women expatriates will be hindered by *cultural and/or gender prejudice* in the host country as an explanation for the low ratio of female expatriates is judged very differently: Whereas companies in the various studies for the most part agreed with this thesis (e.g. Harris, 2002; Ruhe and Allen, 1997), female expatriates themselves reported neutral or even positive experiences in this respect (e.g. Caligiuri, Joshi and Lazarova, 1999; Vance and Paik, 2001). According to Adler (1987, 1994) the rejection of this thesis can be explained by the triple identity of female expatriates: she is seen as a manager in the first instance and as a foreigner and a woman only in the second instance. This is also connected with the lack of *role models*; this means that traditional female role models are seen as incompatible with the managerial role of a female expatriate by the women expatriates themselves (e.g. Linehan and Scullion, 2002ab; Mayrhofer and Scullion, 2002). Concerning the corporate perspective this thesis was confirmed by several studies in the late 1970s and in the 1980s (e.g. Thal and Cateora, 1979) and rejected in a study in the 1990s (Marmer Solomon, 1998). This may indicate a change over time in the conception of the female role model. Additionally, research results suggest that women and men do not differ regarding their *success rate*, that is to say, on their desire to terminate their global assignments or on their supervisor-rated performance (e.g. Caligiuri and Tung, 1999; Selmer and Leung, 2003). Finally, both parties (companies and female managers) unanimously report on difficulties with respect to *family issues* and *dual-career relationships* which may prevent women from moving to another country (e.g. Harris, 2002; Linehan and Scullion 2001ab; Linehan, Scullion and Walsh, 2001; Linehan and Walsh, 1999ab). In recent studies women have reported on the lack of *policies and practices* that would help to solve these and other problems (e.g. Linehan and Scullion, 2001ab).

The above-mentioned empirical studies generally indicate weak corporate support for woman employees in general and female business expatriates in particular. Hence, female managers have to overcome more barriers in their progression to (international) management positions than men. As a result of these additional barriers that exist both inside and outside the work environment, women need more support on the part of the company in developing their (expatriate) careers. Only few (empirical) studies have focused on appropriate approaches and their impact so far (as an exception cf. Linehan and Scullion, 2001ab). Aspects such as the attainment of equal opportunities for women and men and gender diversity, which are central to our study, are not mentioned in any of the studies. Examples of practices that serve to achieve gender diversity include:

- The employment situation of women in the company: increasing the number of women in higher management positions; no differentiation between women and men in part-time or full-time work and on parental leave; realization of equal pay for women and men.
- Staff recruitment and selection: gender neutral job advertisements; same selection criteria and methods for women and men; reintegration of women and men after their parental leave.
- Personnel development and further education: personnel and career development of part-time workers; support of women regarding expatriation as this helps to reach top management positions; equal career paths for women and men; (more or different) career counselling, mentoring and coaching programmes, cross mentoring programmes; support of mixed leadership.
- Flexible working hours: part-time work in higher management positions; enabling change from part-time to full-time work and vice versa.
- Information and communication policy: internal policy on equal opportunities; internal statements of co-operation between women and men in the workplace; institutionalization of equal opportunities and partnership-based behaviour in the workplace.
- Service for families: support of child care; support for families and contact during parental leave; guidelines for coming back after parental leave.
- Flexible job organization: working at home; (mobile) telework; teamwork.

Companies have to be aware of the fact that the failure of organizations to provide such support may deprive women of avenues for organizational success. In addition, companies need to make use of the (international) abilities and experience acquired during the expatriation phase by women in order for foreign assignments to be a step towards management positions. Research is needed on the promotional opportunities for women in the home organization as well as on the impact of gender diversity (achieved via female foreign assignments) on organizational success. This last-mentioned control mechanism is required if we are to find out which of the support mechanisms proves to be the most effective and efficient for companies, and to determine and steer an optimum level of diversity. The lack of research in this area is the starting point of our research project.

## Research question

The aim of the empirical study presented in the following sections is to investigate which initiatives are being taken by companies within selected fields of activity to achieve gender diversity in management ranks in general. We especially focus on female foreign assignments (cf. Figure 7.1).

In order to better steer the activities that serve to achieve gender diversity, their effectiveness and efficiency need to be assessed. A measurement tool to calculate the impact of female foreign assignments and gender diversity in management ranks on organizational success is presented in the subsequent section.

The above mentioned results of the reviewed empirical studies on female foreign assignments lead us to the overall research question of our survey:

> *Do companies in Germany pursue the goal of obtaining equal opportunities and/or do they aim at profiting from gender diversity in their organization?*

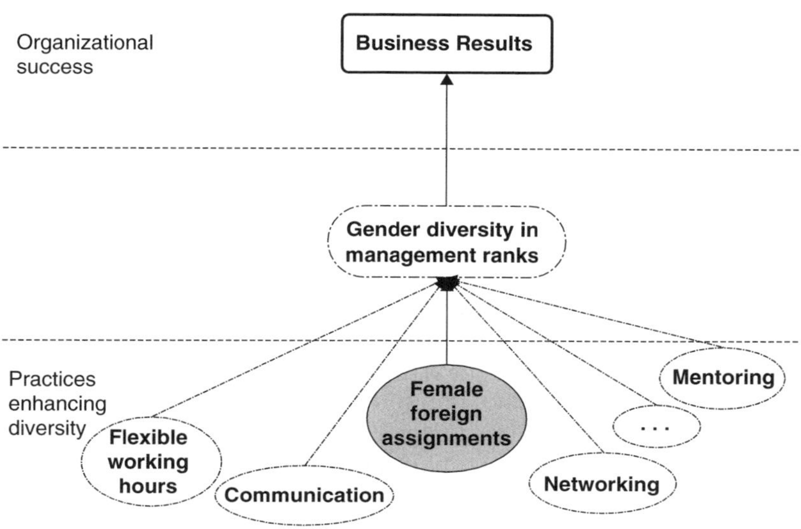


*Figure 7.1:* Female foreign assignments as a means to achieve gender diversity in management ranks
*Source:* Own illustration.

The practices of MNCs described in the various research studies contradict the best interests of globally active firms. Companies may unintentionally create a considerable disadvantage in their internationalization process. MNCs aiming at a maximization of talent cannot afford to limit their pool of talented human resources by excluding particular groups of employees such as women. Hence, qualified women need to be as equally considered as men for international assignments and for management positions. In order to reach this goal MNCs need to attract and motivate female candidates by providing special support and activities in general, and particularly with regard to foreign assignments, which may need to be differently designed than would otherwise be the case for their male counterparts. In order to be able to answer the overall research question, the following sub-questions guided our research:

> *Question 1: Do companies* **communicate** *the goals of equal opportunities and/or gender diversity (a) externally and/or (b) internally?*
> *Question 2: Do companies proactively take initiatives* **in general** *that serve to reach the objectives of equal opportunities and gender diversity?*
> *Question 3: Do companies take special initiatives with respect to* **female foreign assignments** *that serve to reach the objectives of equal opportunities and gender diversity?*

## Practical evidence in German banks and insurance companies

### Survey methodology

The survey started with the analysis of the homepages of the 50 biggest banks and 28 biggest insurance companies in Germany with respect to *public* statements and documents about gender diversity. Banks and insurance companies were chosen because of their high proportion of female staff in general. In addition, we investigated whether the 50 banks and 28 insurance companies implemented activities to support gender diversity in general and/or promoted this topic by communicating it *internally* to their employees and/or implemented measures to support female expatriation. For this investigation we used structured telephone interviews as well as a content analysis of internal documents and brochures of these companies. The survey attained a response rate of 36 per cent for the banks (18 banks in total) and also 36 per cent for the insurance companies (10 insurance companies in total).

*Table 7.1:* Empirical results

| | Banks | Insurance companies |
|---|---|---|
| Statements on their homepage | 5 (n = 50) | 1 (n = 28) |
| Internal communication | 15 (n = 18) | 3 (n = 10) |
| Internal measures to foster gender diversity in general | 12 (n = 18) | 3 (n = 10) |
| Measures to enhance female expatriation | 1 (n = 18) | 0 (n = 10) |

## Results

In most of the banks and insurance companies the large majority of the staff are female. However, the percentage of female managers is no higher than 30 per cent in any of these companies. On average, 7 per cent of top management, 5 to 12 per cent of middle management and up to 35 per cent of the lower management level positions are held by women. These results prove the assumption that companies do not take advantage of the potential of their entire internal staff to fill management positions.

Table 7.1 summarizes the results in relation to external and internal communication of the goal of gender diversity, the implementation of measures to reach the goal of gender diversity, and the realization of measures that serve to support women for foreign assignments.

### External communication

The investigation of the 50 biggest German banks and the 28 biggest German insurance companies regarding statements of gender diversity on their homepage shows that 7.7 per cent of the banks and 3.6 per cent of the insurance companies have placed statements which refer to this topic on their homepage. This kind of external communication is completed by a few of the companies with public events and/or articles placed on the Internet or in newspapers and magazines. On average, nearly 7.7 per cent of the investigated companies communicated their commitment regarding gender diversity and/or equal opportunities externally on their homepage and/or placed statements in newspapers or on the Internet (cf. Table 7.1).

### Internal communication

By analysing the responses of 18 banks and 10 insurance companies with respect to the question as to whether internal statements which declare the support of gender diversity exist and what kind of measures

*Table 7.2:* Levels of intensity

| Levels of intensity |
|---|
| *1. Very high intensity*<br>Companies which communicate gender diversity internally and externally as a company goal, and which additionally implement general measures with respect to gender diversity and provide special support for female expatriation. |
| *2. High intensity*<br>Companies which communicate gender diversity internally and externally as a company goal and which additionally implement general measures with respect to gender diversity, but do not provide special support for female expatriation. |
| *3. Middle intensity*<br>Companies which communicate gender diversity internally and/or externally as a company goal and additionally implement at least one general measure with respect to gender diversity. |
| *4. Low intensity*<br>Companies which communicate gender diversity internally as a company goal but do not carry out any general measures to promote women in managerial positions. |
| *5. Very low intensity*<br>Companies which do not communicate gender diversity as a company goal and do not carry out any measures at all to promote women in managerial positions. |

have been established in the companies, the results showed that internal statements to general gender diversity are made by 83 per cent of the banks and 30 per cent of the insurance companies surveyed. On average, 65 per cent of the companies surveyed communicate the goal of gender diversity internally (cf. Table 7.1). Of those companies that do not give evidence of their commitment on their homepage, some limited their communication to internal interest groups.

## Initiatives regarding equal opportunities and gender diversity in general

Sixty-seven per cent of the banks and 30 per cent of the insurance companies implement specific measures to achieve the objective of gender diversity. On average, 54 per cent of the companies surveyed indicated that they had at least one activity. On the basis of these results five levels of intensity can be derived which are described in Table 7.2.

These intensity levels (especially level 1, 2 and 3) depend on the kind and the number of measures which have been realized in the company, and on the effectiveness of the measures implemented. We assume that

*Table 7.3:* Categorization of the companies surveyed

| Intensity | Very high 1 | High 2 | Middle 3 | Low 4 | Very low 5 |
|---|---|---|---|---|---|
| Banks (n = 18) | 5.6% | 16.7% | 44.4% | 16.7% | 16.7% |
| Insurance companies (n = 10) | 0% | 0% | 30% | 0% | 70% |
| *Total (n = 28)* | 3.6% | 10.7% | 39.3% | 10.7% | 35.7% |

there are only a few companies which implement activities designed to promote equal opportunities, and that these companies very seldom reach the highest intensity level. This means that they will not reach their potential level of success (in terms of gender mix and organizational success).

In order to gain the advantages of gender diversity the organizations in the sample work on several aspects of human resource management. The most important initiative is the implementation of flexible working hours in connection with part-time work, which has also been implemented to some extent in higher management positions. Similarly, a few companies have flexible job organization schemes, providing the possibility to work at home, or telework, as well as special services for families such as child care support, active contact during parental leave and guidelines for coming back after parental leave. Other activities include measures concerning personnel development, such as mentoring and coaching programmes, as well as supporting women's networks within the companies.

On the basis of these results companies can be subdivided into five different groups regarding the degree of intensity related to the goal of gender diversity (Table 7.3).

In a detailed analysis the companies which have a middle, high or very high intensity level have to be split into different sections depending on the amount, content and effectiveness of the implemented measures. This will be theoretically analysed in the last section and will also need to be investigated in further empirical research. However, it is obvious that there are differences between banks and insurance companies. Banks implemented measures to increase the number of female managers more frequently. Most of the companies carry out a minimum of one measure and are classified at intensity level 3.

## Special initiatives with respect to female foreign assignments

Only one of the companies considers female foreign assignments to be an issue. This means that employment abroad is almost totally neglected as a measure.

## Discussion

There are many possible approaches for supporting gender diversity in companies. In this research one of the above-mentioned activities in particular is of major importance: the support of female expatriation in connection with the development of women for top management positions. According to existing research studies presented at the start motivation, the performance and the satisfaction regarding foreign assignments does not differ between men and women. No serious reason for not sending women abroad could be detected. However, in reality the number of women in the expatriation process is still very low in contrast to men working in foreign countries. If intercultural experiences are taken to be one of the prerequisites for reaching top management level, then the huge potential of women is not being given due or sufficient consideration.

However, several companies do use external and/or internal information platforms to communicate the goal of gender diversity to the public and/or to their employees. They also make arrangements for specific activities to implement measures to reach the goal of gender diversity; however, they almost never organize special activities to increase the number of women placed on foreign assignments. There are differences between the companies themselves and between the fields of activity, and these will have to be examined more precisely.

This analysis leads to calculations which form the basis for a visual presentation of the specific advantages enjoyed by companies implementing gender diversity measures; these companies are not only committed to reaching these goals from a marketing point of view.

## The impact of female foreign assignments on organizational success

In order to evaluate the impact of diversity-aimed practices on organizational performance, companies need a measurement tool. Several studies have been conducted in the field of value-oriented human capital management (e.g. Arthur, 1994; MacDuffie, 1995; Huselid, 1995), but there is still little research focusing on the impact of gender diversity. Whereas Kilduff et al. (2000) and Hambrick et al. (1996) argue that age diversity of top-management teams affects overall performance positively, Milliken and Martins (1996) reported generally negative effects of this kind of diversity. Knouse and Dansby (1999) suggest in their study that 50% of gender diversity can be considered as a possible optimum of diversity level regarding group effectiveness. Despite these empirical findings, there is still no answer to the question: 'How can companies measure the impact of foreign assignments as a diversity-aimed practice on organizational success?'

Our intention is to make the first step towards designing a model that determines the impact of female management development on organizational success, based on the assumption that female foreign assignments do contribute to a better gender diversity in management ranks.

According to several researchers and corporate surveys (Handel, 1999; McNulty and Tharenou, 2004) the Return on Investment (ROI) is determined as a suitable means of measurement to assess the success of an international assignment. McNulty and Tharenou (2004) use Flamholtz's (1985) definition of ROI, which defines it as 'a financial ratio that expresses profit in direct relation to investment'. Furthermore the authors suggest a strategic ROI approach rather than a financial one, as the first incorporates both 'financial and non-financial costs and benefits, specific to the strategic objectives of the MNC' and sees its purpose in ensuring the link 'between all of the costs and benefits of the assignment and the purpose of the assignment itself' (McNulty and Tharenou, 2004). Thus we have based our evaluation model on the strategic ROI approach, as we consider this to be the most suitable way to evaluate the impact of FFA on managerial gender diversity and thus on organizational success. The following three steps illustrate the process of determining ROI.

## Step 1: Identifying strategic objectives of FFA

McNulty and Tharenou (2004) argue that the differences among the organizational reasons for using expatriates will lead to different ROI of foreign assignments, 'as the cost and benefits for each purpose will be different'. Thus it is quite important for the decision makers to be aware of the strategic objective of the female expatriation from the very beginning of the calculation process.

There are several classifications of objectives regarding foreign assignments within the expatriate literature that can be grouped into three major reasons for using expatriates: *staffing, management development* and *enabling transfer of a firm's culture* (Edstrom and Galbraith, 1994). In the case of our model we have taken *female management development* as the single purpose of female foreign assignments (cf. Figure 7.2). *The strategic goal of female foreign assignment can be defined as the increase of the gender diversity level in management ranks*. The fulfillment of this goal leads to specific benefits related to the business results.

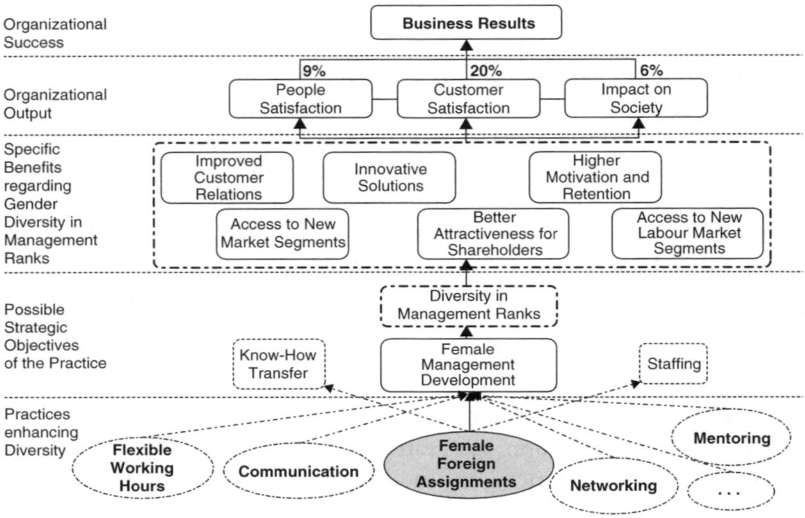


*Figure 7.2:* The impact of FFA on organizational success
*Source:* Own illustration.

## Step 2: Quantifying impact intensity on business results

For the purpose of our model we have considered the beneficial part of the ROI calculation as a percentage of the business result (for example increase in profit). Furthermore, there are three major aspects specifying the relation between FFA, gender diversity in management ranks and organizational success. *First,* female foreign assignments can increase the gender diversity in the management ranks (for example top management team), where this diversity leads to a positive impact on business results (Knouse and Dansby, 1999). *Second,* this positive impact results from the interaction of different benefits regarding gender diversity in general and diversity at managerial level in particular (cf. Figure 7.2). Such benefits, as already mentioned in the theoretical part, can be *improved customer relations, access to new market segments, increased attractiveness for shareholders, access to new labour market segments* and others. *Third,* according to the EFQM Model of Excellence, business results can be improved by increasing *people satisfaction (PS), customer satisfaction (CS)* and *impact on society (IS)* (Zink, 1996). Thus we consider these criteria of excellence (Nabitz et al., 2001; Simon and Nauheim, 1999; Zink, 1996) with their weights 9%, 20% and 6% respectively (Simon and Nauheim, 1999; Zink, 1996) as suitable derivates for organizational success (cf. Figure 7.3).

**Impact Intensity = (CS × 0.2 + PS × 0.09 + IS × 0.06) × ML**

| Impact on | Customer Satisfaction | People Satisfaction | Impact on Society | × Maturity Level | Intensity of Impact % |
|---|---|---|---|---|---|
| Flexible Working Hours | 0.14 | 0.15 | 0.10 | 0.50 | |
| Communication | 0.12 | 0.12 | 0.20 | 0.25 | |
| **Female Foreign Assignments** | **0.15** | **0.20** | **0.09** | **0.75** | **5%** |
| Networking | 0.12 | 0.08 | 0.10 | 1 | |
| Mentoring | 0.06 | 0.10 | 0.05 | 0.25 | |
| Others | 0.41 | 0.35 | 0.46 | | |

*Figure 7.3:* Determining impact intensity of FFA
*Source:* Own illustration.

In order to determine the impact intensity of FFA as a practice increasing the gender diversity, we have made use of the 'paper computer' (Ulrich and Probst, 1991). This instrument illustrates the impact of each gender practice on each criteria of excellence (cf. Figure 7.3). The use of a paper computer implies that the impact intensity has to be estimated by the decision makers. In order to gain a better understanding of this our example includes different practices enhancing gender diversity in general. After estimating the impact intensity regarding the three different criteria of excellence, the decision makers have to define how high the *maturity level* is (cf. Figure 7.3). The success of a practice depends to a great extent on the organizational ability and experience in designing and implementing such practice. In the context of the presented model, we have considered the maturity level as a measure assessing organizational ability in terms of implementing and managing a gender-related practice. For the purpose of defining the maturity level we suggest a five-step per cent scale from 0 to 100 (for example 0%; 25%; 50%; 75%; 100%).

By using the formula,

$$Impact\ Intensity = (CS \times 0.2 + PS \times 0.09 + IS \times 0.06) \times ML,$$

the decision makers can define the impact intensity of FFA as a percentage of the increase in profit.

*Table 7.4:* Measurement of expatriates' performance

| Performance measurement values | Appraisal scale | Weighting factor |
|---|---|---|
| Optimization of material and human resources | (1–10) | 0.16 |
| Knowledge management | (1–10) | 0.07 |
| Planning and development | (1–10) | 0.07 |
| Strategic capability | (1–10) | 0.07 |
| Innovation | (1–10) | 0.30 |
| Leadership | (1–10) | 0.33 |
| *Total performance indicator* | | |

*Source:* Following Handel, 1999.

Additionally, the benefits regarding FAA will, to a great extent, depend on the personal performance of the expatriate. The weighting system of the Georgia Institute of Technology measures the success of the expatriate in his/her assignment by means of relative weighting of his/her key performance indicators, such as, for example: optimization of material and human resources, knowledge management, planning and development, strategic capability, innovation and leadership (Handel, 1999). 'A basic performance evaluation, based on a 1–10 system, grades an employee in each of the above categories, which are then multiplied by the value of the category. All the scores are then added together and divided by ten to determine the employee's performance indicator' (Handel, 1999). Based on the weighting factors developed by the Georgia Institute of Technology (Handel, 1999), we have suggested our own, the sum of which makes one (cf. Table 7.4).

## Step 3: Determining and calculating the costs of female expatriation

The final step of our calculation model focuses on the costs involved in a female foreign assignment. The costs are a major topic in the expatriate research and literature. Based on Peixoto (1999) and Black et al. (1992) we divided the costs incurred during international assignments into two major groups: *fixed costs* as expenses for developing expatriation policies and practices, material expenses, HR services, etc. and '*compensation package including indirect costs'* containing salary, financial rewards and costs related to other expatriation incentives. A broader expatriation package can also include: travel, search, payment of housing, cultural and linguistic training and some periods of holiday at home (Peixoto,

1999). The *indirect costs* depend on the specific situation of the expatriate and compensate him/her for their specific individual needs, such as travel of spouse and children, payment of appropriate family housing, international schools, job search for spouse, etc. (Peixoto, 1999). Finally, it should be mentioned, that the costs of expatriation for the particular group of highly skilled expatriates 'may double ... his/her original payment at home' (Peixoto, 1999).

One result of our empirical study is that with respect to expatriation of female staff the companies do not provide any specific initiatives which help to motivate and support women. A possible explanation for such behaviour can be the emergence of *additional* costs, *specific* for *female expatriation*. Due to such costs the ROI of female expatriation may be lower than the ROI of male expatriation, but this tendency occurs only at the beginning of the expatriation period. However, there is a second difference between the female and male ROI of expatriation. In contrast to the additional costs for motivation and support initiatives, the present 'pay gap' between male and female staff at managerial level lowers the total costs of female expatriation. According to the European Commission (2001) 'the average female rates of pay at managerial level are only 2/3 of those for men'. In almost 60 sectors of the economy female staff earns 70 to 85 per cent of men's rates of pay (Achleitner, 2002). In conclusion we can present the *total costs of female foreign assignments* as the sum of the above mentioned fixed costs, the compensation package including indirect costs and the specific female costs of expatriation. The fixed costs should be determined per individual assignee.

For a better understanding of the three-step calculation process, we will be presenting a case study in the following section. It should be considered as an illustration aimed at ensuring a better understanding of the process. The following example is based on corporate data collected from different workshops and brochures.

## Case study

There are three female expatriates working for a big German bank over the course of one fiscal year. The impact intensity of FFA is 5 per cent of the annual profit increase of the company (cf. Figure 7.3), which is €950,000. The benefit of this practice is measured after the female expatriates have returned and have experienced promotion to higher managerial positions. In other words, the benefit of the FFA regarding gender diversity is €47,500. The personal performance of the current female managers following the completion of their international assignments is graded by their supervisors as follows: two of them have achieved a grade of seven in all categories, and one has achieved grade nine in all categories (cf. Table 7.4). After calculating the total performance indicator for each assignee, we obtained the following results: two of them have a performance indicator of 0.7, and the third female expatriate has a performance indicator of 0.9. This means that we have to multiply the benefit by the average performance of all three assignees, which gives a figure of 0.76. The final benefit brought about by the three female expatriates is therefore €36,100.

Let us assume that the average salary of an expatriate is €40,000 a year. Considering the rule of Peixoto (1999), that the total expatriate's costs may double his/her salary, we can conclude that the total investment amounts to 3 × €80,000 = €240,000.

In this example, the ROI of female foreign assignments regarding gender diversity in managerial ranks is:

$$ROI(FFA) = \frac{36,100}{240,000} = 15\%$$

As the final result of 15 per cent is a relative value it has to be considered in relation to other data. The ROI (FFA) calculation supports the decision-making process regarding the achievement of higher gender diversity as it allows a direct comparison to be made between different alternatives such as FFA, mentoring, networking and so on.

Furthermore, the value can be used within both internal and external benchmarks, either regarding gender diversity or regarding female management development in particular. A further advantage of our model is its ability to quantify the impact of female expatriation or an alternative practice on organizational success. Finally it should also be mentioned that the ROI (FFA) takes into account the female specific costs with respect to international assignments.

## Résumé

The results of research studies on women in global assignments over the last twenty years reflect that women face barriers that limit their national as well as international career opportunities. This means that companies are not exhausting their potential for the achievement of a gender mix, and so do not take advantage of the benefits connected with it. This is even more serious considering the fact that – at least from a resource-based view – companies can no longer afford to refrain from the employment and promotion of women, especially as the struggle to acquire talent makes access to the pool of outstanding individuals difficult.

Whereas there are numerous studies available which explore the barriers for women regarding foreign assignments, we believe there is a need to go one step further and to study (a) how effective female foreign assignments are in achieving gender diversity in management ranks and (b) the impact of gender diversity (achieved via female foreign assignments) on organizational success.

Referring to our empirical study, we are able to state that companies use external and/or internal information platforms to communicate the goal of gender diversity to the public and/or to their employees. They also implement specific activities that serve to achieve the goal of gender diversity; however, almost no special activities designed to increase the number of women in foreign assignments are implemented. Although suggestions on how to ameliorate the situation are frequently given in literature, the number of initiatives introduced by organizations in practice to support the taking up of management positions by their female employees are somewhat sparse and insufficient. It still seems that there are no real equal opportunities regarding the selection for foreign assignments, and that in this way companies are relinquishing their chance to achieve gender diversity in management ranks.

The approach of measuring the impact of female expatriation with respect to gender diversity is based on two strategic considerations. *Firstly*, female foreign assignments in their role as a female management development practice do contribute to a higher gender diversity in management ranks. *Secondly*, an optimum level of gender diversity (Knouse and Dansby, 1999) at managerial level – due to its different benefits – impacts organizational success positively. A three-step ROI calculation is central to this approach. It supports companies by measuring the contribution of each gender-aimed practice to organizational performance.

In the following, suggestions for further research are presented which have been derived from our empirical findings. A more precise investigation regarding the specific benefits and costs of gender diversity at managerial level could be conducted both in a quantitative and qualitative manner. The qualitative investigation could be based on a 360° analysis of a selective practice, including as many perspectives as possible from within the organization (for example employees, management, HR department, works council).

Further research should also involve other industries in order to investigate potential differences between companies with a high, middle or low proportion of female workers. Additionally, measures contributing to gender diversity should be analysed with respect to their efficiency and effectiveness.

Knouse and Dansby (1999) found that a gender diversity level of 50 per cent is a possible optimum level for team effectiveness. There is still a need to determine an optimum level of gender diversity in management ranks with respect to its impact on organizational success.

## References

Achleitner, A. K. (2002): Einsam an der Spitze. *Financial Times Deutschland*, Agenda, 11.11.2002, p. 29.

Adler, N. J. (1984a): Expecting international success: female managers overseas. *Columbia Journal of World Business*, 19 (3), 79–85.

Adler, N. J. (1984b): Women do not want international careers: and other myths about international management. *Organisational Dynamics*, 13 (2), 66–79.

Adler, N. J. (1984c): Women in international management: where are they? *California Management Review*, 26 (4), 78–89.

Adler, N. J. (1987): Pacific basin managers: a gaijin, not a woman. In: N. J. Adler and D. N. Izraeli (eds), *Women in Management Worldwide*, New York: M. E. Sharpe, 226–49.

Adler, N. J. (1993): Women managers in a global economy. *HRMagazine*, September, 52–5.

Adler, N. (1994): Competitive frontiers: women managing across borders. *Journal of Management Development*, 13, 24–41.

Adler, N. (2002): Global managers: no longer men alone. *International Journal of Human Resource Management*, 13 (5), 743–60.

Arthur, J. B. (1994): Effects of human resource systems on manufacturing performance and turnover. *Academy of Management Journal*, 37 (3), 670–87.

Barkema, H. G., Baum, J. A. C. and Mannix, E. A. (2002): Management challenges in a New Time. *Academy of Management Journal*, 45 (5), 916–30.

Bittner, A. and Reisch, B. (1991): *Internationale Personalentwicklung in deutschen Großunternehmen*. Eine Bestandsaufnahme, Bad Honef.

Black, J. S., Gregersen, H. B. and Mendenhall, M. E. (1992): *Global Assignments. Successfully Expatriating and Repatriating International Managers*, San Francisco: Jossey-Bass Publishers.

Black, J. S., Gregersen, H., Mendenhall, M. and Stroh, L. (1999): *Globalizing People through International Assignments*, 1st edn, Reading: Addison-Wesley.

Caliguiri, P. M., Joshi, A. and Lazarova, M. (1999): Factors influencing the adjustment of women on global assignments. *International Journal of Human Resource Management*, 10 (2), 163–79.

Caligiuiri, P. M. and Lazarova, M. (2002): A model for the influence of social interaction and social support on female expatriates' cross-cultural adjustment. *International Journal of Human Resource Management*, 13 (5), 761–72.

Caligiuri, P. M. and Tung, R. L. (1999): Comparing the success of male and female expatriates from a US-based multinational company. *International Journal of Human Resource Management*, 10 (5), 763–82.

Catalyst (2001): Stay-at-home careers? Women want to work overseas. *Global Business*, January, 62.

Domsch, M. E. and Lieberum, U. B. (1997): Weibliche Führungskräfte im Ausland. *Personalwirtschaft, Special Issue: Frauen im Management*, 9, 18–21.
Edstrom, A. and Galbraith, J. (1994): Alternative Policies for International Transfers of Managers. *Management International Review*, 34, 71–82.
European Commission (2001): The gender pay gap. *Gender Equality Magazine*, 11, 5–10.
Flamholtz, E. G. (1985): *Human Resource Accounting, 2* (ed., revd. and expanded edn), San Francisco: Jossey-Bass.
Friday, E. and Friday, S. S. (2003): Managing diversity using a strategic planned change approach. *Journal of Management Development*, 22 (10), 863–80.
Hambrick, D. C., Cho, Th. S. and Chen, M. J. (1996): The influence of top management team heterogeneity on firm's competitive moves. *Administrative Science Quarterly*, 41, 659–84.
Handel, J. (1999): Determining ROI of expatriation assignments. *ACA News*, 42 (7), 22–5.
Harris, H. (1993): Women in management: opportunity or threat? *Women in Management Review*, 8, 9–14.
Harris, H. (1995): Organisational influences on women's career opportunities in international management. *Women in Management Review*, 10, 26–31.
Harris, H. (2002): Think international manager, think male: why are women not selected for international management assignments? *Thunderbird International Business Review*, 44 (2), 175–203.
Harris, H. (2004): Women's role in international management. In: A.-W. Harzing and J. Van Ruysseveldt (eds), *International Human Resource Management*, 2nd edn, London: Sage, 357–86.
Huselid, M. A. (1995): The impact of human resource management practices on turnover, productivity, and corporate financial performance. *Academy of Management Journal*, 38 (3), 635–72.
Izraeli, D. N. and Adler, N. J. (1994): Competitive frontiers: women managers in a global economy. In: N. J. Adler and D. N. Izraeli (eds), *Competitive Frontiers: Women Managers in a Global Economy*, Cambridge: Blackwell Publishers, 3–21.
Izraeli, D. N., Banai, M. and Zeira, Y. (1980): Women executives in MNC subsidiaries. *California Management Review*, 23 (1), 53–63.
Izraeli, D. and Zeira, Y. (1993): Women managers in international business: a research review and appraisal. *Business & The Contemporary World*, Summer, 35–45.
Jain, H. C., Sloane, P. J. and Horwitz, F. M. (2003): *Employment Equity and Affirmative Action: An International Comparison*, Armonk, NY: M. E. Sharpe.
Jelinek, M. and Adler, N. J. (1988): Women: world-class managers for global competition. *Academy of Management Executive*, 2 (1), 11–19.
Kilduff, M., Angelmar, R. and Mehra, A. (2000): Top management-team diversity and firm performance: examining the role of cognitions. *Organisation Science*, 11 (1), 21–34.
Kirk, W. Q. and Maddox, R. C. (1988): International management: the new frontier for women. *Personnel Management*, 65 (3), 46–9.
Knouse, S. B. and Dansby, M. R. (1999): Percentage of work-group diversity and work-group effectiveness. *Journal of Psychology*, 133 (5), 486–94.
Kovach, K. A., Kravitz, D. A. and Hughes, A. A. (2004): Affirmative action: how can we be so lost when we don't even know where we are going? *Labor Law Journal*, 55 (1), 53–61.

Lau, D. and Murnighan, J. K. (1998): Demographic diversity and faultlines: the compositional dynamics of organisational groups. *Academy of Management Review*, 23 (2), 325–40.
Lepak, D. P. and Snell, S. A. (1999): The human resource architecture: toward a theory of human capital allocation and development. *Academy of Management Review*, 24 (1), 31–48.
Linehan, M. and Scullion, H. (2001a): Challenges for female international managers: evidence from Europe. *Journal of Managerial Psychology*, 16 (3), 215–28.
Linehan, M. and Scullion, H. (2001b): European female expatriate careers: critical success factors. *Journal of European Industrial Training*, 25 (8), 392–418.
Linehan, M. and Scullion, H. (2002a): Repatriation of European female corporate executives: an empirical study. *International Journal of Human Resource Management*, 13 (2), 254–67.
Linehan, M. and Scullion, H. (2002b): The repatriation of female international managers. An empirical study. *International Journal of Manpower*, 23 (7), 649–58.
Linehan, M., Scullion, H. and Walsh, J. S. (2001): Barriers to women's participation in international management. *European Business Review*, 13 (1), 10–18.
Linehan, M. and Walsh, J. S. (1999a): Recruiting and developing female managers for international assignments. *Journal of Management Development*, 18 (6), 521–30.
Linehan, M. and Walsh, J. S. (1999b): Senior female international managers: breaking the glass border. *Women in Management Review*, 14 (7), 264–72.
MacDuffie, J. P. (1995): Human resource bundles and manufacturing performance: organisational logic and flexible production systems in the world auto industry. *Industrial and Labor Relations Review*, 48, 197–221.
McNulty, Y. M. and Tharenou, Ph. (2004): Expatriate return on investment. Academy of Management Best Conference Paper IM.
Marmer Solomon, C. (1998): Women expats: shattering the myths. *Global Workforce*, 3 (3), 10–14.
Mayrhofer, W. and Scullion, H. (2002): Female expatriates in international business: empirical evidence from the German clothing industry. *International Journal of Human Resource Management*, 13 (5), 815–36.
Milliken, F. J. and Martins, L. L. (1996): Searching for common threads: understanding the multiple effects of diversity in organisational groups. *Academy of Management Review*, 21 (2), 402–33.
Nabitz, U., Severens, P., Van den Brink, W. and Jansen, P. (2001): Improving the EFQM model: an empirical study on model development and theory building using concept mapping. *Total Quality Management*, 12 (1), 69–81.
Napier, N. K. and Taylor, S. (2002): Experiences of women professionals abroad: comparisons across Japan, China and Turkey. *International Journal of Human Resource Management*, 13 (5), 837–51.
Peixoto, J. (1999): International firms, national managers: the obstacle to migration of highly skilled labour in transnational corporations. *Socius*, 4, 1–15.
Pérotin, V., Robinson, A. and Loundes, J. (2003): Equal opportunities practices and enterprise performance: A comparative investigation on Australian and British data. *International Labour Review*, 142 (4), 471–505.
PricewaterhouseCoopers (2002): International Assignments Global Policy and Practice Key Trends 2002.

Richard, O. C. (2000): Racial diversity, business strategy, and firm performance: a resource-based view. *Academy of Management Journal*, 43, 164–77.
Ruhe, J. A. and Allen, W. R. (1997). Preparing women for careers in international management. *Journal of Education for Business*, 72 (5), 278–83.
Schuler, R. S., Jackson, S. E. and Luo, Y. (2004): *Managing Human Resources in Cross-Border Alliances*, London, New York: Routledge.
Selmer, J. and Leung, A. S. M. (2003): International adjustment of female vs. male business expatriates. *International Journal of Human Resource Management*, 14 (7), 1117–31.
Simon, W. and Nauheim, B. (1999): Das EFQM-Modell: die bessere Alternative zur DIN ISO 9000 ff. *Personal*, 3, 130–13.
Stark, E. (2001). Valuing diversity: strategic business imperative or HR agenda. *Institute of Behavioral and Applied Management Proceedings*, 34–9.
Stroh, L. K. and Caligiuri, P. M. (1998): Strategic human resources: a new source for competitive advantage in the global arena. *International Journal of Human Resource Management*, 9, 1–17.
Stroh, L. K., Varma, A. and Valy-Durbin, S. J. (2000): Why are women left at home: are they unwilling to go on international assignments? *Journal of World Business*, 35 (3), 241–56.
Thal, N. and Cateora, P. (1979): Opportunities for women in international business. *Business Horizons*, 22 (6), 21–7.
Thomas, D. A. and Ely, J. E. (1996). Making differences matter: a new paradigm for managing diversity. *Harvard Business Review*, 74 (9/10), 79–90.
Tung, R. (1988): Career issues in international assignments. *Academy of Management Executive*, 11 (3), 241–4.
Ulrich, H. and Probst, G. J. (1991): *Anleitung zum ganzheitlichen Denken und Handeln*, Bern, Stuttgart: Paul Haupt.
Vance, C. M. and Paik, Y. (2001): Where do American women face their biggest obstacle to expatriate career success? Back in their own backyard. *Cross Cultural Management*, 8 (3–4), 98–116.
Varma, A., Stroh, L. K. and Schmitt, L. B. (2001): Women and international assignments: the impact of supervisor-subordinate relationships. *Journal of World Business*, 36 (4), 380–8.
Wentling, R. M. and Palma-Rivas, N. (2000): Current status of diversity initiatives in selected multinational corporations. *Human Resource Development Quarterly*, 11 (1), 35–60.
Westwood, R. I. and Leung, S. M. (1994): The female expatriate manager experience. *International Studies of Management and Organisation*, 24 (3), 64–85.
Whitehead, S. (2001): Woman as manager: a seductive ontology. *Gender, Work & Organisation*, 8 (1), 84–107.
Wright, P., Ferris, S. P., Hiller, J. S. and Kroll, M. (1995): Competitiveness through management of diversity: effects on stock price valuation. *Academy of Management Journal*, 38 (1), 272–87.
Yurkiewicz, J. and Rosen, B. (1995): Increasing receptivity to expatriate assignments. In: J. Selmer (ed.), *Expatriate Management: New Ideas for International Business*, Westport: Quorum Books.
Zink, K. J. (1996): Total quality management: Das Europäische Modell. *Personalführung*, 1, 8–14.

# 8

# Finnish Business Repatriates' Coping Strategies at Work: Problem-Focused and Emotion-Focused Forms of Coping

*Solja Paganus*

The complexity associated with cross-cultural transfers calls for individuals to cope with various kinds of changes. In this chapter, we focus on the range of coping strategies utilized by a number of Finnish managers and specialists during their repatriation at work. The data presented here is based on 22 depth interviews and 10 follow-up interviews with repatriated employees/managers in a number of Finnish MNCs.

After operating for some time in the foreign location it is common that an individual may have to make significant changes to his or her role behaviour. His or her role conceptions remain influenced by the foreign assignment, which might cause readjustment problems (Dowling, Schuler and Welch, 1999: 211). The study reported here demonstrates how readjustment to work demanded that the repatriates change their work role behaviour thus shaping their coping efforts. The term 'coping efforts' is used to refer both to 'coping strategies' and 'forms of coping'. The repatriates confronted many challenges and changes concerning their work roles and work tasks themselves. Thus, various kinds of coping efforts emerged from the data, when the repatriates strove to improve their performance at their repatriate work or just to adapt to the change.

The first section presents the findings on the usage of emotion-focused coping strategies or reactive work adjustment mode. Specifically it recounts that those specialists who had less opportunities than managers to influence their work roles, were more likely to adopt these coping responses. The second section describes the specific work role changes that the repatriates' problem-focused coping strategies were connected to. These coping strategies could also be identified as a proactive work adjustment mode that was usual among the managers who were in a better position than the specialists to modify their work roles.

## Emotion-focused coping strategies and reactive work adjustment mode

Emotion-focused coping strategies (Lazarus and Folkman, 1984: 150) were found to have occurred when the repatriates, working usually as specialists, continued on almost at the same positions and with the same work tasks as earlier. They felt themselves more restricted, since their work role allowed them little scope for making changes in the work role. Thus, their adjustment to work could also be identified as reactive. The direction of change in reactive coping was addressed to the repatriates' personal development (cf. Nicholson, 1984), as they worked out their personal relationship to work, and reflected the changes of its character. The repatriates used emotion-focused strategies when they were engaged in working with their feelings of frustrations, with values and perhaps also with some identity modifications. Let us explore these strategies and reactive coping efforts in greater depth.

To adapt to the change or to the contrast between the nature of the expatriate and the nature of the repatriate work, which only a few repatriates clearly experienced strongly, it looked like some elements of absorption strategy were manifested in the repatriates' coping efforts. In this reactive coping they mostly assimilated their new skills, social behaviours and frames of references to meet the requirements of the new work situation (Nicholson, 1984: 176). By engaging in emotion-focused coping efforts these repatriates reflected their adjustment demands and tried to analyse their own responses to them. These emotion-focused coping efforts might be directed to handling negative feelings, like frustrations. On the other hand, some of the repatriates might experience a similar type of change in their work positively by applying psychological reappraisal as their way of coping (Lazarus and Folkman, 1984), when for instance, they appreciated having a bit less hectic and less social repatriate job. Satu[1] told about her repatriate job:

> Satu: *This is a kind of period of rest, just the fact that I have a shorter work time, and there are not so much social relationships here at the workplace. I cannot go on that kind of a speed any longer, so in that sense this is good.*

Sami had travelled a lot between the host and the home country during several weeks of the transition phase, and adapting to sitting in one place was difficult for him. At the beginning, when he faced the new working conditions, he had difficulties in concentrating on his work tasks, but by getting used to the change he moved toward a more stable stage in his repatriation. He spoke about his restlessness:

> Sami: *The hardest thing was getting settled in one place, after spending almost a year moving around. Now I am, though of course I travel a lot, but anyway it was a big change. It demanded getting used to. It makes one restless.*

Similarly, Henna suffered from the same kind of 'symptoms' and clearly also from some kind of frustration, calling upon her emotion-focused coping efforts when she had to give up some pleasant features of her expatriate work. She told how her personal life had changed significantly, and, thus, she pointed out that she did not have any special expectations on her repatriate work. However, she obviously also went through a kind of shock phase, when she confronted the reality of her repatriate work for the first time. Nevertheless, she recovered, and by accepting the situation she adapted to the change in the work setting relatively quickly. Henna explained how the change called her to reflect and analyse her relationship to her repatriate work quite heavily at least temporarily:

> Henna: *While I was abroad, I was quite busy in the end, I visited the ship and the office, I took care of things and I moved a lot, and didn't just sit in the front of a computer. When I returned to work I realized that here, I just sit for eight hours in front of the computer and I hardly move at all. I felt very restless; it was difficult for me to sit in one place. It takes a couple of weeks to settle down, to realize that it won't always be like I feared for a moment: will it be like this for the rest of my life? There was a boring moment, but it went over.*

Only very few of the repatriates were slightly disappointed with the content of their work, but by finding out the positive sides of the work and taking advantage of its benefits, in other words, through psychological reappraisal (Feldman and Tompson, 1992) they kept their work motivation. Kari started in a new work role, but at the same position. He was an excellent example of how he saved himself from any frustrations by appreciating his repatriate work as a specialist straight from the beginning:

> Kari: *This is not less interesting, I work with the newest technology in the world. We will produce a new product to the market, and I will work with that. I do not have anything to complain about.*

In the transition phase from the host unit to the home unit a few repatriates were simultaneously involved in work tasks in both units for a certain period of time. Naturally in this kind of situation they could not concentrate well on either finishing their expatriate work or the forthcoming repatriate work and their energy dispersed between these different work roles. Having this kind of dispersed work role for some time in the transition phase seemed to be very constricting.

In the next example because of the situation, the returning expatriate was very restricted to apply any coping strategies, but knowing that the situation was temporal made it easier to stand. But in this case the work role changes demanded adaptation, and the repatriate's coping was focused to regulations of emotions (Lazarus and Folkman, 1984: 150). He recognized the need for letting his old expatriate work role go and pave way to the new repatriate work role. Jani described his transition as 'schizophrenic' and was relieved, when this difficult period turned out to be quite a short time:

> Jani: *It was a little bit of a schizophrenic situation in the beginning, when I travelled to Ireland, and I could not concentrate on the new work tasks. When I was there I took care of the things of this place, and when I was here I took care of things both here and there. Fortunately it didn't last a long time, but it was difficult. I couldn't leave that work and concentrate solely on this.*

The situation, in which the repatriate actually lacked the proper work tasks in the beginning of the return phase was rare, and concerned mostly the project managers. The research results illustrate how two of the repatriates reacted very differently and applied very opposite coping strategies in the similar situation. At first I take a closer look on the case using the reactive coping in the work role change, and later we consider the case, when the repatriate applied proactive coping efforts.

To finish his expatriate job Jouni, a project manager, had used the problem-focused strategy by working longer days (Feldman and Brett, 1983). In the return phase his holiday was disturbed by many phone calls from work and he felt that he had not actually had a real chance to recover from the exhausting expatriate work before entering the home unit. Jouni told how his holiday was spoiled by the many work phone calls:

> Jouni: *After my expatriation I had a very negative experience, when I tried to have some holiday, because I did not take any time off during my expatriation. Anyway I could not take my time, because my colleagues called me*

> *home, about how now they have this and that. I did not have a chance to recover. I was terribly tired and that autumn was very hard, we worked during the weekends and had long days all the time.*

In this first case the repatriate realized his frustration to the lack of work tasks, but he did not actually do anything in order to change the work situation. The workload in the immediate history before the repatriate work might also lie on the background, when he at first remained quite passive at work.

Thus, this project manager remained passive and avoided handling the problem by just letting the time pass. On the other hand, he sought compensation to his frustration at work by turning his attention to, and by investing in, his hobby outside the work sphere (cf. Nicholson, 1984). What is interesting to notice that building a summer cottage still offered this project manager a possibility to continue and to reconfirm his occupational identity as a project manager. Jouni told how he was frustrated at work, but he applied his problem-focused strategy (Lazarus and Folkman, 1984: 152) to handle these feelings, and after all he seemed to be quite happy with his achievements in free-time:

> Jouni: *I did not know what my new job was like, I did not have any idea of it. In the spring I did not have anything meaningful to do, it frustrated me. When I came to work in the morning, and I did not know what to do that day, I had to really find out how to get through the day. It was boring. But I had one big hobby; I built a summer cottage. It was my personal project.*

Another significant element of work roles, which typically can change in work role transitions, is role discretion. Next I look at how the repatriates dealt with the changes concerning work role discretion.

Mainly those repatriates working as specialists and also some managers did not confront any remarkable changes in their role discretion, when they underwent role transition from an expatriate to a repatriate job. Thus, their adjustment strategy perhaps more likely reminded replication (Nicholson, 1984: 176). They apparently only made a few changes in their role behaviour, and mostly performed in much the same manner as in their expatriate jobs. Tero's work role discretion remained on the same level in the work transition. He said:

> Tero: *My work is very independent here, like it was on the assignment. It is not less independent now, it is almost the same.*

Further, these repatriates, who did not experience any significant changes in their work role discretion, quite typically identified their repatriate work role relatively clearly as well. They had a clear conception of their work contents, and by using problem-focused coping they internalized their work tasks relatively quickly (Lazarus and Folkman, 1984: 150). This presumably refers to the use of replication (Nicholson, 1984: 176); they did not have to go through a lot of effort in order to modify their work roles. Instead they could concentrate on the right things straight from the beginning. Kai, a young manager, pointed out how in his opinion the clarity of the work role called for less coping efforts in his repatriate job, because he internalized them quicker.

> Kai: *Of course it is important. The more precisely they are defined, the better you are able to internalize yourself what you are going to do, and the less disappointments there will be.*

The next example illustrates the difficulty of identifying a particular coping effort either as emotion-focused or problem-focused coping. Dealing with lower work role discretion is identified as a form of emotion-focused coping, handling frustrations. But this particular coping attempt in this context could also have been identified as problem-focused coping, if it is interpreted as including motivational and cognitive changes (Edwards, 1988: 240).

Only a small number of repatriates had to struggle in order to find a new balance between their expatriate work role and lower discretion repatriate work role. These coping efforts occurred mainly as cognitive, emotion-focused coping, (Lazarus and Folkman, 1984: 150), dealing with the frustrations because of some kind of loss of role discretion. Besides, Jari's strategy in this situation is reminiscent of replication as well (Nicholson, 1984: 176), in which he in his same specialist position had limited opportunities to affect his work role discretion, but rather he had to submit to the situation. He learned to be more patient, but still passive adaptation was quite hard for him. Jari told:

> Jari: *It was difficult to get used to work with less role discretion. It is irritating when one has to wait to be able to do something. When I work alone, I can do things in the order that I please. Waiting for something demands patience.*

This section showed that the repatriates used emotion-focused coping strategies in those kinds of work role changes when their possibilities to change their roles and situations were limited. Next, I look at in what kind of work role changes the usage of problem-focused strategies seemed to be common.

## Problem-focused coping strategies and proactive work adjustment mode

This section explores particular kinds of work role changes that were linked to problem-focused coping strategies.

Those repatriates who typically worked as managers on higher organizational levels, used many problem-focused strategies (Lazarus and Folkman, 1984: 152). These strategies have similarities with proactive work adjustment mode (Nicholson, 1984) as well; they were directed to the work situation itself and to the change of role requirements. Thus, it was presumably more a question about the utilization of determination and exploration of adjustment modes. Usually the repatriates' relatively high role discretion gave them more room to implement these changes (cf. Suutari and Välimaa, 2002), so that they could better find a suitable match between their new role requirements in changed positions, and their needs, enlarged professional qualifications and changed identity. Next, I look more closely at what kind of work role changes triggered problem-focused coping efforts.

Some of the repatriates' work role discretion decreased, but because of their managerial positions it still remained relatively high. These people were typically managers, who returned from smaller host units to the bigger home unit. They started in new and different positions, so their coping included mostly elements of the proactive strategy (Nicholson, 1984). But concerning especially the diminution of their work role discretion, they used psychological reappraisal (Lazarus and Folkman, 1984: 151) as their problem-focused coping way. The repatriates had learned to know both the positive and negative sides of their expatriate jobs, and by drawing on this experience they made comparisons between the expatriate and repatriate job. In this way they could better identify the positive sides of the repatriate job and value them. Lauri and Sami told how they in their expatriate job had high role discretion and more responsibility. Thus, they experienced a kind of pressure to manage on their own. In return they found it just as alleviating to have their other colleagues' support and a little bit less responsibility at their work:

> Sami: *Of course the role discretion was higher on the assignment. It has its own appeal and it has its own negative sides too. The high role discretion is*

> *appealing, and you pay for that, to get the salary. And there is the risk that you take to the sidetracks.*

> Lauri: *Maybe the role discretion was higher there, but there was no support either. I found it as a better situation, when you have role discretion but you also have support.*

Tapio also worked out the challenges associated with lower work role discretion, but his coping efforts referred more likely to the use of some elements of exploration adjustment strategy (Nicholson, 1984: 176). Thus, there was a question about simultaneously some renegotiations of his identity as a manager and changing his work role parameters. He tried to define the borders of his work role, which in his case meant learning different bureaucratic rules of his home unit's work environment, in comparison to those which he had used as a CEO in his expatriate job. Tapio had worked in a country where there is a great power distance. So he used to use power differently, a style that was not necessarily as functional when he returned. In the beginning he was probably a bit shocked at facing such significant difference of organizational cultures and he probably made some mistakes, breaking the bureaucratic rules of his home unit. By learning he internalized new kinds of power relationships to facilitate his interaction with his colleagues and improve his work performance. Thus, these problem-focused coping efforts (Lazarus and Folkman, 1984: 152) also included learning the work descriptions of other colleagues. Tapio, who returned from a smaller host company unit to the larger home unit, commented on his biggest challenges in the return job in the following way:

> Tapio: *The most difficult part was the adaptation to this kind of line organization. When there are many departments, the management of bureaucracy, so that you know what belongs to whom, and then you have to be cautious, so that you do not step on your colleague's feet. If you do something, which actually does not belong to you, somebody gets angry, 'why does he come here', 'why does he interfere in this'. It demands adapting, because in that kind of small organization you take part in everything and everybody expects it too.*

Kai had higher role discretion in his repatriate job, but he confronted quite similar types of adjustment challenges. It was apparent from his speech that he expected something else than what actually awaited him, when he received his repatriate job. Obviously he rapidly went through a kind of shock, made an evaluation of the situation, and then started to 'fight' in order to clarify his new role and position to his colleagues. In this situation his cognitive coping efforts came close to exploration, as he tried to imprint the stamp of his identity and unique skills upon his role and its surrounding milieu (Nicholson, 1984). He told about how he as a young manager by using problem-focused coping and by redefining his repatriate job (Feldman and Brett, 1983) aimed to clarify to his colleagues his new role and new responsibilities:

> Kai: *When my new job description was defined, and the work contract was assigned, maybe I was a little bit naive when I thought that everything would be clear. Then, upon return, there is somebody who is used to taking care of certain things, and there are certain routines for certain tasks. So having something on paper does not help all that much. It sort of like okay, all these belong to me now, don't tangle this now. You have to honour your own position.*
> SP*: You have to learn the limits?*
> Kai: *The whole organization has to learn them. As in, now we have this person, who takes care of these responsibilities and so on.*

Naturally, already on expatriation, the interviewees had gone through work role changes which brought them into strong identity shaping processes. This kind of development also influenced their coping strategies.

In their 'identity projects' people are always open to both negative and positive experiences, which makes their view of themselves appear as a constant subject to question; how they see themselves dealing with situations in everyday life, and how others view and respond to them. In different socio-cultural environments people are drawn to situations, in which these reflexive identity projects are powerfully influenced by experiences which are defined in a certain cultural context. Thus, peoples' notion of themselves is strongly taken from their cultural knowing – what they have seen, heard and read in their lives (Watson and Harris, 1999; Watson, 1997).

The varied range of new challenges put the expatriates into a very powerful identity formation process. Working in different cultures with different people in new circumstances put new demands on their social identity work. This meant a lot of working out regarding their own sense of themselves, where new experiences, sometimes also difficult matters, had to be dealt with. Jani presented how he saw the challenges of his expatriate work and how it had influenced his personal development and identity shaping:

> Jani: *Of course I have become a more mature personality. I've got more experience, both occupational and otherwise. I had to work with different people from different cultures there. It was a maturing experience.*

Besides the socio-cultural challenges, the expatriates had also enlarged their views on their managerial roles and on doing business in their identity formation processes.

Many expatriates had, by applying perhaps more likely the exploration coping strategy (Nicholson, 1984: 176) tried to actively determine elements in the content or structure of the expatriate work role. Generally, through reconstruction of their managerial role and redefining their work tasks besides the professional development simultaneously the expatriates had clearly increased their self-confidence. Most of the repatriates seemed to be very conscious about this strong positive change. Mauri returned from four and half a years' assignment and described how important it is to believe in yourself in doing challenging work tasks during expatriation:

> Mauri: *My identity has changed. My self-confidence has grown remarkably. When one receives this kind of work, one has to believe in what one is doing 100%. Otherwise it is not possible to get these other people from different cultures involved in it with their whole heart, if you are not convincing yourself. What follows from that is that at first you have to internalize you own work very well and be able to lead the project consistently, otherwise you will lose the ground of the work, which you do with them.*

Many of the repatriates commented how they at their very challenging expatriate work had learned to use high role discretion for modifying their work tasks in order to able to meet the new work requirements. They had, for instance, learned to make decisions much more decisively. This kind of independence also resulted as stronger self-confidence, when they usually could not draw upon existing support, but they had to try to manage even more on their own than earlier in their home country. Teuvo compared the repatriate job to his expatriate job:

> Teuvo: *Both my expatriate and repatriate work is very similar. In America I had more things to do, in that way it was more challenging, I was forced to do everything from the beginning. In this job I have the organization ready, work tools, and so on. I just concentrate on producing.*

Next I examine how the repatriates utilized their rich international work experience and personal development in order to cope with the challenging repatriate work role changes.

Earlier we looked at a case, where the repatriate remained quite passive in the context of lacking the proper work tasks, and he turned his attention to his free-time activities. In a corresponding situation where the repatriate lacked proper work tasks, the other project manager used problem-focused coping efforts (Lazarus and Folkman, 1984: 152). This repatriate's aim was to find and define his work tasks. Mauri told how his first reaction to the lack of work tasks was a kind of panic, but he recovered from it quickly and started to apply problem-focused strategy by trying to face the problem in order to change the situation. This coping mechanism is also comparable to positive denial or reappraisal (Welds, 1991). Through re-evaluating and reinterpreting his work situation, this manager started to see it as a great opportunity to influence his forthcoming work. Mauri strove at coping by thinking strategically, and using his time for learning things, which he had missed during this expatriation. By applying this kind of active problem-focused strategy he could feel better and maintain his self-esteem (Feldman and Brett, 1983), while waiting for his new project. Simultaneously he more likely moved towards cognitive appraisal again, forming expectations of his forthcoming new work tasks.

The problem-focused coping strategy, which the repatriate used in this case, is in line with those arguments on identity constitution, according to which people near draw to situations in which it is possible to show themselves in a positive light and present valuable features, rather than hide or present themselves negatively. People tend to seek esteem-enhancing or positive self-definitions (Ashforth and Kreiner, 1999), and are motivated to maintain and increase their self-esteem (based on a sense of competence and power or achievement) and self-worth (based on a sense of morality and moral worth) (Shamir, 1991).

Using problem-focused coping strategies expressed the repatriates' active strive towards confirmation and reconstruction of their identity. This project manager very consciously took upon himself a role as 'learner' or 'student'. His problem-focused coping (Lazarus and Folkman, 1984: 152) guaranteed himself a possibility to renegotiate his identity and achieve certain coherence in it. When lacking the proper work tasks and using his time for studying, Mauri constituted his identity through identity-enhancing experiences. There was also a strong need to try to fill in the gaps and make sure the continuation of career identity in some way. On the other hand, the manager in this case after the reappraisal found it very good that there was not any available identity position for him in the beginning. So he could let his proper identity formation be still open and as freely negotiable as possible. Being back to Finland in less than three months Mauri explained his viewpoint like this:

> Mauri: *Now I have to learn all these new systems, so that I know what these new methods are. But I have to say that I had a little bit of a negative reaction in the beginning, it was like: 'let's see', so I fought for that quite strongly. But I think that by becoming involved in many things I can also further others' efforts on how to see it. I think I am in a better situation than if I had stepped into a ready-planned box to which somebody had set the boundaries for.*

As a result of pursuing active, problem-focused strategies (Lazarus and Folkman, 1984: 152) to achieve a suitable return position, many of the repatriates had an opportunity to start their repatriate work in a new work role. It was very common that at the beginning the repatriates did not have any clear ideas of the content and the tasks of their new work role.

In pursuing problem-focused strategies, the repatriates conducted various forms of it in their new work role to clarify to themselves their work tasks. These strategies occurred even as an anticipatory adjustment. This kind of preparing and efforts to get a grasp of the repatriate work refers to the utilization of problem-focused coping (Lazarus and Folkman, 1984: 152), when the repatriate tried to evaluate his forthcoming work challenges. One expatriate strove for responsibility and self-initiative in forthcoming repatriate work tasks through strategic planning even before the actual return. Anssi told how he aimed to plan the timing for his return so that he would have better chances to influence and define himself his repatriate work content. This young manager explained how he prepared himself for the repatriate job:

> Anssi: *The beginning of autumn is a good time to return. Then the decisions concerning the plans and budgets for the next year are made. So in the beginning of the next year you can start from an empty table and you can have more influence on things, it is easier for you to commit to them.*

Another repatriate started to orientate to his repatriate work by visiting the home unit; in other words, through problem-focused strategy he tried to gather information to be able to construct a kind of picture of his repatriate work (Lazarus and Folkman, 1984: 152). This kind of information can help the employee to learn the fastest, most effective way of working with the least anxiety (Feldman and Brett, 1983). Tapani also had facilitated his work adjustment by trying to reorientate to it beforehand:

> Tapani: *I visited here in the spring and it smoothed my return. In fact I already started to do some of the home unit's work. I tried to learn a little bit and familiarize myself with that work ahead of time, before my return.*

In their new work role the repatriates working as managers had better possibilities to more effectively utilize their diverse expatriate work experience. A channel was opened for their 'emergent' identity as well and they did not have to identify themselves for any certain identity positions. Instead their identity formation was still left open and these repatriates seemed to be very motivated and content with this kind of situation.

On the other hand, having a new work role also meant a better possibility to create a suitable fit between the repatriate's changed self and his current work. In the new work role the repatriate could identity himself as a developer, as somebody who starts changes, and this way fix some part of himself or herself to the development of business. Through new challenges and possibilities for identification the repatriate created his or her new work role as meaningful and satisfying. In a new work role he or she achieved a better congruence with his enlarged international work experience as well (cf. Downes and Thomas, 1999). So he or she could create a natural path for identity continuation and re-affirmation of some parts of his 'old self'.

These repatriates, who were mostly managers, drew upon their strengthened self-confidence and took a positive attitude to take more responsibility for themselves for achieving their tasks successfully. This refers to what Carver and Scheier (1998: 196) say about how the feeling of doubt stops people to try to move towards their goals, whereas more confident people keep trying.

The repatriates found the unclear, new work role as a challenging opportunity to be creative at their work and define guidelines for the work according to their own opinions. In line with this it was also common to see the situation as a chance for continuous learning, which was associated with better work motivation (cf. Inkpen, 1998). Thus, these kinds of very positive attributions associated with the unclear work tasks come close to argumentation on curiosity (Loewenstein, 1994). In order to experience curiosity, people must experience a contrast between the higher reference point and the lower present knowledge. The lack of correspondence between these elements has a stimulating effect (Carver and Scheier,

1998: 213). Tapio returned when the organization was in a transformation stage and he found this situation to be a great opportunity to effect and define his work content and work tasks. His coping efforts reminded more likely exploration (Nicholson, 1984: 176), as he strove to define his repatriate work role. He told how he had had a possibility to conduct some preliminary work in order to formulate his repatriate work role. Tapio expressed his satisfaction with his work situation as follows:

> Tapio: *It was not clear. Maybe because our organization changed a lot when I returned. In that way it was quite nice that I had impact on the job I received. It was a good time, some kind of developmental phase, I could get involved in it already in the former position.*

At their challenging expatriate work the interviewees had increased their work experience in many different ways by learning new things and using their skills more extensively. Often they had worked in broader sectors and had enlarged their perspectives on their company's business operations. Thus, they had learned to look at business from new and different perspectives. These strategies mainly reminded exploration, in which people use their unique skills to define elements in the content or structure of the role (Nicholson, 1984: 176). Some repatriates quite clearly approached their repatriate work by utilizing their benchmarking knowledge. Through their international work experience they had learned to question more things and to identify problems and potential areas of further development. Anssi used this kind of problem-focused coping, and found benchmarking knowledge and questioning things very valuable at his work. He said:

> Anssi: *It is important for the company to get a repatriate or foreigner either from inside or from outside the company every now and then to question things, then it works well.*

The repatriates utilizing determination or exploration (Nicholson, 1984: 176) continued in a similar vein. They pointed out the involvement of the development perspective, which was an important motivational element in the repatriate job as well. By being able to initiate progress the repatriates felt more committed to their work and to the future of the business of their company. These repatriates used their increased ability to analyse things better and to react to situations quicker. Based on this they were able to make conclusions for further actions. The repatriates' problem-focused coping strategy in the context of a new work role can be described as a continuous shifting between evaluating and shaping their work role. Timo commented on his occupational development, and also Tero talked more about future orientation as an essential element at his work:

> Timo: *You have learned how to analyse things more systematically and to react very quickly when you act in different cultures with different people. And you can make anticipatory evaluation.*

> Tero: *When you know that you will take a certain direction for at least two, three years, and we will try to get the situation to the certain level then, it increases your motivation.*

In their problem-focused strategy (Lazarus and Folkman, 1984) some of the interviewees managed to link their work tasks to their expatriate work experience in a way that the experience was seen and utilized more as a preparatory phase for the repatriate job. In comparable terms some others also mentioned that through their expatriate work experience they had got a more realistic picture on work issues in the host companies' context that was very helpful with their repatriate work tasks. In these types of strategies there was probably a question about exploration, in which the change occurs both in individuals' personal qualities and role parameters. These processes are typical for jobs, in which 'social contracting' and interpersonal role negotiations are central features (Nicholson, 1984). One young manager highlighted the fact that in his job he would not be able to put himself in his client's shoes, without the expatriate work experience. Anssi used this kind of identification with his client's position as a coping mechanism in his new position:

> Anssi: *This current job is such that you would not be able to do it, if you have not worked abroad. All the customs are abroad, and all what I do requires, that you are able to understand and take their position in a different way and see this from outside Finland.*

As a form of problem-focused strategy, problems or just normal work tasks can be brought into more manageable, sequential steps, or on the other hand, difficult tasks can be integrated better. Kari gave the following example of using problem-focused coping in his repatriate job:

> Kari: *If there are problems, I try to split them up, and then to solve them one at a time. Another way can be, that when I concentrate more on the whole thing, then I solve many problems at the same time as a group.*

As a behavioural coping strategy, individuals can ask for help from their supervisors and co-workers (Feldmand and Brett, 1983). Some expatriates had enlarged their networks on the assignment both by getting new contacts with other expatriates and with other colleagues in the host company. When applying these kinds of problem-focused strategies (Feldman and Tompson, 1992) the repatriates used their new contacts to clarify unclear questions in their job (cf. Dougherty, Munir and Subramaniam, 2002). Mauri handled his challenging work tasks through the help of his contact network:

> Mauri: *When you have a difficult problem, and you have this kind of network of specialists from different parts of the world, it makes it always possible to ask for help.*

During the long-term assignments the expatriates' technical skills can become out of date (Black et al., 1992). Even though it was not so common, some of the repatriates admitted they had really had these types of challenges. They needed technical support, and in order to get their tasks done, and they asked help from other colleagues who had these skills and knowledge. Further, besides technical challenges, some repatriates' work was more like team-work, thus in accomplishing their work tasks they needed help from their colleagues. These coping efforts were forms of problem-focused strategy as well (Lazarus and Folkman, 1984: 152). Riku spoke about how team-working was a necessity for him to get his work tasks done in a highly specialized area:

> Riku: *This is quite a little team, which takes care of this grain starch industry, so this is a very tight organization. It would certainly not be successful, if you could not co-operate, you could not manage to do anything alone.*

## Discussion

This chapter described the transactional relationship between the repatriate and his or her work environment. Two main categories of coping were identified: emotion-focused and problem-focused strategies. The forms of emotion-focused coping strategy (Lazarus and Folkman, 1984: 150) occurred in those kind of work role changes, which offered the repatriates less room for change. These repatriates working usually as specialists often continued in similar types of positions and work tasks. Using Nicholson's (1984) terminology, their work adjustment mode was reactive.

By using replication and assimilation, the repatriates mostly continued behaving similarly as before, so they did not significantly modify their work roles. The repatriates analysed their work role changes in many cases in order to achieve a better understanding of the coping demands caused by the work role changes. Greater appreciation of this occurred when the repatriate's coping was significantly directed to valuing their repatriate work role. Besides the specialist, also some managers used the next newly recognized forms of emotion-focused coping (Lazarus and Folkman, 1984: 150), which have not been identified in previous research. These new forms of emotion-focused coping showed in which kind of work role changes the repatriates' adjustment demands were addressed to dealing with emotions that were typically frustrations. By reflecting, and using cognitive coping the repatriates adapted to the clear contrast between their expatriate and repatriate work role. They coped with the lower work role discretion as well by accepting the change. Tolerating the dispersed work role and finding it as a temporary situation also occurred in very few work role transitions. When one project manager lacked the proper work tasks, he remained mostly passive and let the time pass. Thus, he dealt with frustrations by using emotion-focused strategy (Lazarus and Folkman, 1984: 150). On the other hand, this kind of situation was solved by seeking compensation from outside working life, such as building a summer cottage.

Those repatriates, whose positions changed and who started in new work roles, were often managers, and mostly utilized problem-focused coping strategies (Lazarus and Folkman, 1984: 152–3). They used a greater number and a greater variety of different forms of problem-focused strategy than emotion-focused strategy. When using these strategies, the repatriates could draw upon their changed identities, increased self-confidence, and rich work experience. These repatriates had more opportunities to define their work tasks and change the structures of their work roles. Thus, their coping efforts included more likely elements of exploration adjustment mode (Nicholson, 1984). Various newly recognized forms of these problem-focused strategies occurred in the data. The new forms of problem-focused coping strategy in the context of new work roles showed the content of the repatriates' adjustment when they aimed at getting their work tasks done. In order to define and clarify their new work role boundaries, the repatriates' coping efforts were focused to internalizing new power relationships and learning the work descriptions of other colleagues. Even the expression 'fighting' was used in this context, when the repatriates had to establish their new positions. Planning the timing of the return was mentioned as an opportunity to influence forthcoming work tasks.

The lack of proper work tasks, which was very rare, was also seen as an opportunity to influence forthcoming work tasks. The positive attitude was highlighted, and by this way the repatriates found their new, and typically unclear work tasks as an opportunity for continuous learning. Furthermore, the repatriates pointed out comparing expatriate work situations to repatriate work situations, by questioning, identifying, and orientating to the repatriate work tasks beforehand, as well as including a future or developmental perspective on it, when they tried to become more successful at their work. After expatriate work they also had a more realistic view of many things associated to their work that was helpful at repatriate work. The repatriates also applied some behavioural forms of problem-focused coping in work role transitions, like visiting the home unit beforehand in order to orientate to the forthcoming work tasks, and asking help from their co-workers.

To conclude, the research results indicated that the repatriates, especially the managers, used different forms of problem-focused strategy more often than the various forms of emotion-focused strategy. They also used a larger range of problem-focused strategy than emotion-focused strategy. The repatriates shifted between different forms of coping strategies, depending on the situation and the coping demands. Their coping efforts might also accumulate over time.

## References

Ashford, B. E. and Kreiner, G. E. (1999) How can you do it? Dirty work and the challenge of constructing a positive identity. *Academy of Management Review*, 24(3): 413–34.

Black, J. S., Gregersen, H. B. and Mendenhall, M. (1992) *Global Assignments*. San Francisco, Jossey-Bass.

Carver, C. S. and Scheier, M. F. (1998) *On the Self-Regulation of Behavior*. Cambridge, Cambridge University Press.

Dougherty, D., Munir, K. and Subramaniam, M. (2002) Managing technology flows in practice: a grounded theory of sustained innovation. *Academy of Management Proceedings*, 1–7.

Dowling, P. J., Schuler, R. S. and Welch, D. E. (1999) *International Human Resource Management. Managing People in a Multinational Context*. 3rd edn. Cincinnati, OH, South-Western College Publishing.

Downes, M. and Thomas, A. S. (1999) Managing overseas assignments to build organizational knowledge. *Human Resource Planning*, 22(4): 33.

Edwards, J. R. (1988) The determinants and consequences of coping with stress. In: Cooper, C. L. and Payne, K. (eds) *Causes, Coping and Consequences of Stress at Work*. Chichester, John Wiley, pp. 233–63.

Feldman, D. C. and Brett, J. M. (1983) Coping with new jobs: a comparative study of new hires and job changers, *Academy of Management Journal,* 26(2): 258–72.
Feldman, D. C. and Tompson, H. B. (1992) Expatriation, repatriation, and domestic geographical relocation: an empirical investigation of adjustment to new job assignments. *Journal of International Business Studies,* 24(3): 507–29.
Inkpen, A. (1998) Learning and knowledge acquired through strategic alliances. *Academy of Management Executive,* 12(4): 1–12.
Lazarus, R. S. and Folkman, S. (1984) *Stress, Appraisal and Coping.* New York, Springer Publishing Company, Inc. (1984).
Loewenstein, G. (1994) The psychology of curiosity: A review and reinterpretation. *Psychological Bulletin,* 116, 75–98.
Nicholson, N. (1984) A theory of work role transitions. *Administrative Science Quarterly.* 29: 172–91.
Shamir, B. (1991) Meaning, self and motivation in organizations. *Organization Studies,* 12(3): 405–24.
Suutari, V. and Välimaa, K. (2002) Antecedents of repatriation adjustment: new evidence from Finnish repatriates. *International Journal of Manpower,* 23(7): 617–34.
Watson, T. (1997) The labour of division: the manager as 'self' and 'other', In: Hetherington, K. and Munro, R., (eds) *Ideas of Difference. Social Spaces and the Labour of Division.* Oxford, Blackwell.
Watson, T. and Harris, P. (1999) *The Emergent Manager,* London, Sage.
Welds, K. (1991) The return trip, *HRMagazine,* June.

# 9

# Intonations of Repatriation: a Discursive Analysis of Expatriates' Talk of Work After Repatriation

*Tina L. Howell*

## Introduction

Traditionally, the subject of 'repatriation' has been attended to as a concern for expatriate employees (and consequently their employers) at or nearing completion of a 'long-term' (e.g. over one year) international assignment and associated with their impending return to the 'home' organization (e.g. Stroh et al., 2000; Brewster et al., 2001; Lazarova and Caliguiri, 2001; Linehan and Scullion, 2002). However the aim of this chapter will be to explore talk about short-term assignment repatriation and related issues espoused by participants who were currently on, or had recently completed a 'short-term' assignment (e.g. less than one year). The focus of research will be on the problematic nature of short-term repatriation that was evident not only in talk by individuals who had recently returned to work within the 'home' organization, but also emerged as a topic of concern by individuals who had only recently expatriated.

In the main, repatriation research has emanated primarily from a human resource or organizational perspective as opposed to the expatriate's perspective derived from personal experience (Gregerson and Stroh, 1997; Linehan and Scullion, 2002). Although recognized as an area of considerable importance to organizations, the role of repatriation in the expatriation process and its potential impact on the success of international assignments has often been overlooked and under-researched (Black, 1992; Forster, 1994; Bonache et al., 2001). Moreover, and despite recent and substantial growth in the utilization of short-term assignments by organizations in response to increased global working, and also specialized short-term projects, as a less expensive alternative to traditional long-term assignments, relatively few studies have looked at the impact of repatriation on individuals who undertake such assignments (Frazee, 1997; Gregerson and Stroh, 1997; Forster, 2000; Morley and Heraty, 2004). As short-term assignments arguably comprise distinctly different features and demands from traditional long-term assignments, research attention is warranted if we are to advance our understanding about issues and concerns unique to these kinds of assignments (Brewster and Scullion, 1997; Forster, 2000; Brewster et al., 2001; Mayerhofer et al., 2005).

This study attempts to redress the balance within this corpus of work using a constructionist framework and discursive approach to textual analysis (e.g. Potter and Wetherell, 1987; Wetherell, 1998) and analytically explore emerging issues of expectation, change, and organizational belonging in the context of talk about social identity, repatriation and the experience of short-term assignments.

## Method

The participants in this case-study are employed by a large American-owned MNC best known for its research and development of fluid-based lubricants and chemicals for industry and transportation. Operating within 26 countries internationally, the company employs approximately 8,000 people world-wide and claimed annual sales last year of about $3.4bn. The current research was carried out at both the US corporate headquarters and one of the firms' leading research and development sites in the UK. On both of these work sites, the majority of staff were engaged in some aspect of work relating to chemical testing, engineering and technology development within a laboratory environment. The participants were purposely selected by identifying them through the firm's human resources department as having either current, or recent international assignment experience with the organization. No other selection criteria was deemed relevant or necessary to achieve the aims of the research (Silverman, 2001).

Forty-eight semi-structured interviews were carried out over a three-year period with a total of 44 participants. Fifteen of the interviews were conducted in the US and 33 were carried out in the UK. This number of participants provided a theoretically practical sample size that was large enough to ensure a broad data set for analysis and basis for comparison, yet small enough to accommodate the discursive approach to analysis utilized in this research (Potter and Wetherell, 1987; Silverman, 2001). Company tenure amongst the participants ranged from 18 months to 18 years, with a relatively equal number having undertaken either a short-term or long-term assignment.

The data used in this study were taken from transcripts of recorded individual semi-structured interviews that were conducted on-site. An interview schedule of questions was developed around broad areas that concerned expatriation and international assignments in general. The intent of the questions was not to control or limit what topics the participants could talk about, but to guide the interviews towards areas that were both relevant and interesting (Bryman, 1989). The order of questions asked of each participant varied depending on their response when given the opportunity to talk about their own assignment experiences (Wetherell and Potter, 1992). Therefore, it was not uncommon for interviews to veer away from the schedule when other topics of interest emerged that were initiated in talk by the participants themselves (Kvale, 1996). The interviews ranged in length from 45 minutes to an hour and a half, and again this depended on how long a participant was willing to talk. The recorded interview tapes were transcribed verbatim using a combined scaled-down version of transcription notation (e.g. Jefferson 1984b; Wetherell, 1998; Ten Have, 1999). During transcription, pseudonyms were allocated in place of identifiers to ensure anonymity pursuant to the organization's request (Silverman, 2001).

The data were analysed using a social constructionist framework and a discursive analytical approach that draws from discourse analysis (Potter and Wetherell, 1987), conversation analysis (Sacks, 1992), and ethnomethodology (Garfinkel, 1967). Such a research perspective assumes a critical stance towards taken-for-granted meanings, acknowledges the relevance of history and context, and treats talk in interaction as a form of social action (Fairclough, 1992; Rogers et al., 1995; Johnson and Duberley, 2000). Attention was given to the structure and content of the interviews with a view to identifying recurring patterns, repertoires and discourses that were relevant to the interaction at hand (Burr, 1995; Samra-Fredericks, 2003; Coyle, 2000). From this perspective, not only does 'talk' say something about ourselves, but also '*does*' something for us in terms of how we construct ourselves and events in social interaction and endeavour to be heard by others (Potter, 1996, 2001; Chia, 2000; Coupland, 2001; Riley, 2002). Hence, the participants were not viewed as passive members of an organization who merely reacted or responded according to designated company policies and practices (Potter and Wetherell, 1987). Rather and alternatively they were seen as active participants who chose to accept, resist or indeed negotiate, what it means to 'be' a expatriate through varying descriptions of repatriation associated with short-term assignment experience.

## Analysis

During and after transcription, the data were repeatedly read over and annotated for similarity or variability. From these readings, a number of analytical themes or topics emerged that were apparently important and relevant for the participants. One of the most salient was the talk constructed around current and future concerns relative to repatriation and the short-term assignment process. Also of interest was how the participants went about the business of comparing and contrasting themselves to other employees in the company by drawing from an array of rhetorical resources to present own work identities as unique and distinct. Constructing the repatriated working 'self' was often depicted in terms of uncertainty accompanied by implicit frustration with the organizations' apparent inability or unwillingness to confirm or clarify what individual work roles would be upon repatriating back to the home organization. Also manifest within self-ascribed accounts of fractured identities was a constructed lack of agency over unknown or unwelcome changes upon returning home. It is these particular themes that are explored and unpacked in detail in the following analysis of talk.

Transcription notation:

| | |
|---|---|
| (.) | A dot between parentheses indicates a slight pause and more dots indicate longer pauses |
| = | Equal sign indicates no interval or pause between the talk of two people |
| - | A hyphen indicates a change or quick re-wording to what is being said |
| [or] | Left and right hand brackets indicate overlaps in talk by the speakers, at the point that it happens |
| ( ) | Single parentheses indicate verbal behaviour, vocalizations, e.g. cough, laughter. |

### Constructing repatriation: 'anything, something or nothing'

The first segment of talk is taken from an interview with JIM, who has been with the company for 11 years, and had recently returned back to the UK after completing a 3-month short-term assignment in the US. This was his response when asked about his return to work in the UK:

***Extract One***

1. JIM *that was-was probably the hardest part actually (.) uh coming back I think uh*
2. *(.) that's something I always talk to my supervisor uh my boss now (.) but when*
3. *(.) a colleague of mine is out there now it'll be different (.) when I came back (.)*
4. *there wasn't hardly anything to do (.) I mean there was nothing]*
5. INT *[mmm*
6. JIM *and that was ah the hardest thing (.) and I spent the first weeks going around*
7. *with nothing to do and looking for something just going around with my hands*
8. *in my pockets (...) ah cleaning up (.) and getting paid for it which isn't-ah you*
9. *know (.) ah two weeks a highly paid sort of cleaning person (..) that was-that*
10. *was the hardest thing that I-I had to do (..) cause it's a terrible feeling that*
11. *you're not needed (.) in the place where you actually feel most at home kind*
12. *of thing*

In this lengthy extract, the participant constructs a rendition of unwanted change to his working role after repatriation to his usual place of work. Whilst presenting a plausible account, the participant says something about himself, his reception back in work and the organization's hand in the short-term assignment and repatriation process. This is supported by a detailed account of repatriation full of references concerning the adverse impact on quality of work life and the constructed loss of identity and status. The participant pays attention to problematic features of short-term repatriation through talk about undesirable change, loss of agency, and an uncertain future in the home organization.

In the opening line, the participant summarizes the outcome of his repatriation experience as '*probably the hardest part*' of the assignment. However the follow-up description in line 3 implies that the company's repatriation practices have somehow improved or changed since the participant's return in that current expatriates may now ostensibly expect a '*different*' (better?) experience of repatriation to that of his own.

Of interest in this extract is how 'repatriation' is attended to by the participant as simply a matter of '*coming back*' (line 1), or retrospectively '*when I came back*' (line 3). The informality of the description combined with the use of '*I*' attends to the personal nature of the sentiment indicating a high level of stake in what is being talked about (Goffman, 1979). The participant continues on to establish how his own return to work was particularly unpleasant because of having '*hardly anything to do*', and immediately upgrades the description '*there was nothing*' (line 4). The use of '*I mean*' preceding the construction functions to shifts the talk to a more evaluative opinion of a personal situation (Wood, 1995). '*The hardest thing*' (line 6) is an extreme case formulation used to create rhetorical effectiveness by characterizing repatriation as the most difficult part of the short-term assignment. Utilizing detailed temporal terms of '*weeks*' (line 6) and '*two weeks*' (line 9) work to emphasize the lengthiness of the situation in that it lasted weeks as opposed to only days. The account draws attention to the way organizations can effectively forget about, or overlook a returning expatriate's re-entry back into the home organization (Lazarova and Caliguiri, 2001; Morley and Heraty, 2004). As a consequence, identity displacement and a lack of fit in the workplace in this instance is evident through metaphorical descriptions of time spent '*going around with nothing to do and looking for something just going around with my hands in my pockets*' (lines 6–8).

According to Antaki et al. (1996) identities emerge from the listeners' interpretation of the talk presented. For example in this extract the participant constructs and compares his 'new' self-imposed work identity upon returning home to that of a '*highly paid sort of cleaning person*' (line 9). He draws on features commonly associated with the category of a cleaner such as '*cleaning up*' and '*getting paid for it*' (line 8) to position himself convincingly within such an identity (Sacks, 1992). Constructing an alternative work identity enables the participant to portray himself as doing 'something' that was evidently an improvement or alternative to doing 'nothing' (Baruch et al., 2002). Arguably the description also functions to justify his place back at work in the 'home' site. However, his sentiment '*that was-that was the hardest thing that I-I had to do*' (lines 9–10) serves to acknowledge how assuming an unwanted and undesirable work role as a means of passing time brings with it '*a terrible feeling that you're not needed*' (lines 10–11). Arguably this constructed lack of belonging conflicts with the ideology and meaning of work that the participant seemingly attaches to the home organization. This is particularly apparent in line 11 in his portrayal of work as *'the place where you actually feel most at home kind of thing'* (Du Gay, 1996).

According to Edwards (1997) individuals organize their version of events in talk in order to achieve a particular effect. In this extract, the constructed experience of returning home, particularly at the end of undertaking a relatively short-term assignment, is not only portrayed as disconcerting, but arguably unexpected, unplanned, and therefore unwanted (Edwards and Potter, 1992). What is obviously absent from this extract is the construction of usual work-related jobs and tasks that the participant would be expected to be doing, or involved in after spending eleven years working on this site prior to the assignment (Bonache et al., 2001; Baruch et al., 2002). Interestingly, any criticism for job ambiguity and lack of direction in the work place as an implicit consequence of repatriation is never explicitly aimed by the participant towards members of the organization or the company itself. Rather and alternatively, the participant utilizes the interactional setting as a moral arena to construct himself as a 'pioneer' of short-term assignments and add authenticity to the account (Edwards and Potter, 1992). Perhaps it was the context of the interview setting that impacted the way the participant went about presenting this account of repatriation, or it may have been potentially problematic to outwardly cast blame upon the organization when it was clearly apparent that fitting in (or 'back into'?) a previous work identity was a foremost concern for him (Coupland, 2001).

The next extract also concerns the relevance of belonging within the home organization in relation to talk about future expectations of repatriation. Although there are some similarities between this and the preceding extract, topics including uncertainty and agency are dealt with quite differently in this turn. This extract is taken from an interview with LISA, who had been with the company for 18 months, and was halfway through a 4-month short-term assignment in the UK from the US.

### Extract Two

1. LISA *I don't know (.) but ah as far as work wise I'm not sure what I'll be doing when*
2. *I get back (laughter)*
3. INT *Are you concerned about that*
4. LISA *Yeah (..) a little bit (.) I spoke to my supervisor and said 'listen am I still gonna*
5. *have a group to come back to when I get there' and he said ah (...) I think so*

6. *(laughter) (.) so I don't know (.)*
7. INT *And you're not worried*
8. LISA *I'm sure they'll find something for me (laughter)*

In this utterance, the participant constructs a contradictory and dilemmatic version of what she perceives as her future role in work after she completes the current assignment and returns to the home organization (Billig et al., 1988). Interestingly, this participant was only one of two interviewed that had the least tenure with the company (i.e. 18 months). Earlier in the interview she expressed surprise that she had even been considered for an international assignment so early in her career. Such self-ascription resonates with Morley and Heraty (2004) in that expatriate employees no longer tend to fit the traditional mould of well-established and tenured managers associated with the classic long-term assignment.

On the one hand this extract is riddled with talk depicting the problematic aspects associated with getting lost or forgotten in the process of repatriation. This is evidenced by her frequent usage of '*I don't know*' (twice in lines 1 & 6), and '*I'm not sure*' (line 1) (Brewster et al., 2001; Baruch et al., 2002). However in the last line the participant re-evaluates her situation in more confident terms '*I'm sure they'll find something for me*' and works to contradict her earlier talk of unsettlement and uncertainty. When asked '*are you concerned about that*' in line 3, she responds using an extreme case formulation '*yeah (..) a little bit*' (line 4) (Pomerantz, 1986). In this instance the description softens the degree of worry associated with an uncertain future. However, outward insecurity re-emerges in constructing her explicit search for clarification by questioning her supervisor '*listen am I still gonna have a group to come back to when I get there*' (lines 4 & 5). Active voicing '*and he said*' is deployed in constructing his verbatim response '*I think so*' and works to strengthen the plausibility of the account (line 5) (Wooffitt, 1992). However immediately following this up in line 6 with a constructed summarization '*so I don't know*' is indicative of how she nevertheless remains unsure of her post-assignment future. By presenting the talk this way, her discourse of scepticism is legitimized by her supervisor's lack of clarity about the future (Bonache et al., 2001; Lazarova and Caliguiri, 2001). Interestingly, the participant laughs no less than three times in this extract (lines 2, 6 & 8). As it is highly unlikely that anyone would consider the participant's current situation as humorous, perhaps laughter in this instance was used to vocalize trepidation about a future she seemingly has little control over (Jefferson, 1984b).

Expatriate re-integration or re-fit back into the home organization has been compared to expectations that newcomers often have about a new job, although repatriation is generally treated as a process of re-adjustment in reverse (Black and Gregerson, 1999). Carbaugh (1996) claimed that organizations inherently require the management of multiple identities, and whilst some of these will be in harmony, others may be inconsistent and potentially conflicting. In this extract, the onus for creating and managing the participant's expectations of repatriation and sense of self is constructed as clearly resting on the agentic organization and more specifically, on the participant's supervisor (Black, 1992; Forster, 1994; Stroh and Caligiuri, 1998). The constructed nature of the account draws attention to the meaning and relevance of organizational belonging. This is evident in the participant's attempts to maintain consistency by re-establishing her membership within a specific group she had worked with previous to this assignment. The rhetoric deployed in this segment may be likened to the first extract in that 'something' is arguably a preferred option when compared to an alternative of 'nothing'. However interpretation may also be required in this extract as the viewpoint presented may be due in part to the brevity of the relationship between participant and organization (Garsten and Grey, 1997).

As an expatriate, there is a valid expectation or entitlement to know or be assured of what the future in work will hold for you upon repatriation (Lazarova and Caligiuri, 2001). This extract is full of contradiction. For example, whereas the first half implies a lack of clarity about the future, the last line suggests a constructed belief in the organization that the participant will still be valued as a member of the home organization upon her return. The manner in which this extract is presented is indicative of the hegemonic nature of the organization. This is apparent by the way dependency on the organization for responsibility and control over the repatriation process is aligned in talk with how the participant's future role in work may or may not be defined (Fairclough, 1992).

## Resisting, maintaining and negotiating expectations of repatriation

Similar to the two preceding accounts, the following extracts also deal with repatriation, expectation and change. Whereas extract 3 is particularly concerned with resisting change and maintaining a difference in work as a result of expatriation, in contrast extract 4 constructs resistance to change by maintaining an identity argued as unchanged since the onset of his assignment. Of interest in these accounts is how the participants depict the organization as unable or unwilling to recognize and utilize their experience gained from respective assignments (Baruch et al., 2002). Two-sided arguments are used to 'shore up' and support the rationale behind the rhetoric, although each participant deploys a slightly different version and approach to accomplishing this in the talk (Abell and Stokoe, 1999).

The next extract is taken from an interview with IAN, who has been with the company for four years and just returned to the UK from a 3-month short-term assignment in the US. In this account, the experience of repatriation is described as depressing and a letdown due to the apparent and unanticipated lack of positive change and conversely, the imposition of unwanted change to the participant's post-assignment work role. An argument of resistance is presented within a discourse of same and different that functions to differentiate the participant from other organizational members.

### *Extract Three*

1. IAN *when I came back (.) it was almost like an anti-climax because I'd gone back to*
2. *almost exactly what I had been doing only a few months earlier*
3. INT *same type of work=*
4. IAN *=same type of work (.) same everything more or less (.) and that was (..) a*
5. *downer cause (.) you're-you almost are maybe expecting something I mean*
6. *although your life has changed a great deal in 3 months (.) people's lives here*
7. *have stayed the same for those 3 months (.) I don't think you can expect them to*
8. *change for you (.) it's the same when you come home you can't expect to*
9. *change back do you see what I mean*

The extract begins as a story '*when I came back*' (line 1) that precedes a detailed and arguably emotive account of repatriation '*almost like an anti-climax because I'd gone back to almost exactly what I had been doing only a few months earlier*' (lines 1 & 2) (Sacks, 1992). The phrase '*anti-climax*' as an extreme case formulation attends to the constructed nature of short-term repatriation as a disappointing and evidently distressing experience. The participant goes on to describe the lack of any change in his post-assignment work generically '*same type of work*' (line 4). Using vague detail within a neutral description allows the listener to draw certain inferences from talk about the workplace (Potter, 1996). In this case, following up the description by constructing the situation *'same everything more or less'* works to confirm a static and seemingly unchanged work environment.

By evaluating short-term repatriation as *'a downer'* in lines 4–5 not only reinforces the participant's earlier claims but also suggests that the actual assignment when compared to the experience of returning was a seemingly positive experience (Carbaugh, 1996). His deployment of *'maybe expecting something'* (line 5) creates an air of uncertainty about what he expected, but clearly implies that change in some form was anticipated as a consequence of the experience (Forster, 1994; Gregerson and Stroh, 1997).

Temporal descriptions *'only a few months'* (line 2) and *'3 months'* (lines 6 & 7) is an explicit acknowledgement of the relative shortness of the participant's assignment. Hence the prevailing assumption would be that this kind of time frame would (should?) have little, if any impact on a returning short-term expatriate. However, the constructed *'life has changed a great deal'* (line 6) implies that irrespective of assignment length, the participant is orienting to having undergone a significant change and is now evidently different to whom or what he was like prior to the assignment. By positioning himself as having ostensibly changed entitles him to go on and conversely characterize 'other people' in work as having *'stayed the same for those 3 months'* (lines 6 & 7). This works to create an interesting contrast by situating individuals who undertake assignments, albeit in the short-term, as having moved on or altered in some positive manner (Linehan and Scullion, 2002). Whereas those who metaphorically stay behind in the home organization are by implication, inert and static in that change in this context would not be expected or assumed.

The participant's position is further manifest in his justification *'I don't think you can expect them to change for you'* (lines 7–8) to reference to other employees who stay behind. Having gained short-term international assignment experience and constructed himself back to work in the home organization as a seemingly different person enables the participant to present a reciprocal claim that it should be *'the same when you come home you can't expect to change back'* (lines 8–9). The description attends to a two-sided argumentation that works to legitimate a viewpoint that just as imposed change is evidently unwelcome and unwanted by those who do not undertake assignments, it is equally unacceptable to ask the same of those who have (Abell and Stokoe, 1999)." " '

Of particular relevance in this turn of talk is how the participant's expatriation experience is implied as neither acknowledged nor utilized by the organization subsequent to repatriation. However what is evident throughout the account is the participant's constructed resistance to organizational attempts at imposing change in the form of an unwanted previous work role. The extract is full of references concerning the participant's apparent desire to sustain a 'new' work identity depicted as having been developed over the course of his assignment. Thus identity formation relative to the participant's repatriation experience in this instance was continually constructed, changed, maintained or resisted throughout the segment (Edwards and Potter, 1992). The detailed analysis of talk is illustrative of how the problematic nature of describing one's experience of returning to work upon repatriation in the present may lie in conflict with ideologies of the past (Billig et al., 1988). This is an interesting point in that Lazarova and Caligiuri (2001) have suggested that because there is less interruption to work, short-term assignments should be less problematic. Therefore any difficulties associated with re-integrating and re-entry back into the home organization should also be that much easier. Clearly this is not the case in this extract of talk. In the last line of the extract *'Do you see what I mean'* serves to elicit empathy from the listener in understanding the participant's constructed argumentation (Symon, 2000).

This following extract is taken from an interview with DAN, who was midway through a 3-month short-term assignment to the UK from the US having been with the firm for nine and a half years. This is his reply when asked what he thought he would be doing after the assignment:

***Extract Four***

1. DAN *I guess one interesting is (.) which has already come up ah you know my*
2. *supervisor saying 'so ah what do you want to do when you come back' (.) I*
3. *guess initially I assumed that I'd be doing all the same things when I get back*
4. *(.) as when I left so I don't know why I wouldn't be doing more of a similar*
5. *type thing when I got back (.) because the whole point is for me to see how*
6. *people work over here and how I can make things better you know between the*
7. *two areas*

In this segment, the participant constructs and questions the differences between the organization's perspective on repatriation and his own expectations about returning home to work in future (Davies and Harré, 1990).

In the opening line, *'one interesting'* is used as an evaluative comment to introduce an area that has recently *'come up'* and is therefore deemed relevant to the discussion at hand. The participant goes on to explain how he had been asked by his supervisor *'what do you want to do when you come back'* (lines 2–3). Reporting the verbatim words of others is what Hutchby and Wooffitt (1998) identified as 'active voicing'. As a rhetorical tool, this works to add credibility to what is being said and strengthens the speaker's version of events. By implication *'I guess initially I assumed'* in line 2 positions change associated with going back as a non-issue until it was brought up by his supervisor. In contrast to extract 3, the imposition of inevitable but nevertheless ambiguous change to the participant's working self upon returning in this instance is portrayed as an unexpected feature of the short-term assignment process (Forster, 1994, 2000; Lazarova and Caliguiri, 2001).

The participant's description *'doing all the same things when I get back as when I left'* further justifies resistance to such imposition (lines 3–4). Using the follow-up line of reasoning *'I don't know'* injects uncertainty in the talk by creating a dilemmatic situation (Billig et al., 1988). Deploying *'because the whole point'* in line 5 serves as the basis of a two-sided argument used oppose any change to the repatriated working self through a repertoire of sensemaking and pragmatics (Weick, 1995). This is evident in his two-part list *'to see how people work over here'*, and *'how I can make things better you know between the two areas'* (lines 5–7) as the primary reasons for having undertaken the assignment in the first place. This kind of description chimes in with Riusala and Suutari (2005) in that the objectives of the participant's assignment evidently entailed knowledge transfer and enhancement of the working relationship between the home and host site. Hence, the prospect of potentially doing something decidedly different upon repatriation is positioned as unexpected, contradictory and clearly unwarranted (Baruch et al., 2002).

In this extract, the participant draws on a number of discursive tools and repertoires to negotiate a particular rendition of repatriation as a consequence of unforeseen change. The constructed argument functions as a foundation used by the participant to make sense of ambiguity by resisting an imposed change to his working identity (Brown, 2000). As part of this construction, he implores a discourse of continuity as a means of resistance. Hence accounting for a mitigated state leads to inferences that uncertainty associated with unwanted change not only interferes, but undoubtedly impacts on the constructed ability to maintain a coherent accounting of self-identity (Garsten and Grey, 1997).

## Repatriation: constructing membership categories and entitlement

In contrast to the four previous accounts, the final extract deals with repatriation and difference in a somewhat divergent and distinctive manner. This extract is taken from an interview with JO, who had been with the company for 12 years, having recently returned to the UK after completing a 1-year assignment in the US.

What is unique about Jo is that she is engaged with the human resource end of the company and is not involved as the previous four participants with research and development. This turn of talk was selected because it illustrates a particularly interesting way that repatriation experience within this organization may be constructed and legitimated from a dual category of membership.

***Extract Five***

1. INT *did you have any qualms issues concerns about coming back (.) about going*
2. *back to work what you'd be doing*
3. JO *yeah loads (laughter) (..) we don't do a good job (.) of (.) repatriation at all*
4. INT *why do say that (.) from your own experiences*
5. JO *oh (.) oh yeah (..) and people would tell me that and then I actually experienced*
6. *it for myself things like it was a very sloppy-cause things go on but it was just*
7. *very sloppy (.) it regurgitates all that unsettledness that you had ah prior to*
8. *going you know (.) in actual fact I actually feel more- more (.) it's more*
9. *unsettling (.) by far I mean coming back than it was going out*

In the above extract, the participant presents an openly critical evaluation of the organizations' repatriation practices legitimated through constructions of both personal and managerial experience. By responding in line 3 to the interviewer's question using an extreme case formulation *'loads'* draws attention to an upcoming problematic and personal account of repatriation (Pomerantz, 1986). She goes on to summarize company practice through a collective and self-inclusive *'we don't do a good job of repatriation at all'*. Using the pronoun *'we'* is symptomatic of a shared responsibility for the way repatriation is handled by the firm (Edwards and Potter, 1992). As the participant related earlier in the interaction that her current role in the organization was in human resources, deploying *'we'* also functions as a category entitlement for claiming a particular knowledge about international assignments and expatriate-experienced employees (Sacks, 1992).

Dual organizational membership as both a member of HR and a former expatriate is further evident in her constructed understanding of repatriation *'people would tell me that and then I actually experienced it for myself'* (lines 5–6). This is indicative that until she experienced repatriation firsthand, her apparent awareness of inadequate repatriation practices within the organization derived from the conveyed experience of other employees whilst she was working in an HR capacity. The description functions to support and legitimate her entitlement to know about these issues based on her claim to duality as both a member of HR and her experience gained from undertaking a short-term assignment. In so doing, her constructed denigration of company practice associated with problematic repatriation is unlikely to be challenged by others (Potter, 1996).

The shift to using *'myself'* in line 6 moves the talk from generalized company practice to a more personal account of events relative to the participant's own experience of repatriation and related concerns. Although a generic descriptor *'things'* is deployed in line 6, it is apparent that the primary issue for this participant was the apparent mishandling of her own repatriation. The participant constructs and reiterates the experience as *'very sloppy'*. As an extreme case formulation, this functions to persuasively strengthen the way the argument is presented in the talk (Pomerantz, 1986). She goes on to construct repatriation outcome similar to the pre-departure stage of an assignment based on the way it ostensibly *'regurgitates all that unsettledness'* (line 7). As repatriation is all about returning back to one's usual and thus seemingly familiar place of work, constructing it as *'more unsettling'* (lines 8–9) highlights the problematic aspects of assuming that repatriation even after a short-term assignment is simply just a matter of 'coming home'.

The description *'in actual fact I actually feel'* (line 8) although a constructed personal opinion, works to add a sense of fact or reality about the experience. The use of *'I'* moves the talk away from the collective and closer to the participant to imply she is now speaking from an expatriate-experienced position rather than as a member of HR (Goffman, 1979). *'By far I mean coming back than it was going out'* (line 9) as a comparative evaluation again works to upgrade repatriation subsequent to a short-term assignment as a more distressing experience than the anxious and uncertain pre-departure stage of an assignment (Linehan and Scullion, 2002). The participant's talk is indicative of a loss of agency and lack of autonomy over the outcome of her own assignment. This kind of description functions rhetorically as a means to ward off any assumption that as a informed member of HR she would (should?) have had control over her own situation (Stroh et al., 2000; Linehan and Scullion, 2002). Arguably as a discursive tool in talk, this works to preclude the participant from responsibility for the constructed mismanagement of her own short-term repatriation experience. In so doing, accountability for the outcome in this instance rests firmly with the organization (Black and Gregerson, 1999).

## Conclusion

A discursive approach to analysis was used in this organizational-based case study to explore constructions of repatriation expectations and outcomes, and attend to the way future work roles were portrayed by participants that were currently on, or had recently returned from a short-term assignment. Three distinct research themes emerged from the data that included *'Constructing repatriation: anything, something or nothing'*; *'Resisting, maintaining and negotiating expectations of repatriation'*; and *'Constructing membership categories and entitlement'*. Of interest within the detailed and in-depth analysis of the talk presented were accounts of short-term assignment repatriation that were not only constructed as disconcerting in the final stages of a short-term assignment, but also implied by some as a problematic and issue of concern over the course of the assignment. Moreover in this study identity formation was treated not as a static entity, but as a continuing and flexible phenomenon that was created in and for the context of social interaction. Hence, accounting for the self as an expatriate-experienced employee in this particular organization varied considerably depending on the background and knowledge that each participant brought with them to the workplace.

During the analysis, multiple sub-themes and interrelated issues surfaced from the constructed talk. Of particular interest was how constructing criticism or distain about the organization or other members, whether indirect, or unmistakably explicit, was cautiously introduced and carefully negotiated into the talk by the participants. This was manifest for example by the way the participants frequently legitimated claims about re-entry or repatriating back into the home organization as/was the most unpleasant and unsettling aspect of the assignment experience. Although repatriation concerns of this nature are relatively commonplace within the long-term assignment literature, this was a surprising and unanticipated feature of short-term assignments and an area of research in need of further attention. The findings from this study are supportive of the view that short-term assignments may not necessarily alleviate all of the problems traditionally associated with long-term assignments; rather they have the ability to inherently create their own new and unique set of problems (Brewster et al., 2001; Linehan and Mayerhofer, 2005).

Shotter (1993) argued that in order for individuals to be valued and accepted in the workplace, they must be able to demonstrate social competence through their actions. This is usually achieved by fulfilling certain job-related duties and accounting to others for one's membership or role within the organization. In this case, ostensibly becoming, or accounting for a particular work identity was accomplished rhetorically and interactionally by socially constructing one's desire to fit, re-fit and ultimately belong in work after repatriation (Edwards and Potter, 1992). However it was evident that for some participants this created a paradox in that much of their talk about the meaning of work and the way past or current identities were constructed within the context of the home organization contrasted with attempts to make sense of unknown or unexpected change relative to repatriation (Weick, 1995; Glanz et al., 2001).

Although the focus of this study was on talk about short-term assignment outcomes, the findings may be compared to long-term assignment literature in a number of ways. For example, the organization's agentic role in creating or imposing particular expectations about short-term repatriation was implicit (e.g. Black, 1992; Forster, 1994, 2000; Stroh and Caliguiri, 1998; Bonache et al., 2001; Lazarova and Caliguiri, 2001). Moreover and whereas long-term repatriation would undoubtedly represent a potential upheaval for many individuals in terms of 'fitting in' and belonging back in the context of the home organization (Black, 1992; Forster, 1994); in this study concerns of a similar nature were also expressed by short-term experienced expatriates. However and in contrast to repatriation and the long-term assignment, the major issue surrounding short-term repatriation for participants in this study appeared to be not so much of an *'out of sight out of mind'* depiction of how they felt the organization viewed them, but more of a *'out of sight for a little while but nevertheless still in the dark'* repertoire (Forster, 1994; Black and Gregerson, 1999; Baruch et al., 2002). This theme was particularly evident in talk constructed around the loss of autonomy, unmet or undesired change, and a overwhelming lack of consensus about what is, or should be expected from repatriation by individuals undertaking arguably brief stretches of time away from the 'home' organization (Stroh et al., 2000; Linehan and Scullion, 2002; Linehan and Mayerhofer, 2005).

In response to Linehan and Scullion's (2002) call for more in-depth research from the perspective of expatriation-experienced individuals, this case study has presented a collection of relevant and persuasive accounts of short-term international assignment experience, repatriation and related constructions of work place identity. Given the rise in short-term assignments, a consideration of practical implications is warranted with regard to the management of these kinds of assignments in future (Brewster et al., 2001). In particular, attention should be directed to the expressions of doubt manifest in the participants' talk about the constructed value and benefit of accepting and undertaking a short-term international assignment in the first place (Scullion, 1994). Not only does this have the potential to impact on whether or not a returning short-term expatriate chooses to stay with the organization, but it may also play a part in influencing the willingness of others to accept this kind of assignment in future (Suutari and Brewster, 2003).

According to many theorists, authors are selective about the evidence they present and as a consequence, varying interpretations may be constructed out of the same dialogue. What this case-study attempts to provide is a reflexive, alternative and novel version of repatriation relative to short-term assignment experience (Searle, 1995; Brown, 2000; Taylor, 2001). Therefore it is acknowledged and accepted that others may wish to apply different meanings, understandings or interpretations to the collection and analysis of the data presented. The design of this study has represented a significant change to the way accounts of short-term assignments and repatriation have been approached and attended to in the past. Utilizing a discursive approach to analysis has enabled exploration and identification of issues made relevant to the talk by the participants themselves. As a result, the findings have relevance by offering some new perspectives and raising fresh questions about the nature of short-term assignments and repatriation embedded within a framework of social identity construction. Moreover, the findings gleaned from the analysis are supportive of a view that just as short-term assignments are not homogeneous because of considerable variance in length, purpose and context; so too are the individuals who accept and undertake them.

## References

Abell, J. and Stokoe, E. H. (1999) I take full responsibility, I take some responsibility, I'll take half of it but no more than that: Princess Diana and the negotiation of blame in the 'Panorama' interview. *Discourse Studies*, 1(3), 297–319.

Antaki, C., Condor, S. and Levine, M. (1996) Social identities in talk: Speaker's own orientations. *British Journal of Social Psychology*, 35, 473–92.

Baruch, Y., Steele, D. J. and Quantrill, G. A. (2002) Management of expatriation and repatriation for novice global player. *International Journal of Manpower*, 23(7), 659–74.

Billig, M., Condor, S., Edwards, D., Gane, M., Middleton, D. and Radley, A. R. (1988) *Ideological Dilemmas*. London: Sage.

Black, J. S. (1992) Coming home: The relationship of expatriate expectations with repatriation adjustment and job performance. *Human Relations*, 45, 177–92.

Black, J. S. and Gregerson, H. B. (1999) The right way to manage expats. *Harvard Business Review*, 77(2), 52–60.

Bonache, J., Brewster, C. and Suutari, V. (2001) Expatriation: A developing research agenda. *Thunderbird International Business Review*, 43(1), 3–20.

Brewster, C. and Scullion, H. (1997) A review and agenda for expatriate Human Resource Management. *Human Resource Management Journal*, 7(3), 32–41.

Brewster, C., Harris, H. and Petrovic, J. (2001) Globally mobile employees: managing the mix. *Journal of Professional HRM*, 25, 11–15.

Brown, A. D. (2000) Making sense of inquiry sensemaking. *Journal of Management Studies*, 37(1), 45–76.

Bryman, A. (1989) *Research Methods and Organisation Studies*. London: Routledge.

Burr, V. (1995) *An Introduction to Social Constructionism*. London: Routledge.

Carbaugh, D. (1996) *Situating Selves: The communication of social identities in American Scenes*. Albany N.Y.: State University of New York.

Chia, R. (2000) Discourse analysis as organisational analysis. *Organisation*, 7(3), 513–18.

Coupland, C. (2001) Accounting for change: A discourse analysis of graduate trainees' talk of adjustment. *Journal of Management Studies*, 38(8), 1103–19.

Coyle, A. (2000) Discourse analysis. In G. M. Breakwell, S. Hammond and C. Fife-Schaw (eds) *Research Methods in Psychology*. London: Sage (251–68).

Davies, B. and Harré, R. (1990) Positioning: The discursive production of selves. *Journal for the Theory of Social Behaviour*, 20, 43–63.

DuGay, P. (1996) *Consumption and Identity at work*. London: Sage.

Edwards, D. and Potter, J. (1992) *Discursive Psychology*. London: Sage.

Edwards, D. (1997) *Discourse and Cognition*. London: Sage.

Fairclough, N. (1992) *Discourse and Social Change*. Cambridge: Polity Press.

Forster, N. (1994) The forgotten employees?: The experiences of expatriate staff returning to the U.K. *International Journal of Human Resource Management*, 5(2), 405–25.

Forster, N. (2000) Expatriates and the impact of cross-cultural training. *Human Resource Management Journal*, 10(3), 63–79.

Frazee, V. (1997) Short-term assignments grow in popularity. *Workforce*, 76(4), 8.

Garfinkel, H. (1967) *Studies in Ethnomethodology*. Englewood Cliffs N.J.: Prentice Hall.

Garsten, C. and Grey, C. (1997) How to become oneself: discourses of subjectivity in post bureaucratic organisations. *Organisations*, 4(2), 210–28.

Gregerson, H. B. and Stroh, L. S. (1997) Coming home to the Arctic cold: antecedents to Finnish expatriate and spouse repatriation adjustment. *Personnel Psychology*, 50(3), 635–54.

Goffman, E. (1979) 'Footing'. *Semiotica*, 25, 1–29.

Glanz, L., Williams, R. and Hoeksema, L. (2001) Sensemaking in expatriation: a theoretical basis. *Thunderbird International Business Review*, 43(1), 101–19.

Hutchby, I. and Woofitt, R. (1998) *Conversation Analysis*. Cambridge: Polity Press.

Jefferson, G. (1984a) Transcription notation. In J. M. Atkinson and J. Heritage (eds) *Structures of Social Action: Studies in Conversational Analysis*. London: Cambridge University Press (9–16).

Jefferson, G. (1984b) On the organisation of laughter in talk about troubles. In J. M. Atkinson and J. Heritage (eds) *Structures of Social Action: Studies in Conversational Analysis*. London: Cambridge University Press (346–69).

Johnson, P. and Duberley, J. (2000) *Understanding Management Research*. London: Sage.

Kvale, S. (1996) *Interviews: An introduction to qualitative research interviewing*. London: Sage.

Lazarova, M. and Caligiuri, P. (2001) Retaining repatriates: the role of organisational support practices. *Journal of World Business*, 36(4), 389–401.

Linehan, M. and Mayerhofer, W. (2005) International careers and repatriation. In H. Scullion and M. Linehan (eds) *International Human Resource Management: A Critical Text*. Basingstoke: Palgrave Macmillan (131–55).

Linehan, M. and Scullion, H. (2002) Repatriation of European female corporate executives: An empirical study. *International Journal of Human Resource Management*, 13(2), 254–68.

Mayerhofer, W., Hartmann, L. C. and Herbert, A. (2004) Career management issues for flexpatriate international staff. *Thunderbird International Business Review*, 46(6), 647–66.

Morley, M. and Heraty, N. (2004) International assignments and global careers. *Thunderbird International Business Review*, 46(6), 633–46.

Pomerantz, A. (1986) Extreme case formulations: A way of legitimizing claims. *Human Studies*, 9, 219–29.

Potter, J. (1996) *Representing Reality: Discourse, Rhetoric and Social Constructionism*. London: Sage.

Potter, J. (2001) Wittgenstein and Austin. In M. Wetherell, S. Taylor and S. J. Yates (eds) *Discourse Theory and Practice*. London: Sage (39–46).

Potter, J. and Wetherell, M. (1987) *Discourse and Social Psychology: Beyond Attitudes and Behaviour*. London: Sage.

Riley, S. C. E. (2002) Constructions of equality and discrimination in professional men's talk. *British Journal of Social Psychology*, 41, 443–61.

Riusala, K. and Suutari, V. (2005) International knowledge transfers through expatriates. *Thunderbird International Business Review*, 46(6), 743–70.

Rogers, R. S., Stenner, P., Gleeson, K. and Rogers, W. S. (1995) *Social Psychology: A Critical Agenda*. Cambridge: Polity Press.

Sacks, H. (1992) *Lectures on Conversation* (Vol. 1). Oxford: Blackwell.

Samra-Fredericks, D. (2003) Strategizing as lived experience and strategists' everyday efforts to shape strategic direction. *Journal of Management Studies*, 40(1), 141–74.

Scullion, H. (1994) Staffing policies and strategic control in British multinationals. *International Studies of Management and Organisation*, 24(3), 86–104.

Searle, J. R. (1995) *The Construction of Social Reality*. London: Penguin.

Shotter, J. (1993) Becoming someone: identity and belonging. In N. Coupland (ed.) *Discourse and Lifespan Identity*. London: Sage.

Silverman, D. (2001) *Interpreting Qualitative Data*. London: Sage.

Stroh, L. K. and Caligiuri, P. (1998) Increasing global effectiveness through people management. *World Business*, 33(1), 1–17.

Stroh, L. K., Gregersen, H. B. and Black, J. S. (2000) Triumphs and tragedies: expectations and commitments upon repatriation. *International Journal of Human Resource Management*, 11(4), 681–98.

Suutari, V. and Brewster, C. (2003) Repatriation: empirical evidence from a longitudinal study of careers and expectations among Finnish expatriates. *International Journal of Human Resource Management*, 14(7), 1132–51.

Symon, G. (2000) Everyday rhetoric: Argument and persuasion in everyday life. *European Journal of Work and Organisational Psychology*, 9 (4), 477–88.

Taylor, S. (2001) Evaluating and applying discourse analytic research. In M. Wetherell, S. Taylor and S. J. Yates (eds) *Discourse as Data: A guide for analysis*. London: Sage (311–30).

Ten Have, P. (1999) *Doing Conversation Analysis*. London: Sage.

Weick, K. (1995) *Sensemaking in Organisations*. Thousand Oaks, CA: Sage.

Wetherell, M. (1998) Positioning and interpretive repertoires: conversation analysis and post-structuralism in dialogue. *Discourse and Society*, 9(3), 387–412.

Wetherell, M. and Potter, J. (1992) *Mapping the Language of Racism: Discourse and the Legitimation of Exploitation*. Hemel Hempstead: Harvester Wheatsheaf.

Wood, L. A. (1995) Discourse analysis in research on aging. *Canadian Journal on Aging*, 14(1), 82–99.

Wooffitt, R. (1992) *Telling Tales of the Unexpected: The Organisation of Factual Discourse*. Hemel Hempstead: Harvester Wheatsheaf.

# Notes

## 3 The Use of Foreign Assignments and their Relationship with Economic Success and Business Strategy

1 Roughly speaking, the international dollar is a hypothetical currency unit reflecting the worth of local currency unit. It is calculated by using purchasing power parities and allows the comparison between countries and over time.

2 In this case, the median is calculated as the value of the variable at the lower end of the interval that contains the cumulative percentage of 50 per cent plus the distance along this interval required to meet the 50 per cent point.

## 4 Another Scandal in Bohemia? A Look Back on how we Measure Expatriate Adjustment

1 In countries where there were only one or two expatriates, the co-operating company could have deduced from Table 4.1 which individuals participated in this study and which did not. This would have violated the assurance given to all respondents that individuals will not be identifiable. It was therefore decided to code these countries, using generic terms such as EuroWest1 or SAmerica1. Thus the individual's identity is protected while at the same time as much information as possible is retained.

2 'World region' is here used in a descriptive sense and is mostly meant to indicate geographical proximity. Membership of any region follows lexical definition. The only exception is the distinction between Europe (West) and Europe (East), which in light of the radical political changes over the past 20 years in Eastern Europe seems warranted.

3 Although not identical with any of them, this definition draws on definitions by Früh (1989: 23), Holsti (1969: 14) and Krippendorf (1980: 21).

4 Twenty per cent of these were set aside for coder training and test-coding. All frequency counts in the results section of this paper refer to the thus diminished base of domain nominations.

5 Recording units describe 'the specific segment of content that is characterized by placing it in a given category' (Holsti, 1969: 116). These 'specific segments of content' can be single words or symbols, themes, characters, sentences or paragraphs or items (Holsti, 1969). For the purpose of the present study the recording unit was the domain or theme.

6 An entire body of literature has evolved around the question of what constitutes a proper inter-coder reliability coefficient (for a review, see Friede, 1981). The problem with almost all coefficients put forward in the literature is that none of them enjoys a long history of usage. The one exception is the simplest and most commonly used coefficient, calculating the percentage of coding decision on which the coders are in agreement relative to the total number of coding decisions: $R = (2M/(N_1 + N_2)$ with

$M$ = Number of coding decisions on which the two coders are in agreement
$N_1$ = Number of coding decisions made by coder 1
$N_2$ = Number of coding decisions made by coder 2

7 Even if one concedes that there are leisure time activities that are of a solitary nature, most of them usually involve considerable social contact.

## 6 The Effect of Culture of Origin on the Adjustment Process

1 'Scandinavian' includes 35 Danish, 13 Swedish and 9 Norwegian expatriates.

2 $$F = \frac{(SSE_{cum} - SSE_K - SSE_F)/(k)}{(SSE_K + SSE_F)/(n - 2 * k)}$$

When it is significant (large F test and low level of significance), the null hypothesis equal regression coefficients in the different samples (can be safely rejected and interaction is demonstrated.

## 8 Finnish Business Repatriates' Coping Strategies at Work: Problem-Focused and Emotion-Focused Forms of Coping

1 The names have been changed to guarantee the anonymity of the interviewees.

# Index